101

Bike Routes in Scotland

HARRY HENNIKER

MAINSTREAM
PUBLISHING

EDINBURGH AND LONDON

First published in Great Britain in 1996 by
MAINSTREAM PUBLISHING COMPANY (EDINBURGH) LTD
7 Albany Street
Edinburgh EH1 3UG

ISBN 1 85158 785 3

A catalogue record for this book is available from the British Library.

Typeset by the author, using an Atari ST computer and That's Writ 3 Software. Drawings by Sally Harrower, and imported in IMG format. Maps drawn by the author and published by permission of the BikeBus.

Printed in Finland by Werner Söderström Oy.

CONTENTS

INTRODUCTION

Acknowledgments

My first acknowledgment must be to members, past and present, of Spokes Events Group. As well as campaigning for better facilities for cyclists around Edinburgh, members of Spokes, The Lothian Cycle Campaign, have over the years biked in many of the best places in Scotland. To a great extent it is their explorations that I have drawn on when writing this book.

In particular I'd like to thank Sally Harrower for her amusing cartoon drawings. I'd also like to thank Dave McArthur, my companion for many a mile, for his help with the mountain bike routes, and Peter Hawkins for his help in checking out bike routes in the north of Scotland.

I should also thank Miss Tracy of Forest Enterprise, South Scotland; Jackie Grant for taking notes for me in Islay, Colonsay and Jura; Richard Grant for help with the Orkney Islands; Louise Sharpe for help with the Cairngorms; Ewan Tait for help in working out the route mileages; the lads from Livingston, James Catton and James Bain, for riding over Mount Keen; and Fiona Ritchie for help with the islands and for lots of support.

This book started as a series of individual route cards which were sold in bike shops in Edinburgh. I should like to thank Mike Sweatman for his general encouragement, and Edinburgh Bicycle Co-operative in particular for selling so many of them, which kept me going while I struggled with the computer software.

As far as computer software is concerned, most of all I thank my brother Dave, who persuaded me to get a computer in the first place, and answered all my dumb questions; without that, this project would never have started.

Finally there are a lot of other people who I haven't mentioned, some I've known for years, and cycled with regularly, others I've only met briefly. All of them have shared some knowledge with me. I hope you all enjoy the book.

Using the Book

Choose a route to suit your ability by using the route grading symbols (see page 7), and reading the description.

Nearly all the routes connect up to each other, so you can combine them to make them longer, or mix and match as you please.

If you need to use a hostel, B&B, hotel or ferry, phone the number given to make sure there is a place for you. (Phone tourist information for bed and breakfast or hotels.)

Have some food and drink with you, the tea rooms and pubs described in the text are not guaranteed to be open. Take waterproof clothing and a bike repair kit.

Have a map of the general area to provide additional information, and in case you wander off the route (OS maps are best). North on maps in this book is at the top of the page.

Most of the routes are suitable for experienced older children. Young children should use routes marked with a child symbol. Children should be accompanied by an adult.

The routes in this book were carefully checked at the time of writing. Inevitably some of the information will become out of date, and some routes may be extended, altered or withdrawn.

The mileages given in the book are intended as a general guide to distances, but should be accurate to within 10%.

Map Symbols (unless indicated otherwise on map)

Main Route → → Alternate Route ⇒ ⇒ Forest

Hostel (YH) ▲ Mountain △ Bike Path ....

On Mountain Bike Maps
Public Road _____ Dirt Track ========

On Road Cycling Maps
Busy (class A) road Quieter Road

Notes for Off-Road Cycling

Unless you are the fortunate owner of a highland estate, it's a virtual certainty that you are going to have to cycle/mountain bike on someone else's property. In Scotland this is often less of a problem than you might think, but there are a few rules to bear in mind to keep you safe and avoid antagonising others.

At the time of writing it was possible to ride a bike over all the routes in this book. Many of the routes are rights of way, but in other cases the landowner naturally has the right to prohibit biking if cyclists cause damage, or are a nuisance. If cyclists and mountain bikers are considerate this is less likely to happen. The advice given below by the Scottish Sports Council is a useful guide.

Of course any route through the hills is only a bike route if it is possible to ride a bike along it. Naturally some routes are easier than others. We have checked out all the routes in the book, if we couldn't ride at least 80% of any route it didn't qualify to go in the book. A few routes only just met this criteria, but the majority are 100% bikeable.

Mountain Biking Code of Conduct (Scottish Sports Council)

Think about others
Ride with consideration for others, give way to walkers and horse riders, and to farm and forestry workers. Give friendly greeting to people you approach and thank those who give way to you. Watch your speed when close to others. Try to avoid places that are used heavily by pedestrians, especially families. Walk through congested areas, don't come up silently behind people. Respect the work of the land, avoid forestry operations, don't disturb sheep gathering or game shooting.

Care for the environment
Keep to hard tracks and paths, don't cut corners. Walk over soft ground. Avoid fierce braking and skidding. Don't take bikes on to fragile mountaintops and plateaux. Take litter home.

Look after yourself
Watch your speed on loose surfaces and when going downhill. Match your speed to the track surface and your skill. Scotland can be rough and remote, bike within your abilities

as an accident or a breakdown in a remote area could be serious. Take a companion in remote areas. Crossing burns and rivers in spate is dangerous. Take a map and compass and know how to navigate. Carry warm waterproof clothing, emergency food and a lamp. Take tools and a repair kit. Wear a helmet.

To the above I would add that your tool kit should include a chain tool, and that you can often bike safely in busier areas by choosing your time of day.

The position regarding access to land in Scotland is sometimes misunderstood. There is no right of access to private land, except where there is a right of way or where access has been negotiated. In practice the majority of landowners do not object to one or two people crossing their land providing no damage is done. If they do object, one would expect a notice saying so. Large groups of people should restrict themselves to signposted mountain bike routes, such as those provided by the Forestry Commission. The Forestry Commission have asked me to include the following advice, which is in addition to the mountain bike code of conduct:

'Remember the forest is a work place. Respect warning signs and keep clear of operations and machinery. Although forest roads are quiet you should remain alert for other vehicles and timber lorries using the routes. Please note that waymarked routes and other forest roads may be temporarily closed for essential forest operations. Do not cycle on waymarked forest walking trails.'

Route Grading Symbols

Road Cycling

Fairly easy road cycling, some hills but they will not be very steep or long.

Varied cycling with some hills, either steep but short, or longer but easier.

Serious hills that are sufficiently frequent that getting off and walking is not really an option. Low gears, and being fit is the only answer!

Off-Road Cycling

Route is reasonably smooth, not specially hilly; motor traffic is mostly absent. Suitable for young children.

Off-road route on old railway line or canal towpath, a bit bumpy only, could be ridden on any bike.

Mountain bike route, forest trails or Land Rover track, not particularly hilly and not technically difficult.

Mountain bike route, contains steep sections that are hard work to get up and fast or difficult to descend.

Mountain bike route, some parts not bikeable. You may have to walk up to 20% of the route.

Mountain bike route, you will need to walk for up to 20% of the route and carry your bike for some of this.

Note that the mountain bike gradings only apply in reasonably dry conditions. Routes recommended for children may have some road crossings, or be used by service vehicles. Read the route description before starting.

DUMFRIES AND GALLOWAY

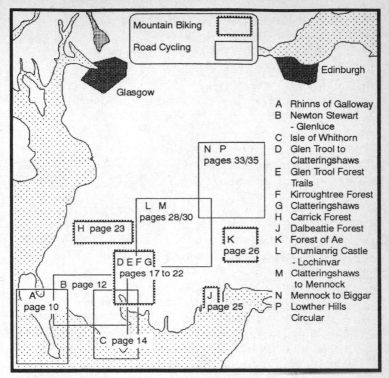

Mountain Biking

Road Cycling

Edinburgh

Glasgow

A	Rhinns of Galloway
B	Newton Stewart - Glenluce
C	Isle of Whithorn
D	Glen Trool to Clatteringshaws
E	Glen Trool Forest Trails
F	Kirroughtree Forest
G	Clatteringshaws
H	Carrick Forest
J	Dalbeattie Forest
K	Forest of Ae
L	Drumlanrig Castle - Lochinvar
M	Clatteringshaws to Mennock
N	Mennock to Biggar
P	Lowther Hills Circular

N P pages 33/35

L M pages 28/30

H page 23

K page 26

D E F G pages 17 to 22

B page 12

A page 10

J page 25

C page 14

'Scotland's surprising south-west'. This slogan is more apt than you might think. It certainly surprised me. I cycled along the A712 for 10 minutes - no cars! Admittedly it was a Sunday morning but even so.

Many of the A roads in Dumfries and Galloway are quiet, the exceptions are the A75, A76 and A77. If there is a road cycling paradise, this is the place; there's some pretty good mountain biking too. One cloud on the horizon is that this is a high rainfall area. It is my impression though that there aren't many more wet days; but when it rains, it really rains.

The Mull of Galloway, Scotland's own Land's End, is the starting point for our long distance route, The Southern Scotland Coast to Coast. This very roughly follows the route of the Southern Upland Way walking route, but ends at Holy Island in Northumberland, instead of Cockburnspath. If you like a challenge perhaps this 249 mile long route is for you. You can do it all on roads, or take in several mountain bike routes along the way if you prefer. If not there is still a host of shorter on-road and off-road routes to follow, all in fine varied scenery.

Rhinns of Galloway

(Southern Scotland Coast to Coast)

The Rhinns of Galloway is the peninsula at the extreme south-west of Scotland. The very tip is the Mull of Galloway. This is an area of unspoiled beaches and lush gardens, road traffic will be light even on main roads. It is the starting point for our coast to coast route: Mull of Galloway to Holy Island. There is also a day ride to Portpatrick, starting from Stranraer.

Mull of Galloway to Glenluce (25 miles)

Start at the mighty cliffs of the Mull of Galloway, nesting site for thousands of sea-birds. The first part of the route is on a hilly minor road which becomes the B7041. This turns right for Drummore, but you should continue straight on, using the B7065 to head for Port Logan.

An interesting place to visit at the north end of Port Logan Bay is the Logan Fish Pond. Unlike most, which only have goldfish, this one is populated by cod. They are so tame that they come to be fed by hand. The pond, which is 30 feet deep, was completed in 1800 as a fresh fish larder for Logan House. A mile north of the Logan Fish Pond, is the Logan Botanic Garden. This has a tea room and lots of tree ferns which flourish in the mild climate. Admission: garden & tea room £2.

Continue north on the B7065. Two miles after Port Logan, near the east coast, this road ends; turn left on to the A716. This is flatter and reasonably quiet; it runs past sand and shingle beaches for four miles to Sandhead, giving good views of Luce Bay. Here either continue north-east to Glenluce on the B7084 (coast to coast), or if you like, turn left to the B7042 to join the circular route described below. If going to Glenluce, turn off the busy A75 after half a mile to go via Glenluce Abbey (see map).

Stranraer - Portpatrick - Stranraer (32 miles circular)

Stranraer is the ferry terminal for Ireland. It's also a busy town with every facility, including a tourist office (01776-702595).

Leave the town, travelling south on the A77. Ignore two left turns for the Industrial Estate, but once you are clear of the town take the first left to a minor road by a large triangle of grass. This road turns sharply north, reversing direction, but soon turns south again. Continue south-east for just over a mile, then turn left at a T junction with a give way sign. After a further half mile take the first right on to a narrow road with passing places. Cross the B7077 on a staggered junction, signed West Freugh, then after just over a mile turn right at a T junction towards Stoneykirk (no sign).

In Stoneykirk bear left through the village to North Milmain, then cross the A716 at the junction to the south of the village. This minor road joins the B7042, it is signposted right for Portpatrick; ignore this, follow the sign for Sandhead, but at the next junction turn right off the B7042 just before a sharp left bend, towards Cairngarroch.

In Cairngarroch turn right at the crossroads signed Portpatrick. This road winds high above the shore towards Portpatrick giving fine views. Keep left for three miles, until you see a sign: Knockinaam Lodge. Continue straight on here, descending to cross a burn, then continue on to Portpatrick.

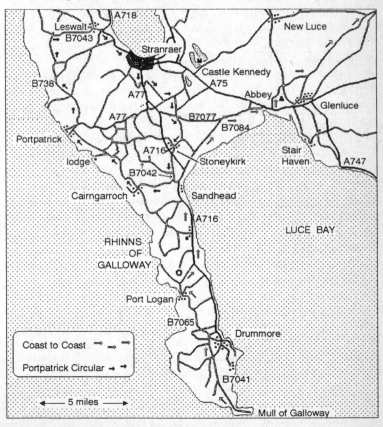

Portpatrick is a lovely little village with an excellent pub. Leave Portpatrick on the A77 but turn left on to the B738, signed Leswalt (A764 on some maps). Continue north on the B738 for six miles, following signs for Leswalt, turn right on to the B7043. In Leswalt follow signs for Stranraer. The last two miles to Stranraer are on the A718.

Newton Stewart to Glenluce

An attractive circular route with good views of the forests, hills and coastline of Galloway. Total distance 47 miles. This also forms part of the Southern Scotland Coast to Coast route, with a choice of going by Loch Ronald or Spittal.

Newton Stewart to
Glenluce (20 miles)

Start in Newton Stewart, in the main street, by the bridge over the River Cree. Bike north upstream, river on your right, using the A714 until you are clear of the town. After two miles turn sharp left on to the B7027 by a church. The road climbs steadily entering trees. After this there is a fast downhill, then a flatter section; you pass two small lochs on the left.

Turn left over a small stone bridge, and cross the River Bladnoch on a minor road. Riding through forest you climb gently for five miles, keep straight on at the junction with the phone box. When the ascent is over there is a caravan park opposite some lochs. A mile after this, ignore the right turn for New Luce. Just after this junction you might like to ride down a bumpy lane to the hotel on the right which does morning coffee, bar meals, etc. Otherwise keep on south-west, gathering speed as the road starts to drop towards the coast.

This road runs straight into the village of Glenluce, however if you intend to visit Glenluce Abbey you need to turn right a mile before the town by some farm buildings. This is another fast descent, the Abbey is straight ahead at the foot of the hill. Glenluce Abbey is a ruin, but parts are still intact, the fine vaulted chapter house is of architectural interest. The abbey was founded in 1192 by the Cistercian Order.

Also of interest nearby, although at the time of visiting it was not yet open, is the Castle of Park. This is a tall imposing castellated mansion house built in 1590. It is still complete and is just off the A75 west of Glenluce. As you cross the A75 on the route look right and you should see it.

Glenluce is an attractive village with a choice of places to eat and shops of various kinds; probably the best place to stop for lunch. If you want somewhere to picnic it's best to continue past Glenluce to the minor road by Luce Bay, stopping by the sea at Luce Sands just before you get to Stair Haven.

Glenluce to
Newton Stewart (27 miles)

After Glenluce take care crossing the A75 and continue south on a minor road by the sea. Turn left up a steep hill at Stair Haven and after the hill, turn first right, to eventually join the A747 two miles further south. Roll along, sea on your right for three miles then turn left on to the B7005. This road climbs through trees at first, then levels off in open country.

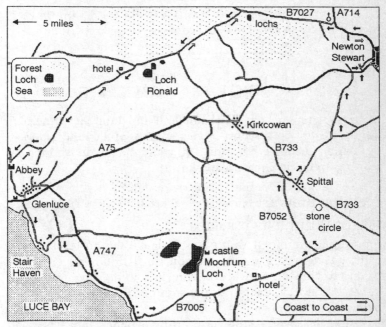

If you have plenty of time, you might like to make a two mile diversion north at the first left turn, to look at the Old Place of Mochrum. Also known as Drumwalt Castle, this is a 15th and 16th century building with picturesque towers. The building itself is not open to the public.

Continuing along the B7005 you have a gentle downhill

run though mixed woodland. If you need a cup of tea the Corsemaizie House Hotel can provide one; it's quite grand with peacocks on the lawn, but they make you welcome.

The next turn you need to make is a left on to the B7052 to travel north. Three miles after this, turn right towards Spittal on the B733, then half a mile later, in Spittal, turn left to a minor road to head towards Newton Stewart.

There is a Bronze Age stone circle one mile south-east of Spittal, just off the B733 (see map). This consists of 19 boulders surrounding a low mound.

The last section is in lovely rolling country with the hills of Cairnsmore of Fleet forming a scenic backdrop. Turn left at the fork in the road after Spittal (see map); shortly after you will meet the A75 where you turn right. A short section on the A75 is unavoidable, but take the first left off it then immediately turn right, using a back road into the town to avoid the A75 roundabout. You arrive back at your starting point near the tourist information office.

Newton Stewart Tourist Information: 01671-402431. Minnigaff Youth Hostel: 01671-402211.

Isle of Whithorn

An easy circular route starting and finishing at Minnigaff Youth Hostel or Newton Stewart. Lots of historic interest. Maximum distance 52 miles, it could be made shorter by starting and finishing at Wigtown.

Newton Stewart to
Isle of Whithorn (24 miles)

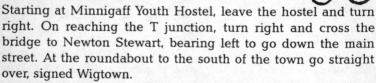

Starting at Minnigaff Youth Hostel, leave the hostel and turn right. On reaching the T junction, turn right and cross the bridge to Newton Stewart, bearing left to go down the main street. At the roundabout to the south of the town go straight over, signed Wigtown.

After just over a mile turn left by a phone box. The road sweeps to the east with views of the Cree estuary. Just before Wigtown bear left. After half a mile there is a lay-by, with a path to the Martyr's Stake.

This is a monument to Margaret McLaughlin and Margaret Wilson (aged 18), who were drowned at the stake here by the incoming tide for refusing to renounce their religion. The graves of other Covenanters can be seen in the churchyard just above, together with a sad piece of poetry reflecting on human cruelty done in the name of religion.

After this continue up into the town square. Leave the town by turning left on to a little lane which is in fact the A714, signed Whithorn. The tea room at this junction does good toasted teacakes.

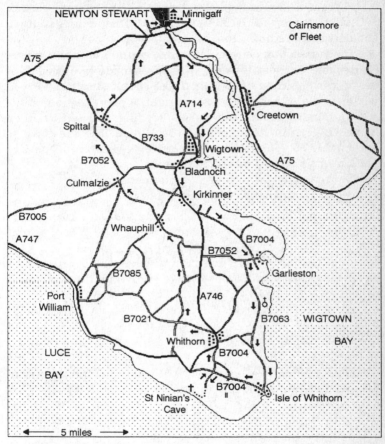

The road winds down to the River Bladnoch, turn left by the distillery and cross the river. Climb the hill and bear left on to the A746 (Whithorn). After Kirkinner, bear left again on to the B7004. Roll along this straight section to the next T junction and turn right at a bridge. Left at the next turning and after a mile bear left on to the B7063 (Isle of Whithorn).

A mile on, just beyond Cruggleton Farm, is a little church in a field, surrounded by a castellated wall. The congregation is long gone but the church is there still, mute testament to a more religious age. Norman (12th century) it was renovated in the 19th. A stout little building, slits for windows, but beautiful decorative ironwork on the doors. There are stile stones in the wall which children would enjoy. Key at Cruggleton Farm, 300m north.

After this continue along the B7063, keeping left by the sea, to the Isle of Whithorn. This delightful little village, with its harbour full of boats, is also the site of St Ninian's Chapel. St Ninian brought Christianity to Scotland in the fifth century. The chapel is signposted, it marks where earlier tourists (pilgrims) gave thanks for their safe arrival. You might prefer to eat first though, the Steam Packet Inn does good food at reasonable prices, there is a shop if you prefer to picnic.

Isle of Whithorn - Whithorn - Newton Stewart (28 miles)

The next attraction is St Ninian's Cave. This is reached by leaving the Isle of Whithorn on the B7004. Don't turn right to Whithorn, but continue beyond this junction for a further mile and turn left (signposted). A short run down by beech trees and you are directed down a leafy lane to the beach.

It doesn't look much, but pilgrims have walked down here for fifteen centuries to visit the cave. Suddenly there is a wild pebble beach and you understand why St Ninian liked coming here. The crosses that were in the cave are now at Whithorn, but there are other recent crosses made out of driftwood. Perhaps we're not completely soulless nowadays after all.

After leaving the cave retrace your way, go straight over at the junction you previously turned left at, then left at the next junction and on to the B7004; this takes you to Whithorn. Whithorn has a number of attractions, first is the Whithorn dig, and its visitor centre and museum.

Being taken round the dig is worth while. The guides are excellent and the tour is full of human interest about the doings and ailments of these people who lived here so long ago. The tour will take at least an hour. The combined ticket covering tour, visitor centre and museum is best value. Also worth looking at is the church and graveyard which is free.

To leave Whithorn take the first left at the north edge of the village, immediately after the police station, on to the B7021. After two miles turn right at the cross-roads at Craig Cottage. After a further mile bear right, signed Wigtown.

16

Shortly after turn left, signed Whauphill. Next turn left on to the B7052. At Whauphill cross over the B7085 and continue along the B7052 to Culmalzie. Turn right here, and after a short distance left again. After just over three miles turn sharp right for Spittal, turning left at Spittal itself on to a minor road going north-east.

After that it's two more miles then another left turn, with the hill of Barraer Fell on the left. At the A75 turn right. After a short distance avoid cycling on this main road by turning left then immediately right for a back road to Newton Stewart. Minnigaff Hostel: 01671-402211. Tourist Info: 01671-402431.

Glen Trool to Clatteringshaws

A mountain bike route, but with some road sections to create a circular route. The route is also part of the Southern Scotland Coast to Coast and offers the alternatives of travelling on forest tracks via Loch Trool, or using the A712 which is reasonably quiet. It will be necessary to walk a little if you go by Loch Trool (see text).

The description assumes starting at Newton Stewart, but an alternative starting point is Clatteringshaws Forest Wildlife Centre. This has a tea room and is open 10am to 5pm, Easter to end of September. Refer to maps on pages 18, 20 and 23.

Newton Stewart to
Glen Trool (12 miles)

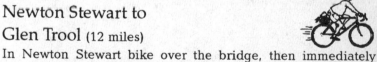

In Newton Stewart bike over the bridge, then immediately turn left into Minnigaff. Cycle past the youth hostel and turn left (north). The road winds up past a church, and along the east bank of the River Cree through mixed woodland and farmland. After three miles it passes the Wood of Cree Nature Reserve (Royal Society for the Protection of Birds).

Continue along on the public road, crossing the Water of Trool; half a mile after this turn right at a T junction. Should you need to eat at this point you could leave the route, turning left then right to go to the hotel which is marked on the map.

Otherwise continue north-east for two miles and cross the Water of Minnoch; turn right here by the Forest Visitor Centre and tea room. There is an information board giving other mountain bike routes here, these are also described in this book (page 19). About two miles after the visitor centre, just before Loch Trool, there is a right turn leading to the very attractive Forestry Commission camp site, this also has a shop.

Glen Trool to Clatteringshaws Loch (15 miles)

Continue up Glen Trool climbing steeply, and keep straight on at the end of the road. A short walk to the top of the hill on your right here reveals the Bruce's Stone, commemorating Robert the Bruce's first victory on the road to Scottish independence. It's worth climbing up there even if you are not a Scottish patriot, because the view is tremendous; it also enables you to see the next part of the route.

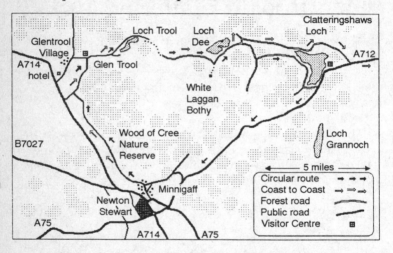

At the end of the public road continue along the stoney track which plunges steeply. Cross a little bridge near a waterfall. The track briefly climbs to a gate, then drops steeply again to loch level, crossing two cattle grids. Go over a bridge and enter oak woods.

Shortly after this you will cross a third cattle grid, and then see an abandoned china sink on your right. Look for an inconspicuous green waymark post. Leave the track here and bike or walk towards the stream on your right (Glenhead Burn). If you encounter a cottage and some corrugated iron outbuildings you have gone too far.

On reaching the burn go upstream towards the new footbridge. Cross the burn then turn left, continuing upstream. There is a sign here: *Cyclists dismount,* you should do this. Cross two stiles then enter plantation forest on duckboards. Continue walking over the mossy pine-needle carpet until you reach the forest road where you turn left.

Go uphill to emerge from the forest by a gate. The surface is reasonable becoming better. Continue climbing to a concrete bridge, after which there is a fast descent, with views over Loch Dee towards the Silver Flowe. At the end of the descent you enter a more open forest area, cross White Laggan Burn (the bothy is a little way upstream on a footpath). Climb again to an angler's hut.

After this there is another fast descent. At the end of this do not turn left to cross the River Dee, but bear right, to keep on the south side of the river. *If you are not returning to Newton Stewart, but are continuing east on the Coast to Coast, cross the river and turn right (see map page 23).*

Descend on the south side of the river to a locked steel gate. Cross by the stile. Shortly after this you will be on a surfaced forest road; follow this for five miles to reach the A712. Clatteringshaws Visitor Centre and Tea Room is a left turn. Turn right to return to Newton Stewart (12 miles, lots of descent).

Glen Trool Forest Trails

The Forestry Commission has created four mountain bike routes in Glen Trool, all starting from Glen Trool Visitor Centre. Please bear in mind that forestry operations may mean that some sections are occasionally closed.

There is a tea room in the visitor centre, and a notice board describing the trails on the other side of the road. There is an attractive camp site with a shop, further up the glen, and a hotel serving bar food just south of Glentrool Village.

Visitors should not be under the illusion that they are biking in a natural forest. Scotland's natural forest started disappearing about AD800 and was mostly gone by the end of the 18th century. The final destruction was caused by the demand for timber during two world wars.

The Forestry Commission has its roots in the fact that much timber had to be convoyed across the Atlantic during the First World War. It was established in 1919 with the aim of making Britain more self-sufficient in timber. The uncharitable describe its operations as tree farming, the quick growing sitka spruce is the most common tree.

Fortunately nowadays there is more emphasis on the recreational use of forest, and a wider variety of trees is being planted, with more consideration being given to landscaping.

Too often we only appreciate what we once had after we have lost it. Perhaps one day we will have our ancient woodlands back.

Minniwick Route -

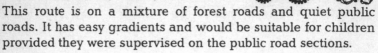

Red Markers (5 miles)

This route is on a mixture of forest roads and quiet public roads. It has easy gradients and would be suitable for children provided they were supervised on the public road sections.

Other Routes

The Balunton Hill Route is 7 miles long and has blue markers.

The Palgowan Route is 8 miles and has green markers.

The Borgan Route is 10 miles and has purple markers.

All of these routes are graded moderate by the Forestry Commision. This means any steep hills will be quite short, and that the route is on forest roads. Probably suitable for older children.

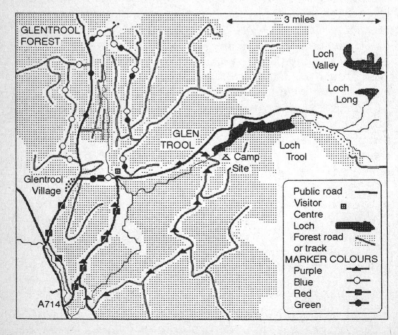

Kirroughtree Forest

This is one of the oldest forests in south-west Scotland, planting began in 1921. There are four marked mountain bike routes. There is more variety than in most plantation forest, and the routes offer views of the hills of Cairnsmore of Fleet and Bargally Glen. Starting point Kirroughtree Visitor Centre, off the A75, this has a tea room.

Kirroughtree Routes

Palnure Burn, 4 miles, an easy route all on quiet public roads: blue markers.

Larg Hill, moderately easy, 7 miles, follow green markers.

Dallash, moderately easy, 10 miles, purple markers.

Old Edinburgh Route, 18 miles, red markers, part on public roads.

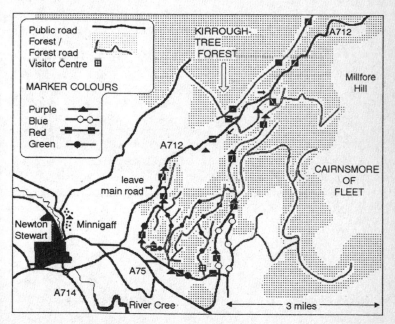

The routes shown on the north of the map connect to other routes in Clatteringshaws, see page 22.

Clatteringshaws Trails

The routes here have Clatteringshaws Loch as their focal point, and offer fine views of the loch and the Galloway hills. Near to the loch and the A712 is Clatteringshaws Forest Wildlife Centre. This has a tea room, and a set of high-quality displays illustrating local wildlife. This area is well known for wild goats, and red deer are also common.

One of the forest routes, The Raiders Road, is promoted as a forest drive. The Forestry Commission leaflet also suggests using this as a bike route. For me one of the main attractions of off-road biking is that there are no cars, so this would not be top of my list. However there is a wide choice of other routes, so this is not really a problem.

Clatteringshaws Loch
Route (14 miles)

Graded easy, and signed with green markers, this goes round the loch and climbs a little way up the River Dee. Part of the route is also the Southern Scotland Coast to Coast. Two miles of it are on the A712. Like many class A roads in Dumfries and Galloway, this is not particularly busy.

Craignell Hill
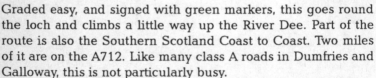
Route (15 miles)

Graded moderate, and signed with purple markers this goes round Craignell Hill (see map) and involves some climb. About half of the route is on a tarmac surface and this includes three miles on the A712.

Deer Range
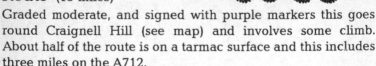
Route (9 miles)

This is graded demanding, and is signed with blue markers. Probably best done anticlockwise as this ensures that the steepest part is a downhill. Again the return is on the A712.

Benniguinea Hill
Route (4 miles)

This is just north of Raiders Road and has red markers. A stiff climb to the top and a very quick descent - great view!

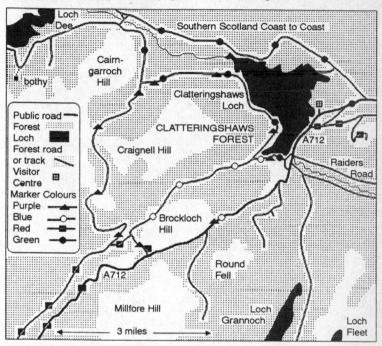

Carrick Forest

This last mountain biking route in Galloway Forest Park is one of the best. It runs from the village of Barr in Ayrshire and reaches Dumfries and Galloway at Loch Doon. The Banks and Braes o' Bonny Doon are still as lovely as when Robert Burns sang of them, though no doubt now they are a little changed. While the route finishes at Loch Doon, the nearest river most of the time is in fact the River Stinchar.

The waymarked route is not circular, so if you have to return to a car you may choose to bike it in both directions. Other alternatives are to join or leave the route at the Straiton -Bargrennan road, or the Crosshill-Bargrennan road (Nick o' the Balloch). Two circular routes are shown on the map, one returning to Barr using the minor road via the River Stinchar which is very pleasant. The other suggested circular route uses the hilly Nick o' the Balloch road.

Barr to Loch Doon (20 miles)

Start in the village of Barr, which is five miles east of Girvan. In the village, bike east away from the river, the forest entry is a left turn after half a mile. The route is waymarked with red marker posts and is comparatively easy to follow.

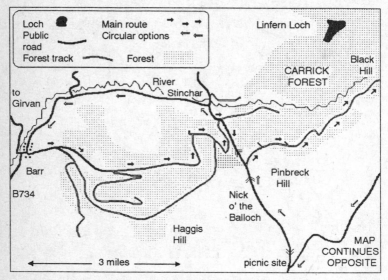

The first two miles are a steady climb to the top of Balloch Hill, after which there is a fast descent, crossing Balloch Burn at the bottom. After crossing the burn there is a sharp left bend to turn north.

After biking north for half a mile you have the option of returning on the River Stinchar road. If you wish to do this, turn left then left again, crossing the Balloch Burn, but keeping on the south bank of the river. Circular distance, 11 miles.

To continue on the main route, bear right to follow the route as it doubles back on itself, climbing steeply south on the Nick o' the Balloch road. After a mile, as you leave the forest, turn sharp left to go round Pinbreck Hill on a forest road. If you meet a bridge over the burn (Witches Bridge) you have gone too far.

The route follows the contour along the edge of the hill giving fine views, the river far below. After passing Black Hill it crosses the Straiton-Bargrennan road, before meeting Loch Bradan.

Here you have the option again of making a circular route using the public road. Turn south, ignoring the left turn at Stinchar Bridge, to continue south for five miles, turning north again to the Nick o' the Balloch road near a picnic site. This option involves a considerable climb in either direction.

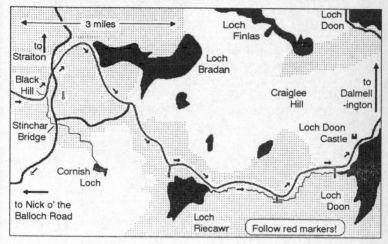

To continue to Loch Doon follow the waymarked route south-east, past Loch Bradan, Loch Riecawr and Carrick Lane (river). The route ends at Loch Doon Castle. The minor road north of this is open to motor traffic but has some fine views.

Dalbeattie Forest

Dalbeattie Forest lies on the hills to the south of the town of Dalbeattie. It is close to the Solway Firth and the attractive coastal villages of Rockcliffe and Kippford. Routes start from the Richorn car park at the north-west corner of the forest, but they can also be joined from the town of Dalbeattie, or from Barnbarroch.

The routes form a figure of eight through the forest, and offer fine views of the pleasant countryside and the Solway coast. Dalbeattie itself is of rather austere appearance, being built of granite, quarried locally. It was this same granite that the town's fortune was built on, and it was used to build London's embankment.

Moyle Hill

Route (7 miles)

This is graded easy by the Forestry Commission. Suitable for younger children, and marked with green markers.

Ironhash Hill

Route (11 miles)

Graded as moderate this is a little longer and more difficult with some short steeper sections; purple markers.

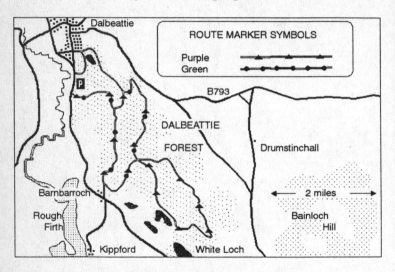

Forest of Ae

The Forest of Ae is north of Dumfries, just off the A701. The routes all begin just north of the village of Ae, and run alongside the Water of Ae, before entering the forest. Glen Ae, at the start of the routes, has attractive picnic spots. There is a historic collection of forest ploughs nearby.

The forest is bisected by a public road, which runs north-south. The terrain to the east of this tends to have steeper hills. The trees are mainly coniferous, with sitka spruce being the most common. There are three waymarked routes, though you need not restrict youself to these. It is however very easy to get lost in a forest of this type!

Windy Hill

Route (10 miles)

Graded easy, this should be suitable for children. It is marked with green markers. The route is mainly on forest roads with gentle gradients.

Greenhill & Whaup
Knowe Route (7.5 miles)

Upper Ae
Route (15 miles)

Both of these routes are graded moderate. The Greenhill and Whaup Knowe Route is signposted with purple markers, and the Upper Ae route with red markers.

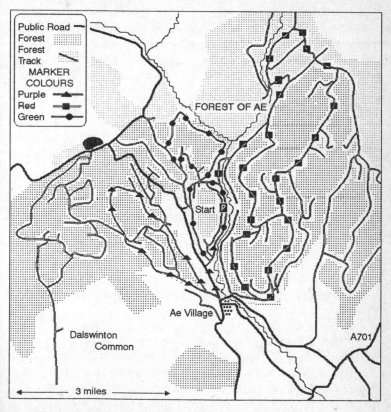

Drumlanrig Castle - Lochinvar

This is a lovely area, with beautiful unspoilt country roads. This bike route is a scenic 55 mile circular route starting from Drumlanrig Castle. If this seems a bit far for you it would be easy to shorten it (see map).

Drumlanrig Castle is intimately connected with the bicycle. There is a cycle museum in an old stable in the castle courtyard; this includes a reproduction of the first pedal driven bicycle, invented by Kirkpatrick MacMillan at nearby Keir Mill, about 150 years ago. The Cyclists Touring Club celebrates this every year, with a series of bike rides based on Drumlanrig Castle. This is usually towards the end of May, and during this time the castle grounds are studded with small tents.

Drumlanrig Castle
to Lochinvar (22 miles)

Approach the castle by the main driveway. Turn right directly in front of the castle, passing a woodland walks map board. Cycle through the woods (watch out for the road humps), passing a pond. At the public road turn left, following a small sign: Penpont. Bear left at the next two junctions, following signs for Penpont.

In Penpont (Volunteer Arms, food shop), turn right on to the A702, sign Moniaive. Ignore the first turn to the right for Scaur Water, but take the second right, signed Tynron. There is a gentle climb then a descent into Tynron.

In Tynron go past the church and over the bridge. Turn right in front of the war memorial, then bear left at the next junction (ignore the turn for Shinnel Glen). There is a steep climb, lovely views, then an even steeper descent to Moniaive.

In Moniaive (two hotels, three shops), cross the bridge turning right, then follow the sign for Carsphairn B729, passing in front of a house with a clock tower. There is a flat section past woods and farms, then a steady climb through a forest.

At the top of the hill the forest ends, and you cross a cattle grid. Turn left to a minor road, signed Fingland (farm). If you see a sign for Stewartry council, you have missed the turning. There is a short climb followed by a gentle descent, with fine views westward towards the massive hill of Corserine.

Turn left at the next junction, signed Lochinvar. Just

before you reach the loch at Lochinvar you pass the ruin of a tiny schoolhouse.

Lochinvar to Drumlanrig Castle via Dunscore (33 miles)

Continue south from Lochinvar and turn right on to the A702, signed St John's Town of Dalry. After a mile, at the bottom of a hill, turn left on to the B7075, signed Balmaclellan. In just over a mile turn left again, signed Balmaclellan. There is a clog and shoe workshop here, and a village shop.

In Balmaclellan, turn left, signed Crocketford & Dumfries. Turn left at the A712 by the war memorial (no sign). Continue

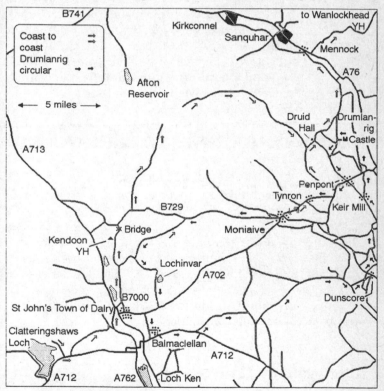

along the A712 for just over two miles, then turn left on to a minor road, at a sign: 'Unfenced road, beware of animals'. If you pass Bread & Beer Cottage you've missed it.

Pass through farmland then forest, right at the next T junction (no sign), left at the next junction over a bridge, signed Dunscore. Keep straight on, ignoring all side turnings for six miles. Pass Glaisters Forest, lots of dry stane dykes, a crossroads with a signpost Dunscore 2 (straight over). Turn left at the next T junction, passing a phone box, signed Dunscore.

Cross a bridge, bear left, then left again at a Holistic Centre cottage. If you want to go to Dunscore itself (village shop, real ale in the George Hotel), bear right at this cottage and cycle towards a church with a tower.

Straight across the B729, signed Low Kirkbridge Farm B&B and KM (bike sign). Go past a pond and a ruined tower, turn sharp left at a triangular patch of grass, climb a hill then turn right at a painted stone cottage.

After this there is a long descent with a stunning view, but keep on watching the road. Turn left opposite a field gate (no sign), then turn right in Keir Mill by a phone box (KM sign). Cross a steel bridge, and bike on to join the A702 at Burnhead.

Turn left on to the A702 (KM sign points right), then shortly after, right down the side of a white cottage (30mph sign). Keep straight on to return to Drumlanrig Castle, bearing left at the castle opening times notice board.

Clatteringshaws to Mennock

(Part of Coast to Coast)

This section of the Southern Scotland Coast to Coast again offers you the choice of a route with an off-road section, or a completely on-roads route. The road route is in part the same as the previous route (Drumlanrig Circular), but is in the opposite direction. The other route runs close to the Southern Upland Way walking route for much of the time, and even follows it occasionally. The off-road section is quite short, just over a mile; anyone on a touring machine would definitely have to push their bike. Map on page 29.

Clatteringshaws Loch to High Bridge of Ken (12 miles)

If you have come round the east side of Clatteringshaws Loch, you will emerge on to the A712 by the sign for Craigenbay. If you are travelling on the public road, look out for this just east of the loch. Turn left up a minor road 400m east of the Craigenbay sign. There is no sign, but the road is opposite a sign 'The Queen's Way'.

There is a short climb, then a long switchback descent. Turn right at the T junction at the bottom, opposite a red post box. When you meet the A762 turn left, sign Ayr. Cross the river, then after a mile, by the power station, turn right, signed Castle Douglas/Crocketford. Immediately after this, after the bridge, turn left up a minor road, signed Milton Park Hotel. Climb through mature trees, there's a view of Earlstoun Loch on the left. Turn left on to the B7000 at a T junction.

Those wishing to avoid the off-road section should turn right two miles after this, sign Lochinvar. Those wanting to include the off-road keep straight on (sign Moniaive) to the High Bridge of Ken, which incidentally isn't particularly high but is quite narrow.

Kendoon Youth Hostel (no phone, address: Dalry, Castle Douglas, DG7 3UD) is roughly halfway between the High Bridge of Ken and the Lochinvar turn off. St John's Town of Dalry is quite near of course. This is an attractive village with B&Bs, hotels and tea rooms.

High Bridge of Ken
to Druid Hall
(off-road route)

(20 miles cycling,
1.2 miles walking)

Continue north from the bridge to a T junction and turn right, signed B729 Moniaive. Continue along for a little over a mile then turn left, signed Holm of Dalquhairn. This is a lovely remote road. After a while the V of the pass becomes visible ahead, and the road becomes bumpy, with grass in the middle; continue on to the end.

Where the tarmac runs out at the end there is a stone bridge, and 400m ahead of this is a white cottage. Follow the dirt track for 100m after the bridge, then fork right on to a faint grassy path.

Cross a fence on a stile and continue up between the dyke and the burn. When the dyke ends turn left through an opening then, keeping a fence on your right, continue up the hill and enter the forest. Follow the path through the forest and turn left when you meet a forest road.

Westbound (opposite direction): When the tarmac road ends, go along a dirt road for 400m to a vehicle turning space. Cross a stile, over a concrete bridge. 300m after this, turn right off the dirt road to a grassy footpath, signed Lorg. Don't cross a second concrete bridge; don't turn right up a hill on a dirt road.

East of the off-road section, what road there is is just a narrow strip of tarmac with no passing places. If two cars met here, one might have to reverse for a long way. The surface is quite good though, and it's mostly downhill. There are a couple of gates to open and shut, then it's more like a normal road.

After ten miles you eventually come to a road junction with a triangular patch of grass in the middle, and a cul-de-sac sign referring to where you've just come from. This is where the on-road and off-road routes meet again. Bear left, Druid Hall is at the next junction.

High Bridge of Ken
to Druid Hall
(road route)

(24 miles)

In fact this section really starts at the junction, signposted Lochinvar, three miles south of the High Bridge of Ken. Follow the sign for Lochinvar, but at the next junction, where a sign says Lochinvar, go the opposite way, turning left to go over a cattle grid.

You will probably encounter lots of cattle on this next section, so the debris on the road is likely to be worse than mere mud; another good reason for having mudguards or fenders on your bike. After this you pass over another cattle grid and it's sheep again, at least they are a bit more willing to get out of your way.

At the next junction turn right on to the B729, crossing another cattle grid and entering a forest. There is a descent, then a flat section, and you are in Moniaive.

Straight on in Moniaive, passing in front of the Craigdarroch Arms Hotel (afternoon teas), signed Thornhill; immediately after turn left, signed Tynron. Go up a very steep hill, then steeply down the other side. Ignore the sign for Shinnel Glen, turn left over the bridge to Tynron, up a gentle hill, and down again to the A702.

Turn left on to the A702, signed Penpont 1; but before Penpont turn left up a minor road, signed Scaur Water. Bike up this lovely little winding road for four miles, turn right over a bridge, and climb to a T junction with a little triangle of grass in the middle, and a cul-de-sac sign. This is where the off-road and on-road routes merge. Turn right, Druid Hall is at the next junction.

Druid Hall to
Mennock (10 miles)

Continue straight on at the Druid Hall junction. You ride through some woods, then there is a panoramic view towards the Lowther Hills. Keep straight on again at the next junction, then descend to a T junction with a red phone box and turn left (no sign).

Now riding north, keep straight on at Burnsands (no sign). A mile after this the road runs up the west bank of the River Nith with the A76 on the other side. You continue up on the quiet minor road. Do not cross over to the A76 at a stone bridge near a bungalow with a slate roof, stay on the west bank until you reach the bridge just beyond Mennock. This can be identified by a bus shelter on the A76 side. Turn right on to the A76 and enter Mennock (Mennock Lodge Hotel & Restaurant).

Mennock to Biggar

(Part of Coast to Coast)

This part of the Southern Scotland Coast to Coast passes through the Lowther Hills, so it involves a serious climb. The high parts of the route are quite bleak and exposed, though they are likely to be pleasant in the summer with open views.

Along the way you pass through Wanlockhead, Scotland's highest village. Wanlockhead was at one time a lead mining area, and there is a mining museum in the village. You can go down the mine, or if that seems a little claustrophobic, try your hand at gold panning in a nearby burn.

There is also an open air museum, with beam engines; a smelt mill, and period furnished cottages dating from 1740 and 1890. There is a youth hostel in the village (01659-74252), and a number of other places to stay and eat. Just beyond Wanlockhead is Leadhills, gold and lead were mined here from Roman times, and gold from this area is incorporated in the Crown of Scotland.

After the Lowther Hills the route passes under the M74 to Crawford and Abington, using minor roads to the east of the motorway. Between Abington and Symington, it is necessary to cycle on the A73 for six miles, the only alternative being the A702 which is very busy.

Mennock to
Leadhills (9 miles)

Just south of Mennock, turn left on to the B797, signed Wanlockhead/Leadhills/Mining Museum. There is a gentle start, then a long well-graded climb of nearly 300m. The bottom section is quite pretty, with the river tumbling through woodland, but as you climb the terrain becomes bleaker. There is a descent into Wanlockhead (hostel 01659-74252), then a climb and a descent to Leadhills (tea room in square).

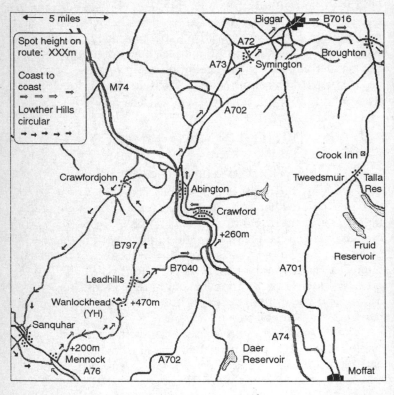

Leadhills to
Biggar (24 miles)

In Leadhills turn right on to the B7040 Elvanfoot Road. This is a fast downhill, but watch out for rocks at the edge of the road. There is a five mile descent to Elvanfoot, where you turn left on to the A702, signed Abington. The motorway will be visible and audible by now. At a roundabout just before it, take the first exit and ride underneath the motorway then turn left, signed Crawford/Abington/A702.

Take the next right, signed Crawford. Crawford has several transport cafes, hotels doing bar food, shops, etc; mostly serving motorway customers. Ride through Crawford, and at the north end of the main street, take a right turn by a stone pillar, signed Camps Reservoir. Cross the River Clyde, then immediately turn left. This single track road goes over then under the railway, then ends near Abington. When you come to a T junction (sign 13' 6" one mile), turn left to cross the Clyde again and enter Abington.

Turn right at the police station (shop nearby), and leave the town following the sign for A702/Edinburgh. This is quiet initially, but it becomes busy when traffic from the motorway joins it at a roundabout. There is a tourist information office at the service station here: 01864-502436.

You need to take the last exit on the roundabout, passing to the right of the service station. Avoid cycling through the roundabout by filtering on to the right-hand side pavement just before it, then using the pedestrian crossing to regain the left-hand side of the A702. After a mile, take the left fork, signed Lanark/A73. Keep on the A73 for six miles until you see a sign for Symington.

Turn right at the sign for Symington, pass under the railway and along a lane with hedges either side. Turn right at a T junction, by number 66 Kirk Bauk, bear left at a grassy patch with children's swings. Turn left in front of a 'Private Road' sign, right at the next junction, then right on to the A72 near a cottage (no sign). After a mile on the A72 you cross the River Clyde. Turn left at the crossroads here, then first right to enter Biggar on a back road. There are plenty of eating establishments in Biggar; tourist information 01899-21066.

Lowther Hills Circular

This is a circular route of 32 miles, visiting the villages of Wanlockhead, Leadhills, and Sanquhar. The section between Mennock and Leadhills is used on the Coast to Coast, but the rest is different. The route is hilly, there are some fast downhills with fine open views. There is more information on Wanlockhead and Leadhills in the previous route. Being circular you can start this route at any point, but the description starts at Mennock. Map on page 34.

Mennock to
Crawfordjohn (15 miles)

Just south of Mennock, turn left on to the B797, signed Wanlockhead/Leadhills/Mining Museum. There is a gentle start, then a long well-graded climb of nearly 300m. The bottom section is quite pleasing, with the river tumbling through woodland, but as you climb the terrain becomes bleaker. There is a final gentle descent into Wanlockhead (youth hostel 01659-74252), then a gentler climb and a descent to Leadhills (tea room in square).

In Leadhills bear left, keeping on the B797. After nearly three miles, bear left to a minor road, signed Crawfordjohn. There is a short climb, then a long descent with open views. Cross the river to Crawfordjohn, then turn left, signed Sanquhar.

Crawfordjohn - Sanquhar
-Mennock (17 miles)

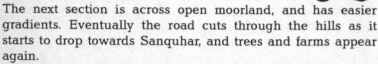

The next section is across open moorland, and has easier gradients. Eventually the road cuts through the hills as it starts to drop towards Sanquhar, and trees and farms appear again.

Just before Sanquhar you pass under a stone arch railway bridge. Immediately after this, turn left off the road and cross Crawick Water on a metal footbridge. Turn right after this, pass behind a housing estate, and continue straight on towards the church ahead of you. Cross the main road and follow the sign for tourist information, following the one way system past Burns Lodge. Turn left on to Queens Road opposite a pond; pass bungalows, then a park on the left. Turn left over the bridge to cross the River Nith.

Sanquhar is notable for having the oldest post office in Britain. It has been functioning since 1763. The town hall is an interesting building with a clock tower. The Tolbooth dates from 1735 and was designed by William Adam, part of it is now a museum. There is a tourist office (01659-50185).

After crossing the River Nith, immediately turn left at a post box, to travel downstream on the west bank of the river. The road runs past woods and farms, when you meet another bridge over the river, turn left to cross it and then turn right to enter Mennock.

THE BORDERS

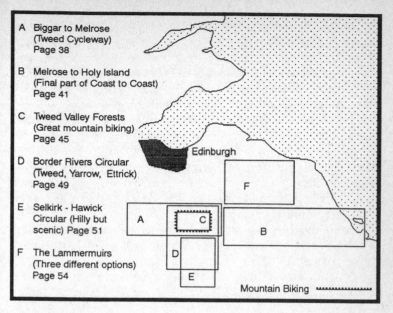

A Biggar to Melrose
   (Tweed Cycleway)
   Page 38

B Melrose to Holy Island
   (Final part of Coast to Coast)
   Page 41

C Tweed Valley Forests
   (Great mountain biking)
   Page 45

D Border Rivers Circular
   (Tweed, Yarrow, Ettrick)
   Page 49

E Selkirk - Hawick
   Circular (Hilly but
   scenic) Page 51

F The Lammermuirs
   (Three different options)
   Page 54

Edinburgh

Mountain Biking ▪▪▪▪▪▪▪▪▪▪▪▪▪▪

Once the scene of fierce conflict, the Borders still has a culture that is distinctively its own. This is most apparent during the annual Common Riding, where the Borderers ride on horseback to preserve their boundaries. The one held at Selkirk dates from the Battle of Flodden in 1513. This is not a spectacle for tourists, but an annual event in which the whole community takes part.

As far as cycling is concerned, the Borders has an excellent network of minor roads, which offer quiet rides in lovely scenery. There are plenty of things to look at, including abbeys and great houses; and there is no lack of cosy pubs and tea rooms. The gradients are reasonably gentle in the river valleys, but crossing between them will involve a climb. Most of the class A roads are not particularly quiet, and should be avoided where possible. The Tweed valley forests have some excellent mountain biking, with panoramic views from the hilltops.

The last two sections of our Southern Scotland Coast to Coast are in the Borders. The first part, from Biggar to Melrose, follows the Tweed Cycleway. The second part, from Melrose to Holy Island, leaves the Tweed Cycleway at Kelso and dips into England for its last few miles to Holy Island. All of the other routes are circular, and there are plenty of ways to mix and match them to make them shorter or longer.

Biggar to Melrose

Part of the Coast to Coast & Tweed Cycleway

Because of its name, the Tweed Cycleway might give you the impression that it is a cycle path, but virtually all of the route is on public roads. As it turns out this is no problem, as minor roads in the Borders are very quiet. This route also forms part of our Southern Scotland Coast to Coast.

The Tweed Cycleway doesn't actually follow the River Tweed all the time. There are some lovely long sections by the river, mostly not too hilly and ideal for families. When the route climbs away from the river the hills are more serious. However there are some fast downhill runs, with splendid views of the hills and forests. The forests also offer some excellent mountain biking

Along the way you can visit the small towns of Peebles, Galashiels and Melrose. These former mill towns still have a distinctive culture dating from the turbulent times when this land was an area of dispute between England and Scotland. There are many places to visit and lots of pubs and tea rooms, ideal cycling country!

Biggar to Peebles

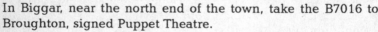

(20 miles, maps on pages 34 and 39)
In Biggar, near the north end of the town, take the B7016 to Broughton, signed Puppet Theatre.

In Broughton turn right on to the A701, signed Moffat. Immediately after, turn left on to Dreva Road. Broughton is famous for being associated with the author John Buchan, and for the real ale Greenmantle. This is brewed locally, and called after one of his novels. Visit the John Buchan Centre in the village if you have time. There is a village shop, and the Laurel Bank Tea Room is on the route.

The Dreva road climbs steadily, ignore the right turn for Rachan just beyond the top of the hill. On the descent you get a first view of the River Tweed, far below on the right. Turn left at the next junction on to the B712, signed Tweed Cycleway. There are bike route signs at many of the road junctions from now on, but don't rely on these only.

After three miles bear right, signed Lyne Station. When you come to a humped bridge, don't cross it, but turn right and go under another bridge, signed: 'Height 16 feet'. This becomes a track then a footpath. Cross the river on a

footbridge and go downstream, between a field and the river.
Watch out for low branches.

The footpath becomes a track. Turn right by a cottage on
to the public road. Climb up this, and at the next junction turn
left, signed Peebles. At the next junction turn right to cross the
Manor Water, signed Peebles via Cademuir. This is a scenic

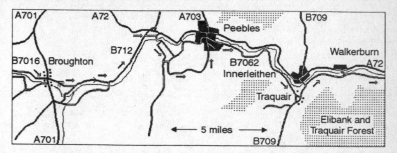

ride, passing Cademuir Hill on the left, and ending in
Peebles.

On entering Peebles turn right on to Springwood Road,
then left at the T junction on to Springhill Road. At the River
Tweed and the B7062, turn right to continue on the route, or
cross the bridge to enter the town (tourist info 01721-720138).

Peebles to
Melrose (25 miles)

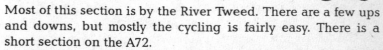

Most of this section is by the River Tweed. There are a few ups
and downs, but mostly the cycling is fairly easy. There is a
short section on the A72.

Continue east from Peebles on the B7062; travelling
downstream by the south bank of the River Tweed to Traquair.
In Traquair turn left at the war memorial, signed Innerleithen,
then right at the next junction, signed Elibank. On the way
you will pass Traquair House, which dates from the 12th
century. Twenty-seven kings and queens have visited it, and it
is open in summer. There is a tea room; pubs and a tea room
in Innerleithen too.

The minor road continues downstream between the river,
and Elibank and Traquair Forest. (It is possible to travel from
Traquair past Elibank on a mountain bike route and this is
described on page 47.) The road route ends at an interesting
old bridge, from here you have to cycle on the A707 for a little
way.

Turn right on to the A707. After 2.5 miles, just before a bridge with traffic lights, bear left on to the B7060. Climb up a hill, when you get to the top turn left just after farm buildings, then after half a mile turn right by an ornamental pond and descend to the A7. This is a busy road, join a footpath 50m ahead on the other side.

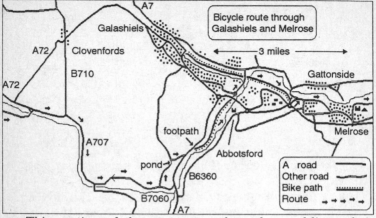

This section of the route runs through a public park in Galashiels by the River Tweed. Initially it is footpath, but it becomes the park road, there is no through access to motor traffic. This is a good spot for a picnic. Abbotsford, home of Sir Walter Scott is on the other side of the river.

To leave the park continue downstream, and pass under a flyover to a roundabout. Take the second exit to Winston Road, and continue up past the circular gasometer. Turn right to a bike path under some power lines (taking the left bike path takes you into the centre of Galashiels).

This bike path takes you across the river, the Eildon Hills can be seen ahead. Keep on for a mile to the end of the path, following posts with thistle markings. Turn right on to the public road, then at the roundabout take the first exit, signed Melrose. To get to Melrose simply follow the road and you end up in the town square, or more accurately the town triangle. Turn left to pass round the north side of the abbey.

Melrose Abbey was founded in 1136 and was finally destroyed by the Earl of Hertford in 1544. The remains are impressive, look for a figure of a pig playing the bagpipes. The former railway station has been restored and now contains a tea room and craft shop, though it would be better if it was still a railway station. Other options are the Abbey Coffee Shop, or Marmion's Brasserie. The youth hostel (01896-822521) is behind the abbey. Tourist information 01896-822555.

Melrose to Holy Island

This final section of the coast to coast route follows the Tweed Cycleway initially, but after Kelso it turns away from the Tweed towards the Cheviot Hills and Kirk Yetholm. It is possible to stay with the Tweed as far as Coldstream, but if you are going to Holy Island you will definitely have to say goodbye to the river there, as at Coldstream the Tweed turns north to meet the sea at Berwick.

Our route skirts the Cheviot Hills, entering England just after Kirk Yetholm. From there we pass by the battlefield at Flodden, then it's on through Branxton, Crookham, and Lowick. Shortly after there is a panoramic view of the Northumberland coast, with Holy Island laid out below. All of the route is on quiet roads.

Melrose to
Kirk Yetholm (25 miles)

Leave Melrose on the B6361 passing between the abbey and the river. The road leads round to the village of Newstead, bear left here, then left again at a health centre. A mile later by an old railway viaduct, turn left through bollards, and cross the River Tweed on the old road bridge, between the viaduct and the modern bridge carrying the A68.

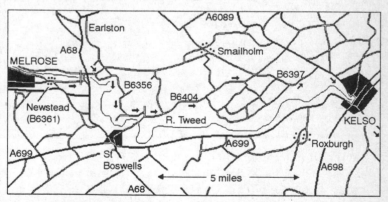

Turn right after the bridge, and right again, following signs for Scott's View. This was the favourite view of Sir Walter Scott, taking in a panorama of the Eildon Hills and the River Tweed. Fortunately modern developments have not changed it too much.

After Scott's View continue on past a sign for the Wallace Statue. This is an oversize statue of Scottish patriot William Wallace, portrayed by Mel Gibson in the film *Braveheart*. The statue stands in trees and is nothing special.

Turn left at the bottom of a hill, signed B6356 Kelso 10; then left again, signed B6404 Kelso 9. After four miles on the B6404, turn right at a crossroads on to the B6397, signed Kelso. After this turn right on to the A6089 and follow this for two miles into Kelso. In Kelso follow the signs for the town centre and the Tweed Cycleway. In the cobbled town square, turn left opposite the Cross Keys Hotel and cross the River Tweed.

Kelso is worth lingering in (tourist info 01573-223464). The town square is particularly elegant, and the bridge over the River Tweed is modelled on the Waterloo Bridge on the River Thames, being designed by the same engineer, John Rennie. Floors Castle is just to the north, originally designed by William Adam; it was used as the setting for Tarzan's ancestral home in the film *Greystoke*.

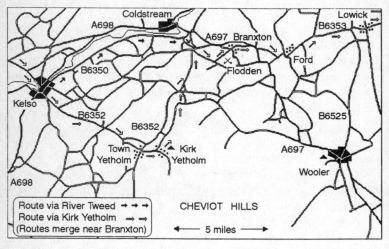

After crossing the Tweed you can either carry straight on, using the B6352 for Kirk Yetholm, or turn left on to the B6350 to continue on the official Tweed Cycleway. The B6350 is flat, and has fine views over the River Tweed. The B6352 is hilly, and has splendid views of the Cheviot Hills. Of course if you are planning on staying at Kirk Yetholm Youth Hostel, you don't have any choice about the matter.

Route via River Tweed: continue along the B6350 by the river for nine miles. A mile after Wark, turn right at a sign: East Learmouth 1, West Learmouth 1. Bear left to pass under the left viaduct, then turn right at a war memorial, signed Yetholm. Take the first left, signed Branxton 2; the two options merge again at this point (see the point marked # below).

Route via Kirk Yetholm: the B6352 begins with a climb, and it continues to be hilly. In Town Yetholm follow the signs for Kirk Yetholm, which is on the other side of the river. Kirk Yetholm and Town Yetholm were once heavily involved in smuggling whisky, they were also the home of the Faas, the gypsy royal family. Nowadays Kirk Yetholm is the northern end of the long distance walk, the Pennine Way. Walkers and cyclists can stay at the youth hostel (01573-420631) or the Border Hotel; there is also a camp site.

Kirk Yetholm to
Holy Island (28 miles)

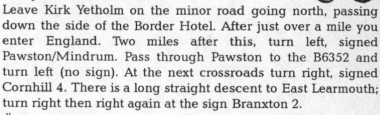

Leave Kirk Yetholm on the minor road going north, passing down the side of the Border Hotel. After just over a mile you enter England. Two miles after this, turn left, signed Pawston/Mindrum. Pass through Pawston to the B6352 and turn left (no sign). At the next crossroads turn right, signed Cornhill 4. There is a long straight descent to East Learmouth; turn right then right again at the sign Branxton 2.
#
There is a gentle climb then you turn left, signed Branxton 1.5. After a mile you pass a sign for Flodden Battlefield. Here in 1513, the flower of Scotland's manhood, led by King James IV, went to die at the battle of Flodden. An indicator board gives more detail. If you need cheering up after this sad tale you should visit the cement menagerie in Branxton, as this is certain to raise a smile. Continue on and bear right in Branxton, signed Crookham 1.5. The menagerie is opposite the red phone box.

After the menagerie, continue on in the same direction to the A697. Turn right, but after a very little way take the second left, signed Crookham. The Bluebell Inn near this junction can provide bar meals, etc. Turn left at the next junction, signed Ford. Turn right opposite an ornamental gateway (Ford). On the way through Ford you pass Ford Castle which is just like an outsize replica of a child's toy castle.

Leave Ford climbing steadily on the B6353, the Friendly Hound Inn is at the top of the hill. Just after this you get your first glimpse of the sea. Turn left on to the B6525, then right off it, signed Lowick. There is a village shop in Lowick, plus the Black Bull Inn, which does lunch and evening meals.

Keep straight on through Lowick, but after a mile turn left at crossroads, signed Haggerston 3. After half a mile turn right, signed Beal. As you bike along this road, the whole of the east coast, from Berwick on Tweed to Bamburgh becomes visible. The outline of Holy Island is instantly recognisable, and you will be able to see whether the tidal causeway is open or not. To find out about this in advance phone Coldstream Tourist Office: 01890-882607.

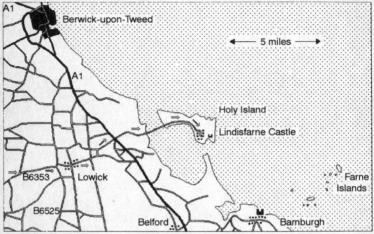

There is a rapid descent to the A1, take care crossing. Holy Island is straight over. The Plough Hotel at the junction can provide food, though there are lots of eating places on the island itself. There is often an ice cream van parked just before the causeway. If you have not previously checked the times of high tide you should do this now at the causeway notice board, to make sure you can get back.

Holy Island was the site of a Christian priory established by St Aidan in 653 until it was eventually abandoned owing to Viking raids. The priory was developed by St Cuthbert and St Wilfred, and during the latter's time the Lindisfarne Gospel was produced. This is now in the British Museum, with a replica in the priory church.

The priory is now in ruins, but the abbey church is still intact. Both can be visited, as can Lindisfarne Castle. The priory also produced mead, and this activity at least is still ongoing, even if not carried out by monks. There is a handful of pleasant pubs and tea rooms. Half of the island is now a bird sanctuary.

Should you need to cycle to Berwick to catch a train, this can be done on the network of minor roads to the west of the A1. Cycling on the A1 is not advised.

Tweed Valley Forests

The forests of the Tweed Valley offer interesting mountain biking, together with good views. They are located on steep-sided hills rising to over 500m, so there is always a climb to start with. There are four forest areas: Cardrona and Yair Hill which are relatively small; Glentress which has a bike hire centre; and Elibank and Traquair Forest which is the largest.

The Ridge Route from Traquair to Yair Hill Forest is also an option for those doing the Southern Scotland Coast to Coast on mountain bikes. Do this instead of using the public road by the River Tweed. The route is difficult, and is on rough paths, not forest roads. It is very steep at times and is not advised if you have a lot of luggage. It also forms part of the Southern Upland Way walking route, and is signposted as such with the usual thistle symbols.

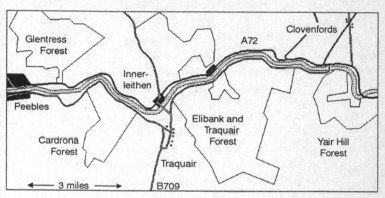

Glentress
and Cardrona

Glentress is just east of Peebles and if you need to hire a bike this is the place to go (01721-720336). There are two marked routes here. The easiest is the Anderson Trail, which is three miles long and has red markers. The Dunslair Trail (purple markers) is eleven miles, and is quite demanding. The routes in Glentress Forest are well signposted, and there are maps on notice boards at the major forest road junctions. This is a popular area.

Cardrona Forest likewise has two marked routes, the red route is just over four miles and is fairly easy; the green route is seven miles and is more demanding.

The Minch
Moor Trail (12 miles)

Elibank and Traquair Forest offers the longest rides. With Minch Moor rising to 567m it also offers the best views. The Minch Moor Trail starts from the minor road on the south bank of the River Tweed. The starting point is just west of the bridge crossing the river at Walkerburn. There are a few mountain bike signposts on the route, but they are quite infrequent. Having Ordnance Survey, Landranger map, sheet 73 with you is a good idea

The route begins as a wide forest road, signed Elibank and Traquair Forest. There is a steady climb through sitka spruce, then a gentle descent to open country, with birch trees and a view of Innerleithen. Turn right at the first T junction. There are good views of the River Tweed through gaps in the trees, then a fast descent.

At the bottom bear left at a junction to climb again, with the village of Traquair below on the right. You cross the Southern Upland Way (thistle emblem), then there is another fast descent to a sharp bend. Keep left here.

Following this there is another rise, another descent, then a short climb to a wide area for forestry vehicles to turn. Turn left at the bike route sign, leaving the forest road. On this section you may need to get off and push. After a short way there is another bike signpost where you turn left, climbing steeply. This is definitely for walking, but after 25m bear right (sign), and you will be able to ride again.

After this the path follows a dyke north through the forest, to the summit of Minch Moor. The top of the hill is visible some way off. At the top the panorama of the rolling Border hills is visible all round. The three bumps to the east are the Eildon Hills.

Following this there is another fast descent to rejoin the Southern Upland Way. Turn right (east) here, to follow the ridge route until you meet a forest road. At this point turn left (north) to zoom down the hill again towards the River Tweed. Right at the first junction halfway down the hill, left at the next, then keep left by Bold Burn to rejoin the public road at four wooden forestry houses.

To return to your starting point turn left up the minor road. To do the route in the reverse direction you of course start at the four wooden houses.

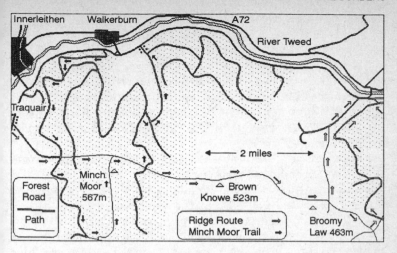

Ridge Route to Yair Hill Forest (9 or 12 miles)

This starts in the village of Traquair; again having OS Landranger map Sheet 73 with you is a good idea. At the cross roads in the village take the cul-de-sac heading south east following the Southern Upland Way signpost. After 150m the road becomes a gravel track and climbs steeply. Shortly after it becomes a simple track.

Climb to the first gate, cross a field, and enter the forest by a fire sign. Continue up, cross a forest road (the other route) then climb steeply up through dense trees, cross a small burn and then another forest road, the climb becomes less steep and then leaves the forest in heather near the top of the hill.

After this you will pass the Cheese Well, so called because drovers used to drop crumbs of cheese into it in the hope of favours from the fairies who were said to haunt it. Soon after you pass the summit of Minch Moor on your right. About here the path becomes smoother, flattening out. It then starts a long fast descent before climbing again to Hare Law (509m). Be careful of ruts in the track which can catch your front wheel. At the bottom there is another forest road which you should cross to continue along the ridgeway.

Continue east along this old drove road, crossing Hare Law. There is a right fork (Minchmoor Road) which you should ignore, bearing left here to keep on high ground. After this the route crosses Brown Knowe, its highest point. Here the Eildon Hills near Melrose come into view ahead. The first 100m after the Brown Knowe summit can be a bit boggy (keep by the fence), but after this there is a descent of about a mile.

At the bottom there is a sign telling you that this is not the turn off for Broadmeadows Youth Hostel, which is a mile and a half further on. In any case we keep straight on, climbing again with trees on our right, going round the north side of Broomy Law on a wide path. The village of Clovenfords can be seen on the left.

Soon you will encounter the sign telling you to turn right (south) for Broadmeadows Youth Hostel. Just ahead is Yair Hill Forest. At the sign for Broadmeadows it's possible to go directly down the hill to join the public road by the River Tweed, or you can continue along the path to Yair.

To go to the River Tweed road, go in the opposite direction to the way the hostel sign points. Leave the trail and bike down the hill towards the River Tweed. Keep about 100m away from Yair Hill Forest to avoid the burn. It is not difficult to bike down this mixed meadow and bracken but keep your speed down in case of unseen hazards.

The descent gradually steepens and eventually you will see signs of a path ahead. It's probably best to ignore this but keep near it. There is a monument marked: this is where, by tradition, W. Hope-Douglas was slain.

Continue down, go through a gate by trees and cross a burn to reach a farm road. Turn right on to this and descend to the public road. Watch out for cattle grids, some of which are in poor condition. When you reach the road turn left to return to Traquair, or turn right for Melrose on the Coast to Coast route.

To continue to Yair Hill ignore the Broadmeadows sign, and keep along the track to the Three Brethern cairns. After this turn left into the Yair Hill Forest. This is reasonably straightforward, but if you miss the left turn after the three cairns you may end up in Selkirk. The descent to Yair Forest has loose scree and needs care.

You end east of Yair, from where it may be possible to travel east on the south side of the Tweed on farm tracks. The alternative is the A707. Anyone doing the Coast to Coast needs to cross over to the B7060 on the north side of the River Tweed.

Border Rivers Circular

This is a ride that follows three border river systems, the River Tweed, Yarrow Water and Ettrick Water. The Yarrow flows into the Ettrick, which in turn is a tributary of the Tweed. The route is fairly hilly at times with some steady climbs as you cross between the river valleys - total distance 38 miles with a longer option of 44 miles.

The route is described starting from Selkirk but you could start at any point. It follows Ettrick Water to Ettrickbridge, where you turn north, crossing over to Yarrow Water. Alternately for the 44 mile option you continue following Ettrick Water to the Tushielaw Inn, turning north near there.

Both routes meet again at the Gordon Arms Hotel, after which there is a steady climb, then a descent to Traquair. Return to Selkirk is by the River Tweed.

Selkirk to Ettrickbridge (7 miles)

Start in Selkirk by the statue of Sir Walter Scott, one time sheriff of the county, and proceed downhill, signed Bowhill 3, and Peebles/Moffat. Turn left near the bottom of the hill to the B7009, signed Ettrickbridge. This road is fairly flat at first, though there is a hill just before Ettrickbridge. Ettrickbridge is the home of David Steel, the former Liberal leader. There is a story that the original bridge was built by Walter Harden, following an incident when a baby was drowned when his horse stumbled crossing the river. There is a commemorative stone.

Ettrickbridge to the Gordon Arms via Yarrow (8 miles)

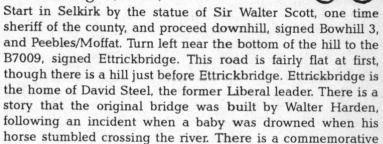

Continue upstream through Ettrickbridge; half a mile beyond the village, turn right, signed Yarrow Valley. There is a climb over about two miles, then a fast descent with fine views. At Yarrow turn left on to the A708, signed Moffat. Yarrow was the home ground of James Hogg, another of Scotland's literary giants. Though not so well known as Walter Scott, his work has perhaps stood the test of time better, his best known being: *Private Memoirs* and *Confessions of a Justified Sinner.*

The next section is a four mile ride on the A708 to the Gordon Arms. This road is usually reasonably quiet. The Gordon Arms serves bar food; there is a plaque on the outside wall indicating that Walter Scott and James Hogg met for the last time there.

Ettrickbridge to
the Gordon Arms

via Tushielaw (14 miles)

This is an attractive ride as the upper reaches of Ettrick Water are really lovely. Ignore the sign for the Yarrow valley and continue south-west. The river meanders by on the left and there is a gentle climb through steep-sided hills to the junction of the B709 and B7009. Turn right here, unless you are planning to be a customer of the Tushielaw Inn. If you are, you have to continue on for half a mile beyond the junction. This is recommended as the Tushielaw Inn serves excellent bar lunches.

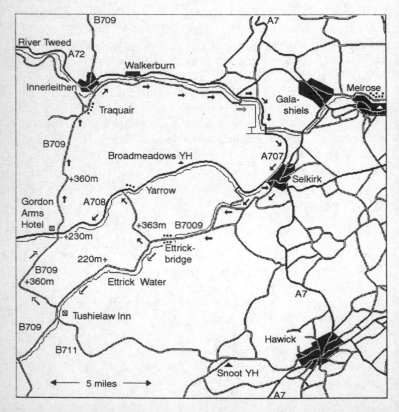

Crossing over to the Yarrow valley starts with a climb by plantation forest. Following that there is a fast descent with lovely views, ending at the Gordon Arms. Look out for the bend at the bottom.

Gordon Arms
to Selkirk
via Traquair (23 miles)

Pass down the side of the Gordon Arms following the sign for Innerleithen. There is a steady climb rather than a stiff one, then a gentle descent past bracken-covered hillside down to Traquair. Bear right through Traquair village, then right again at the next junction, signed Elibank.

Eventually you come to the end of this minor road on the south bank of the River Tweed and an attractive stone bridge carries you over to the A707. You have to turn right and cycle on this to get back to Selkirk. The A707 is reasonably quiet, but it may be possible to miss out half of the distance on it, by using farm tracks on the south side of the river.

This off-road section is currently under investigation by the local council; hopefully it could be signposted as part of the Tweed Cycleway soon. It begins as a dirt track just before the bridge and continues downstream. If this route is open to cyclists it will of course be signposted as a bike route.

If using the A707, cross back over the River Tweed on a bridge with traffic lights. After this it is another four miles to Selkirk town.

Selkirk - Hawick Circular

This is another circular route, which could be started from Selkirk or Hawick. Again there are three river valleys, the Tweed valley of course, but this time the tributaries are the River Teviot and Ale Water. There are some steep climbs, but with splendid views. The route is on quiet roads.

This route could easily be combined with the previous one for a longer tour, possibly staying at the two youth hostels nearby. These are Snoot Hostel near Roberton (01450-880259), which is a converted church in a lovely location, and Broadmeadows (01750-76262), five miles west of Selkirk. If this is not for you the tourist offices in Hawick (01450-372547) or Selkirk (01750-20054) can offer a variety of alternatives.

Selkirk to Hawick
via Minto (18 miles)

In Selkirk town square pass in front of the County Hotel following the sign for Hawick; immediately after the hotel turn left towards a church. Pass the church and a police station, then turn right up Shawpark Road, immediately after Ettrick Forest Bowling Club. Climb steeply for a mile to a radio mast, then turn right at a T junction (half-crown corner).

After a further mile you meet the A699. Turn right then first left to the B6453, signed Midlem. Follow the B6453 through Midlem; go straight over the bridge at the next crossroads, signed Lilliesleaf. At the next junction ignore the right turn for Lilliesleaf and bear left, continuing along the B6400, signed Ancrum.

After less than half a mile, turn right at a sharp left bend, signed Standhill. After this keep straight on towards the dome-shaped Minto Hills and Minto village. Minto village is notable for the church designed by William Playfair, and for the oddly named Fatlips Castle, a folly or peel tower which stands to the east of the village.

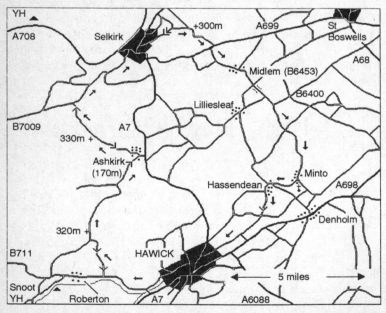

In Minto take the first right by a house called Templecroft, passing round the southern edge of the Minto Hills. Turn right on to the B6405 and pass under an old rail bridge to

Hassendean. Turn left on to the B6359, signed Hawick; but after 100m at a sharp right bend, turn left to a minor road between a byre and a field gate and cross the old railway line.

This road runs parallel to the A698 and descends into Hawick. A mile after Hassendean bear right over a bridge, and a further mile after this, turn right at a give way sign. When you start to enter the town, just after the 30 mph sign, turn left towards the brown brick Slumberdown building. At the bottom of the hill bear right towards a gasometer following the river, then at traffic lights turn left over the bridge to the town centre.

Hawick to Selkirk
via Ashkirk (18 miles)

It is possible to leave Hawick on the main road south, the A7, but the best method is to cross over on to the west side of the river and leave Hawick on minor roads. In either case there is a right turn on to the B711 (signed Roberton from the A7).

Continue down the main street in Hawick (A7) until you come to a mini-roundabout by two public telephone boxes. Turn right here and cross the River Teviot. Turn left immediately after the bridge. Keep turning left at public road junctions to follow the west bank of the river upstream. When you meet the B711 turn right (left sign: give way 50yds).

Bike west by Borthwick Water for two miles. After passing Highchesters Farm, turn right, signed Harden and Borthwickshiels. At the top of the hill, turn right at the T junction, signed Ashkirk. There is a high-level ride over the hills for three miles then a descent into Ashkirk.

Bike through Ashkirk, don't go near the A7, but take the minor road leading north-west from the village, signed Ettrickbridge. There is another stiff climb over the Woll Rigg road, then a descent to a T junction where you turn right, signed Selkirk. Turn right at the next junction and follow the Ettrick Water to Selkirk, turn right to enter the town.

If you have time to spare, Halliwell House Museum, situated off the main square in Selkirk is worth visiting. The building consists of an 18th century row of dwelling houses, renovated to house a museum of Selkirk's history. The town suffered repeatedly from the English invasions, and was destroyed by the English army after the Battle of Flodden in 1513.

The Lammermuirs

The northern part of this route is quite near to Edinburgh, to join it from Edinburgh, see under Gifford (page 59), in the Edinburgh chapter.

The Lammermuir Hills are surprisingly quiet. To the north, east and south there is an attractive network of minor roads. From the hills there are sweeping views over East Lothian and the Borders. There is a youth hostel in Abbey St Bathans (01361-840245), B&Bs in Duns and elsewhere. You could also start by travelling by train from Edinburgh to Longniddry, Drem or Dunbar (reserve a bike space). Tourist information: 01890-750678.

The route can be done as a northern loop of 30 miles, or a southern loop of 29 miles, going right round the whole thing is 49 miles. The text describes the long way round, with a section at the end telling you how to shorten it.

Gifford to
Abbey St Bathans
via Hungry Snout (21 miles)

Leave Gifford on the B6355, signed Garvald, bearing right by Yester Church with its attractive bell tower (1708, worth visiting). At the top of the hill bear left to the B6370 for Garvald. This ridge road gives great views over the sea towards the Bass Rock and other extinct volcanos such as North Berwick Law and Traprain Law.

At the sign, turn right for Garvald, which has a hotel. In Garvald follow the sign for Nunraw, up a very steep hill. At the top pass the abbey (not a ruin!), and continue on still climbing, to White Castle Fort. This iron age hill fort is worth looking over if only for the stunning view.

There is only a short climb after the fort then a long descent. Watch for loose cattle grids and sheep. The road winds through the hills; at Whiteadder Reservoir turn left on to the B6355. Pass the reservoir climbing The Hungry Snout, be careful on the very steep fast descent the other side.

There is a tea room about three miles after, Cranshaw's Smiddy Tea Room. Serious hills are over now. If you are bound for the youth hostel at Abbey St Bathans continue on for three miles only after the tea room, to a stone bridge over the River Whiteadder. After crossing the river turn left on to a rough track. Sign opposite: Whitchester & Longformacus.

The track follows the river for two miles to the youth hostel. The road alternative is over a steep hill. You will need to use the public phone box to summon the warden. If you are looking for a B&B it's probably best to ignore the track and continue along the road to Duns unless you have booked somewhere in advance.

Abbey St Bathans is notable for its ancient oak woods, there are some lovely walks, and a church on the site of a 12th century Cistercian priory. The hostel is owned by the local estate, advance booking is desirable (phone first). The hostel is in the SYHA handbook but more relaxed rules apply. There is a tea room in the village, also a trout farm.

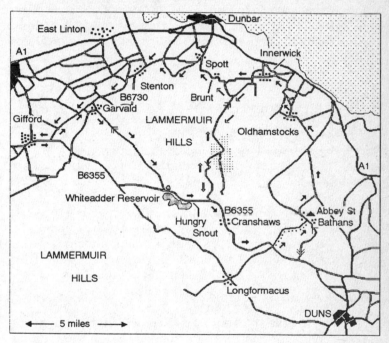

Abbey St Bathans to Gifford via Oldhamstocks (28 miles)

Leave Abbey St Bathans by following the road east (upstream) from the youth hostel. Ignore the left turn for Monynut and climb out of the river valley. Turn left at the T junction after the driving school, ignore a left turn for Monynut but take the next left signed Oldhamstocks.

In Oldhamstocks turn right by the phone box, signed Innerwick. Follow signs for Innerwick. If you fancy a detour, go and see ruined Innerwick Castle, this is down a rough path a few hundred yards after crossing a high stone bridge at a T junction.

The large building in the distance by the sea is Torness Nuclear Power Station. Keep straight on through Innerwick. On the far side look for a piece of poetry by the roadside. Just beyond this, at the T junction turn left, signed Elmscleugh. Shortly after turn right, signed The Brunt.

This road descends rapidly to a river ford then climbs up to The Brunt, eventually dropping to Spott. In Spott at the bottom of the hill turn left opposite a modern bungalow. Soon after Spott, at a major road, turn left, signed Gifford/Garvald/Stenton. After this the route is along the B6370 to Gifford.

Northern Loop (30 miles)
Southern Loop (29 miles)

Both of these routes take advantage of a minor road that runs across the eastern Lammermuirs from Innerwick to Cranshaws. This effectively turns the longer circular route into a figure of eight.

At the southern side, entry to the minor road is a left turn, one mile east of the steep descent of the Hungry Snout and Whiteadder Reservoir. At the northern side, after Innerwick, do not turn right for The Brunt, but continue straight on, turning right at the next T junction, and bearing left after this. From Spott follow the sign for Brunt near a phone box then bear right at the next two junctions.

Whichever side you start from there will be more than one serious hill, from the eastern side there is a climb of over 200m as you are starting from lower down. Avoid a fork in the road leading south in forest as this is a farm road (see map).

ROUTES FROM EDINBURGH

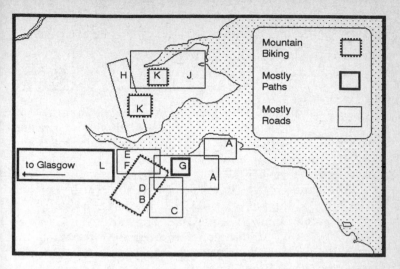

Edinburgh to East Lothian

North Berwick, Haddington, Gifford, and the Pencaitland and Longniddry Railway Paths

(distances in text)

These are circular routes beginning in central Edinburgh. You start on the Innocent Railway Path, and travel to peaceful countryside in East Lothian. As far as possible quiet roads and trails are used. They would make good all day outings for someone living in Edinburgh, the off-road parts would be ideal for children. Destinations could be, North Berwick (26 miles), Haddington (22 miles), or Gifford (27 miles).

Start at the Commonwealth Pool, Dalkeith Road. Go down Holyrood Park Road between the swimming pool and the glass building. Immediately after turn left down East Parkside (before the park). After 50m turn right on to a red brick path, reversing direction. The Innocent Railway Tunnel (now a cycle path) will be ahead. An alternative starting point is the Engine Shed Café, in St Leonard's Lane. Follow the track at the far end of their car park, and whenever you see red brick pavement cycle on it until you reach the tunnel (the Engine Shed Café route is currently blocked by a building site).

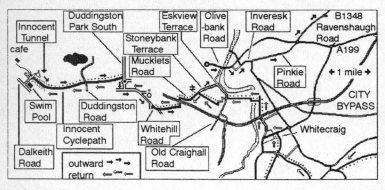

Whizz through the tunnel, at the other side go down the cycle path to Duddingston Road. A plaque can be seen here giving the history of the Innocent Railway, which was opened in 1831 to carry coal to the city. Riding on the horse-drawn trains became popular and the railway company rapidly converted wagons to coaches to carry passengers. The line was converted to a cycle path in 1985 after a long campaign by local cyclists (Spokes, The Lothian Cycle Campaign).

Cross Duddingston Road and continue along to the end of the cycle path - it emerges on to Duddingston Park South. Turn right on to the road here. Ignore the bike route signpost on the far side of the road - this just goes to a supermarket at present.*

Cycle south along Duddingston Park South. Go straight over at the roundabout (children use right pavement) and under the rail bridge to traffic lights at Niddrie Mains Road/ Newcraighall and turn left. You will see a new housing estate on your right, Quarry Cottages on your left. Shortly after turn right by a church, to Whitehill Road. Soon you are in open countryside. Ignore right turns, pass over railway sidings, and under the city bypass. Turn right on to the cycle path on the other side to Mucklets Road.

Continue down past Musselburgh Station. Keep straight on, ignore the cycle path sign for Monktonhall and the River Esk (this is our return route). Go straight over at the roundabout and down Stoneybank Terrace to the T junction at Eskview Terrace (little baker shop on left). Turn left; then right at the bottom at the traffic lights, on to Olive Bank Road.

After a few hundred metres ignore the cycle path sign for the River Esk Walkway, but take the right after it, going down a cul-de-sac between the Riverside Bar and Brunton's Works. Cycle through the traffic bollards to Inveresk Road.

There is a possible diversion here, turning left down Newbigging to Musselburgh High Street and Luca's ice cream parlour; or visit the old village of Inveresk (right turn). Otherwise keep straight on for a mile. Inveresk Road becomes Pinkie Rd; at a roundabout go along Ravenshaugh Road (B1348) by the sea to Prestonpans. Pass Cockenzie Power Station then go through Port Seton. You pass a supermarket; when you see a beach ahead turn right up Fishers Road. If you pass a caravan park you have missed the turning.

After about a mile turn left at a T junction on to the A198. This becomes a dual carriageway with a cycle path. Look right for a railway level-crossing, cross the road and the railway.

The road on the other side continues gently uphill. After a mile or so cross the B6363 at an ivy covered dead tree. Keep going, but after a mile, when you start to descend, look out for the bridge which carries the Longniddry - Haddington railway path. The path entry is signposted. It's occasionally used by horses so the surface may be bumpy at times. If you are going to North Berwick do not join the railway path (see page 62).

---

* It is expected that the bike path over the road will be extended past the supermarket to Musselburgh Station in 1997. If this is done it will be signposted *East Lothian*, or similar. In the absence of this, follow the directions in the main text.

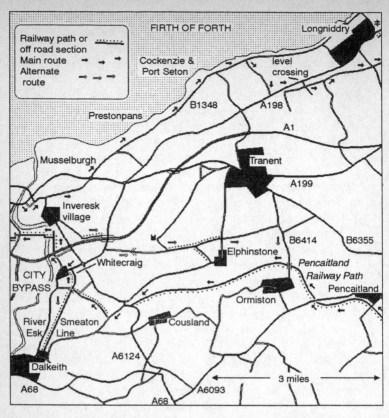

The railway path of course begins at Longniddry, while we have joined it further on. Joining it at Longniddry means more cycling on the A198, and the whole purpose of this guide is to keep you off such roads if possible. The railway path passes through pleasant countryside to Haddington. In Haddington it runs by a housing development and ends shortly after this. Exit to the left, and turn right crossing a bridge over the railway path. When you get to the main road turn left to enter the town.

Haddington is a well-conserved county town with an attractive park. If you are looking for somewhere to eat and price is not a consideration the Waterside Bistro is splendid, it can be busy on Sundays and it is best to book in advance (01620-825674). Another place is Peter Potters in Church Street, this is an art gallery, but with a tea room above. Even cheaper, St Mary's Church does teas in the afternoon. Cheapest of all is the Tesco supermarket (on the left as you enter the town square). The park is down a lane on the other side of the road.

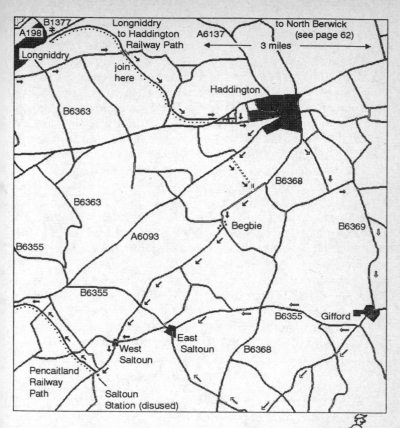

Haddington
to Gifford (5 miles)

You can continue to Gifford by going through the town and turning right on to the B6368 (B6369). Gifford is an attractive village set beside the Lammermuir Hills. Worth a visit here is Yester Parish Church (1708). A tablet nearby commemorates the Rev John Witherspoon, one of the signatories of the American Declaration of Independence.

A pleasant place to eat in Gifford is the Goblin Ha Hotel. There is a beer garden at the back, and they serve food outside in sunny weather. The Goblin Ha is named after Goblin Hall, an undergound vaulted hall nearby, said to have been built by goblins. Two different return routes from Gifford are suggested on the map. The southerly one involves a bit of a climb as you approach the Lammermuir Hills, but the minor roads around here are very quiet and quite pretty, with occasional fine views over the Forth Estuary.

North Berwick

As mentioned earlier, if you are going to the seaside town of North Berwick, don't join the railwaypath near Longdiddry but keep on the road. Turn right at the T junction ahead, go on a little way, under a small electricity line, and take the left fork in the road up a hill. Left at the top. At a T junction turn left to the A6137, then take the first right after a short distance.

On the right here is the Hopetoun Monument. This remnant of a more deferential age was built by a grateful tenantry to the 4th Earl of Hopetoun (1765-1823). It stands on the 168m high Garleton Hill. The view from the top is the best in the Lothians - well worth the climb. Continue east, at the next junction you have the choice of going to North Berwick by Drem (shorter), or Athelstaneford.

Drem route: turn left here, right by the railway, left in Drem by a phone box. Cross the A198 to Dirleton. Dirleton Castle (AD1225) is worth visiting (Adult £1, child 50p). There is a sandy beach and barbeque site at nearby Yellow Craig. After Dirleton, continue to North Berwick on the A198.

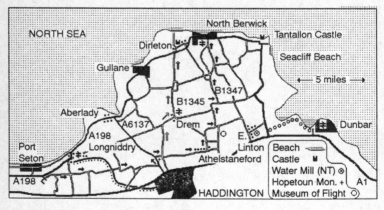

Athelstaneford route: right and left, left in Athelstaneford after the school by a shop. Straight on at the next junction, left at the next on to the B1347 by a grey metal box. The Museum of Flight (see map) is worth a visit (tea room; opening times phone 01620-880308). Keep on the B1347, heading towards North Berwick Law (hill).

Train times (from N. Berwick) MON to SAT:- 1420, 1520, 1620, 1720, 1820, 1920, 2020, 2215. SUNDAYS:- 1320, 1520, 1720. (1996 timetable) Trains stop at, Drem, Longniddry, Prestonpans, Musselburgh, & Edinburgh (0131-556 2451).

Haddington to Edinburgh Railway Path (22 miles)

To return from Haddington leave on the A6093, which is a left fork at a red sandstone church. Bike out on this for just over a mile until you are clear of the town. There is a right turn down a minor road which you ignore; then just after this, opposite a barn (no sign), turn left down a track into a wood. Keep straight on ignoring a right bend, to a small footbridge over a burn, cross this to a minor road and turn right (west). If coming in the opposite direction, look for a right of way sign.

Travelling south-west, bear left and right through Begbie, bear right at the next junction, then cross the B6355 for West Saltoun. In West Saltoun keep straight on at the cross-roads on the staggered junction. The road crosses a hump bridge, there is a line of electricity pylons ahead. The start of the Pencaitland Railway Path is just before the pylons at 'Saltoun Station'.

The path surface is a bit bumpy at first but becomes easier. Pass a wooden bridge and skirt Pencaitland. After this the path is broken by the A6093, take care crossing. Around here there are several plaques giving information about the coal mining companies that the railway line served. Eventually you catch sight of the Pentland Hills ahead, electricity pylons approach from both sides, and you emerge on to the A6124 at Crossgatehall.

Turn right on to the A6124, but left at the traffic lights before the metal bridge. After a quarter mile turn right at the sign for Whitecraig. Just under a mile then you'll see the Smeaton cycle path. Descend on steps before the bridge. Turn right under the bridge, then when the path ends turn left into Whitecraig. At Cowpits Road you'll see the bike sign for the River Esk. Right here, then under the dual carriageway on the bike path at the bend. Follow this, then turn left over a metal footbridge crossing the River Esk. On the other side this becomes a track passing under the east coast rail line. You pass Monktonhall golf course, then run through a new housing development on to Old Craighall Road.

Go straight over Old Craighall Road at a mini roundabout by more houses. First left under pylons, under the rail line again on a gravel path, and then under the rail line a second time (not under the motorway). After a little way you arrive at Mucklets Road by the cycle path sign - you've completed the circle! Return to central Edinburgh the way you came out.

Round Edinburgh Off-Road

This route is 70% off road. It uses four former railway lines, a canal towpath, and crosses the Pentland Hills. The circuit goes round the south side of the city, and the Pentland Hills Park. It will seem that you are in the countryside, even the urban sections are mostly in parks. The first part, to Balerno, could be done on any kind of bike, a mountain bike would be best after this. The route is given anti-clockwise, canal towpath section in the morning, for fewer pedestrians.

Tollcross - Balerno - Penicuik - Dalkeith - - Meadows (37 miles)

Start at the King's Theatre, go up Gilmore Place opposite, first right by a church to Lower Gilmore Place, over Leamington Lift Bridge to the canal. Eventually you will go over a high aqueduct. Shortly after cross a footbridge over the canal and Lanark Road.

Keep right, going along a disused railway line by trees and the Water of Leith. Through a tunnel, under a stone bridge, Spylaw Public Park on left. The path joins an access road crossing the river, turn right, then immediately right again on to a dirt path signed Juniper Green. Continue to Balerno, crossing the river several times, ending by Balerno High School in Bridge Road.

Left on Bridge Road, then after the school left up Bavelaw Road. Straight on up the hill to leave Balerno. At the top of the hill, a mile after Balerno, take the left fork towards the hills. Cross Threipmuir reservoir, then go up Beech Avenue. At the T junction at the top turn right, and then left, following the right of way sign.

After a climb, pass between West Kip on your left and Cap Law. Keep to the main path, dropping to Eastside Farm. There is a brief rise, then it drops again to the A702. Turn left here. You could cycle along the footpath by the side of the road, watch out for boulders. At Silverburn turn right for Penicuik, then left on to the fairly quiet A766 towards the town.

At Penicuik pass houses to the left, then at the bottom of the hill, playing fields on the right. First right after the 30mph sign, between playing fields, signed Penicuik. At The Square turn right by the Olympic Café, signed Peebles. At the bottom of the hill, before the river, turn left down Valleyfield Road to the Penicuik-Dalkeith railway path.

There is a narrow section at Auchendinny, and then a tunnel. The path skirts Roslin Glen giving good views, then leaves the old rail route to avoid a mining development. The path is briefly broken by a road junction at Rosewell - just cross over and you will see it again. After this it passes under the A6094.

At Bonnyrigg the dirt track ends. It seems as if the railway line has disappeared, as indeed it has. However keep straight on. Cross Campview Road and go down the side of a swing park passing a station platform converted to flower beds. Cross Dundas Street, down Waverley Court (new houses). This turns into a cycle path with the usual barrier. The path is carried over a bypass road, and ends in a garage yard. Turn right to go down a dirt track and after a little turn left, go through another cycle path barrier. Continue straight on, under a bridge, to an old station platform.

Currently the surfaced path ends here and the next section may be muddy. You can either carry on, passing under two more bridges, or filter up a ramp to the right. This takes you into the former Eskbank railway station yard. Bike through this, cross Lasswade Road by a shop, and bike through the garage forecourt opposite to Melville Road. Turn left on to this, and after passing the telephone exchange, turn

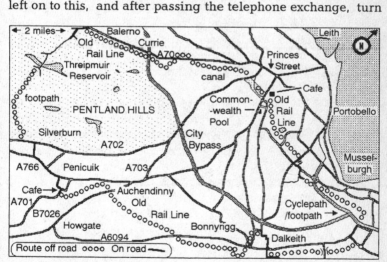

right through a gate to meet the rail line again. Whichever way you've gone you'll meet another cycle path. Turn left and cross the River Esk on the high Glen Esk Viaduct. This was built in 1847 and recently restored (see indicator board). Immediately after the viaduct, leave the cycle path. Turn right up steps past the indicator board. At more steps, turn left through trees, go along a bit, then drop to a public road. Bear right here - you can cycle down the side of the road on a footpath, but you will have to join it at the bridge (Bridgend).

Bear left past Bridgend Court to traffic lights at the junction of Edinburgh Road and Dalkeith High Street and turn left. Follow the main road round (signed Whitecraig, Musselburgh) crossing the River South Esk to a roundabout. Second exit to Thornybank Industrial Site. By playing fields, turn left on to the B6414 (bike sign). 200m beyond the chain link fence, turn left to the Smeaton cycle path. The cycle path turns into a dirt track at a bridge then ends at Whitecraig.

At the public road turn left following the cycle route sign for Musselburgh. After a quarter mile turn right down Cowpits Road, signed River Esk Walkway 2.5. At the next bend leave the road, signed River Esk Walkway 2. Go under the bypass to a metal footbridge, signed Monktonhall 0.5. Cross the river, passing a golf course and under a railway line to a mini-roundabout; go straight over into a cul-de-sac (new houses).

In the cul-de-sac turn left, right, then left and under the railway. Keep right and go under another rail line (not the bypass) to emerge at Musselburgh Station. Left here to pass through the cycle path barrier to Mucklets Path. Left under the city bypass, signed Niddrie, then keep right to emerge at Newcraighall by a church building. Turn left here, then right at traffic lights to Duddingston Park South and pass under a rail bridge. (You can avoid the traffic lights by going right into Peacocktail Close, then across the grass to Cleekim Drive, turning right at Duddingston Inn.)

Just after the roundabout turn left to the Innocent Railway Line at the bike route sign. Follow this, crossing Duddingston Road, then cycle through the tunnel. End here, or to return to the start turn right through the housing estate, follow the red brick path to The Engine Shed Cafe. Turn left to St Leonards Lane, down Rankeillor Street, cross Clerk Street, down a path to Gifford Street, then left and right, through bollards to The Meadows cycle path, and Tollcross/King's Theatre.

West Linton and Temple

Set between the Moorfoot and Pentland Hills, the countryside south of Edinburgh is attractive. We start in central Edinburgh, and use quiet streets where possible to reach the village of Lasswade. After this the route passes Roslin and Penicuik on quiet roads or cycle paths to West Linton. After lunch we turn east, passing Gladhouse Reservoir, before turning north to return to the city via Temple and Carrington.

Route from City Centre

From the west end of Princes Street go south up Lothian Road, between the Caledonian Hotel & St John's Church. First left to Kings Stables Road, then left to the Grassmarket. Up by shops then right up Candlemaker Row. At the top, by Greyfriars Bobby dog statue, join the right hand pavement. Walk the wide pavement in Forrest Road to The Meadows Cycle Path.

Go straight down the cycle path to a light controlled crossing. Straight over to Argyle Place, cross Warrender Park Road into Chalmers Crescent but immediately turn left into Hatton Place, then second right to Lauder Road. Bike the length of Lauder Road and South Lauder Road, crossing the main Grange Road (now see # below)

Edinburgh (Bruntsfield) to West Linton (21 miles)

Start at Edinburgh Bicycle in Whitehouse Loan (by Bruntsfield Links). Go south along Whitehouse Loan (bike shop on left) to traffic lights. Straight over, then second left into Blackford Road. Cross Kilgraston Road to Dick Place, right into Lauder Road at cross roads, this becomes South Lauder Road. #

At a T junction turn left to Relugas Road. At the end of Relugas Road right into busy Mayfield Road, second left after shops and a bus stop into West Saville Road then first right into Granby Road. Go straight along Granby Road (3 cross roads) and at the T junction turn left into Esslemont Road. At the bend turn right by iron railings into Gordon Terrace. Along Gordon Terrace then right into busy Liberton Road. At the traffic lights bear left up Kirk Brae. Kirk Brae becomes Lasswade Road, follow Lasswade road for 4 miles to Lasswade.

In Lasswade turn right after crossing the river into Polton Road, signed High School. Keep straight on for two miles to open country. After a timbered house on the left, turn right, signed Auchendinny and Penicuik. An option here is to follow a cycle path route to Penicuik. This is flat and attractive. It is easy to follow, but might be muddy in places. The road route is quiet but hilly, with good views.

Road route: the road runs beside the cycle path then drops to Roslin Glen. Just before the bottom of the hill turn left uphill by a stone cottage, signed Roslinlee Hospital. At a staggered junction turn right then left. Turn left at the hospital crossroads by a phone box (Farm Road), then immediately right by two stone cottages (Firth Road). Right at Firth Mains Farm, left at a private road sign, then pass farm buildings to turn right on to the B7026. Go downhill for 200m then turn left by Maybank Cottage. At the foot of the hill join the cycle path by turning left; but turn *right* on to it; do not go under a bridge. Cross a river, bear right by an ornamental pond and go through a gate to join the A701 south of Penicuik.

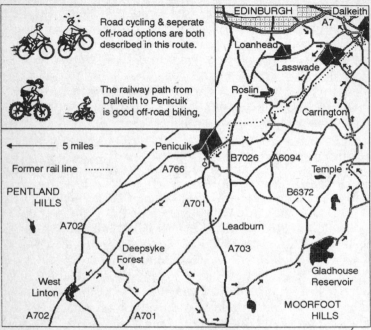

You can get food in Penicuik at the Olympic Café by turning right (delicatessen round the corner). Otherwise turn left to go south on the A701, signed Peebles. Turn right off the A701 at the top of the hill, signed West Linton. This quiet road crosses Auchencorth Moss giving views of the hills. Go straight on at the next junction to West Linton. This attractive village has a tea room, and two hotels which do bar lunches.

West Linton - Gladhouse - Edinburgh (32 miles)

Leave West Linton the way you entered, on Deanfoot Road. At the first crossroads, by Deepsyke Forest, turn right signed Lamanca. The former railway which you cross is not bikeable. At the A701 turn left, then after two miles turn right, signed Eddleston via Shiplaw. Turn left on to the A703 for 1.5 miles then turn right off it, signed Temple and Gorebridge.

Ignore a right turn for Moorfoot (farm) but turn right after this signed Gladhouse. Pass the reservoir, at a T junction with a stop sign turn left, signed Temple/Gorebridge. After Temple turn left over a bridge, then right, signed Carrington. In Carrington follow signs for Cockpen/Dalkeith.

After Carrington there is a fast tree-lined section, you pass a sawmill. Turn left on to the B704 by a church and graveyard, towards Bonnyrigg/Lasswade. When you pass a school look for a cycle path sign on the left next to an old railway platform, now landscaped. Turn right through a new housing estate (The Riggs) to another cycle path. This ends in a yard, turn right here then after 200m, left to another cycle path.

After 400m leave this on a ramp to the right. Pass Eskbank Trading Store, cross Lasswade Road (go through garage forecourt to avoid roundabout), left to Melville Road to return to Edinburgh. Return on the A772, past Butterfly World and over the bypass via Gilmerton. Outwith rush hour this road is reasonably quiet, parts of the road are painted as cycle lanes - often used by motorists as convenient parking spaces.

Pentland Hill Tracks

These tracks have been biked on for many years, but pressure on the Pentlands is now vastly increased, walkers, runners, and mountain bikers use these hills in large numbers. Be considerate, and stop to let walkers pass.

The routes are signposted as rights of way, keep to these. The Pentlands are just half an hour from the city, yet they can seem as remote and beautiful as any of Scotland's hills. Try to keep them that way - avoid fierce braking on wet grass. Tell someone where you're going, wear a helmet.

Route A (4 miles)
Eight Mile Burn to
Threipmuir Reservoir.

At the south end the route starts 1.3 miles north east of the junction of the A702 and A766, west of Penicuik. Sign: Public Path to Balerno, also: Eastside Farm. At the north end start at the bridge over Threipmuir Reservoir as indicated on the map. Turn right at the top of Beech Ave after the reservoir, then left before the private sign. There is a grassy spur leading to Nine Mile Burn just south of the path summit.

Route B (2.5 miles + 3.5 on road)
Threipmuir Reservoir
to Flotterstone.

At the south end start at Flotterstone Inn off the A702 north of Penicuik. The visitor centre is across the road from the inn. At the north end start at Threipmuir as in route A, but turn left instead of right at the top of Beech Ave. There are two high stiles.

There is another path leading north, round Black Hill at the second stile going east, do not go this way, the farmer here is not fond of mountain bikers. It is possible to get from Flotterstone to Eight Mile Burn by cycling on the footpath by the side of the A702.

Route C (2 miles)
Loganlea Reservoir
to A702

This is very steep and needs care, particularly in the wet. At the south end it is signposted: Public Footpath to Colinton and Balerno. If you meet water here go left into the field. The path leads over meadow to a gate, by way of Charlie's Loup (lift your bike over). After this it is a track through heather which becomes progressively steeper. At the north end it starts at the west end of Loganlea Reservoir, and is signposted Old Kirk Road to Penicuik.

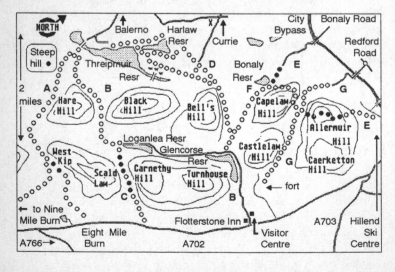

Route D (2.5 miles)
Harlaw Reservoir to
Glencorse Reservoir.

At the north end this is best approached from the crossroads at Wester Kinleith (marked X on map). In Balerno, turn left off Bavelaw Rd into Harlaw Rd, up to the crossroads, then turn right towards the hills. From the Glencorse end the route is signposted Public Footpath to Balerno, Colinton and Currie.

Route E (3 miles)
Bonaly to
Swanston

The most difficult route, although it is easy of access from the city. Best done west to east. Access via Colinton Rd, Woodhall Rd, left up Bonaly Road and over the city bypass to the park. Straight up past the car park, lift bikes over a gate and up through trees to Bonaly Reservoir (easily missed as you don't see it until you've passed it).

At a gate by the reservoir, turn left by a red military area sign, and follow a rough track round the north side of Capelaw Hill. At the first cattle grid turn right uphill. At the second cattle grid go left, crossing it to go up Allermuir Hill. Follow the fence to the trig point on top.

At the top, cross the stile and go past the visual indicator. Keep by the fence to descend, then when the fence climbs, turn left to leave it. Descend towards the ski centre. Do not enter the gate into the golf course, take the track to the right. After the gate turn left past white thatched cottages to Swanston Road. Alternately continue straight on to Hillend Ski Centre.

Route F (2.5 miles)
Bonaly to
Glencorse Reservoir.

This is the same as route E except that at Bonaly Reservoir you turn right at the red military area sign instead of left. After this continue straight on descending all the way to Glencorse. In the opposite direction start the same way as the Glencorse end of route D, but fork right for Colinton after a short climb.

71

Route G   (2.5 miles)
Dreghorn to
Castlelaw.

You cross this route at the second cattle grid on route E. Alternately access at the north end of the route is from Redford Road then cross the city bypass, or at the south end from Castlelaw Hill Fort off the A702.

Route H   (7 miles)
West Linton to Harperrig
Reservoir via Cauldstane Slap.

This route is not on the map. Start on the A702 in West Linton. Go up Medwyn Road (signed Baddinsgill). Keep straight on, the route becomes a track then a footpath. The summit of this old drove road is the Cauldstane Slap. The A70, leading to Balerno is visible ahead (right for Balerno) and seems quite near, but the last mile before the reservoir is boggy and will mean you have to carry your bike a lot. Wet feet are guaranteed if there has been recent rain! It is usually best to do the route as West Linton to Cauldstane Slap and return.

Edinburgh - Hopetoun House

This route uses minor roads, a disused railway, and parts of the Union Canal towpath to get to Hopetoun House near South Queensferry. Distance 23 miles. On any path shared with walkers don't go fast, use a bell or say 'excuse me', try to avoid Sunday afternoons. Sections could be muddy in winter. Return to Edinburgh could be by train, cycling back via Barnton (see route on page 75), or by returning the way you came. The canal towpath is not suitable for large groups.

Edinburgh (Tollcross)
to South Queensferry
(Hopetoun House) (23 miles)

Start at the King's Theatre, Leven Street. Go up Gilmore Place opposite, first right by a church into Lower Gilmore Place, then over Leamington Lift Bridge. Turn left on to the canal towpath. Eventually pass over a high aqueduct leading over the Water of Leith. Shortly after this you will see a footbridge going over the canal. At the footbridge leave the towpath, using the bridge to cross over the canal and Lanark Road.

Keep right, along a disused railway line by the Water of Leith. Go through a tunnel, under a stone bridge, Spylaw Public Park on left. The route crosses access roads a couple of times, continue in the same direction looking for the continuation of the dirt path on the other side. We go under the city bypass. Note that the path continues to Balerno, but we leave it a mile after the city bypass.

Soon, on the left, you'll see a footbridge over the river; ignore it, but when you encounter asphalt again, pass between some large boulders. After 50m bear right by two large boulders on to the dirt path. Shortly after we cross the river to the left bank. Soon after this we meet an arched stone bridge. This is where we leave the river.

Is this the right bridge? On the riverbank there will be steps leading down to the river. On the left are other steps, curving up to the bridge. Carry your bike up, turning left over the bridge, and bike up to Lanark Road West. Turn right, then

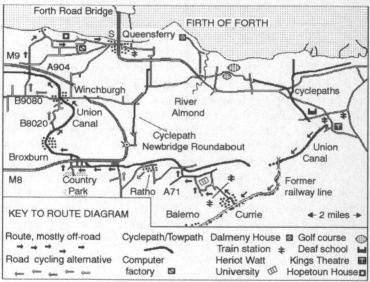

immediately left on to Muirwood Road (cycle route sign Riccarton/Heriot Watt). Muirwood Road turns left by some pylons. Here is another bike sign: Riccarton, Heriot Watt, Wester Hailes, go down the lane. Ignore the sign for Wester Hailes further on - keep straight on and cross the railway. At the major road turn right, then left at the roundabout into Heriot Watt University.

After entering the university grounds, near a bus shelter, take the first right to Boundary Road East. Follow the road round as it curves to the west, passing over three road humps.

When you see a yellow painted vehicle barrier, continue straight on, cycling round it on to a potholed access road. Continue on leaving the university, turning right on to the public road at the give way signs.

This road joins the busy A71. We turn left here, signed Kilmarnock, but carefully cross the main road and cycle along the footpath until you come to Addiston Farm Road, go down there to meet the canal again; continue west by crossing the bridge and turning left on to the canal towpath.

When the canal was built the bridges over it were numbered, the numbers are above each arch. Cross the River Almond on a high aqueduct then to get round the motorway, (the canal is piped underneath) leave the canal at the first bridge (20), crossing it to continue west. The road runs parallel to a railway line for a mile, passing two right turn-offs before coming to a crossroads.

At the crossroads there is a left turn to Almondell Country Park - turn right. Go under a railway and the M8 motorway, to meet the canal again. Here at Learielaw Farm Road cross the bridge and join the the towpath again for a traffic-free route through Broxburn.

Keep on the towpath, the canal is cut by the B8020. Cross this carefully and rejoin the towpath on the other side. After this carry on for 3.7 miles to bridge 35. This stone bridge has black iron railings, the monogram 'HH' is carved in stone. Leave the canal turning right (north) on to the road.

Continuing north we go under another motorway, the M9, and then meet the A904. Cross over and go down the minor road by Abercorn Primary School, signed Hopetoun House 2 miles. This great Adam mansion is open to the public Easter to September. Tel: 0131-331 2451. Turn left into Hopetoun House grounds to enter by the west gate.

Cycling through the grounds to South Queensferry is quite straightforward. It is reasonable to do this if you intend to visit the house or be a customer of the garden centre which is open all year. The garden centre has a tea room. If you want to visit the house itself you will have to pay an admission charge at a small kiosk which guards access to the house itself.

Leave Hopetoun House by the main east gate and continue east by the shore road to South Queensferry, passing Port Edgar Water Sports Centre, and ending up underneath the Forth Road Bridge. Here you have a number of options: to cross the bridge to Fife bike up to the bridge on the cycle path; to return to Edinburgh, go straight over underneath the bridge to Stewart Terrace and continue up the hill, turning right then left into Burgess Road. This leads to Station Road and the train station where you might be able to get on a train, or cycle back via Dalmeny and Barnton, see next route.

Edinburgh to S. Queensferry

This route is a quiet and direct way of getting to the Forth Road Bridge. It is an attractive cycle ride on its own, but may be useful on longer tours to avoid the very heavy traffic on Queensferry Road. About 30% of the route is on cycle paths, the remainder is quiet roads.

Edinburgh (Haymarket)
to Forth Road Bridge (10 miles)

Start at Donaldson's School for the Deaf, an ornate turreted building in playing fields. This is in West Coates, which is 500m west of Haymarket railway station, or one mile west of Princes Street. Look west, just beyond a church (National Bible Society), is a gaily painted bridge. Just before you get to it, turn left at a filling station, into Balbirnie Place.

After 50 metres, turn right on to a cycle path, keeping right to cross the bridge. An alternative starting point is the cycle path entry in Russell Road just south of the above bridge. Reach Russell Road via Dalry Road and Murieston Crescent.

The cycle path crosses the Water of Leith at high level, goes under two road bridges, over a road, passes an old railway platform, then goes under Queensferry Road. Immediately after this, near Sainbury's filling station, there is a left fork which you should take. The cycle entrance to the path here is from Maidencraig Crescent or Groathill Avenue.

The path climbs gently, passing under a red brick bridge. After a while pass under a second red brick bridge and then under a steel bridge. The end of the cycle path can be seen, marked with bollards. A hundred metres before the end of the cycle path turn left on to a dirt track going under another metal bridge. After a little way you will find yourself in Safeway's car park.

Cycle through the car park and turn right on to Cramond Road South. Immediately turn left, opposite a glass building, on to Barnton Avenue. Keep straight on, ignoring all turn-offs.

The road becomes rough and potholed, then turns into a path opposite a red brick house with a veranda. Keep on, passing between two golf courses and enter Barnton Avenue West.

Cross Whitehouse Road, going down into Braepark Road. Keep straight on until you cross the Old Cramond Bridge. Cycle up past a hotel car park, do not enter the main road (A90). Before the main road, between it and a sign: 'Private No Entry', is a further cycle path. Cycle up here to emerge on a minor road by a bus stop. Opposite is a pedestrian/cyclist's underpass going under the A90. Use it, then turn left, left, and left again; to reach the bus stop on the other side. Continue up the lay-by and take the left fork, signed Kirkliston.

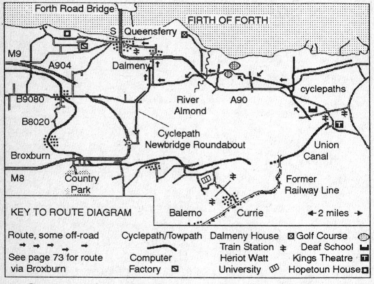

Continue along this for two miles. Shortly after passing under a railway bridge take a right turn going up a hill. Alternately continue on past this junction, to the cycle path 200m beyond and turn right on to this. Whichever way you go, keep straight on under the motorway to Dalmeny Village.

In Dalmeny turn right, then immediately left. Briefly descend and after 500m turn left towards Dalmeny Station. Pass this, entering the housing estate on Station Road. After passing a school turn left into Burgess Road. At the end of this, on reaching Kirkliston Road, turn right. If this is the end of your journey continue down the hill to South Queensferry where there are shops, pubs, tea rooms etc.

If you intend crossing the bridge to go further north, turn immediately left after turning right, to go down Stewart Terrace. The Forth Road Bridge will be visible ahead. At the bottom of Stewart Terrace you will be immediately underneath the Forth Road Bridge. A cycle path leads up from here to the bridge, bear right to cross the bridge on the west cycle path. The cycle path continues for half a mile on the other side after the bridge to the first road junction (see page 80).

To return to Edinburgh you can either go back the way you came, or take the train from Dalmeny Station, assuming there is room for your bike. An alternative, and longer route back, is via Hopetoun House, Abercorn, Winchburgh, Kirkliston, Ratho and the Union Canal towpath. See page 72.

Children's Edinburgh

These are routes with no motor traffic. They are mostly cycle paths, but a canal towpath and a beach esplanade are also used. They are shared with pedestrians, please be considerate. The cycle paths give a completely new view of the city. Swing parks and tea rooms by the routes are also described; entry points that involve carrying bikes down steps are not given. Enjoy taking your child cycling!

Section A to B
Cramond to Granton.

This section is on the Esplanade. Join at the west (beach) end from Cramond Glebe Road, or further east at Silverknowes Road/Marine Drive, or West Shore Road. To avoid cycling West Shore Road, follow the path by the sea. The east end is by a GEC/Marconi building. The start of section B to C is across the road from this, 75m west. Children's attractions: walking to Cramond Island when the tide is out; ice cream van in summer at the Cramond end; tea room by River Almond in Cramond; there is a cheaper tea room and toilets near the Silverknowes Road entrance.

Section B to C
Granton to Crewe Toll.

This forms a useful link but is not attractive. At the sea end start at West Shore Road, by the gasometer, opposite GEC/Marconi Avionics; or use a new link, recently completed by Spokes path builders from Granton Square. Access at the south end, from Ferry Road, just west of Crewe Toll. Section A to B starts just east of the GEC/Marconi building.

Section C to F
Crewe Toll to Roseburn.

At Roseburn join at Balbirnie Place (West Coates), or Russell Road. Going north join from Wester Coates Terrace, Ravelston Dykes (near Garscube Terrace), Maidencraig Crescent, South Groathill Ave (near Sainsbury's), or Drylaw Park (Telford Road) or Crewe Toll.

Section D to E
Davidsons Mains to Craigleith.

Going out of town join this by bearing left at the cycle path junction opposite Sainsbury's (entry also from Maidencraig Crescent). Continuing west access from Telford Road, Wester Drylaw Drive and Ferry Road/Davidsons Mains. It is road cycling to Cramond from here but there are quiet pavements.

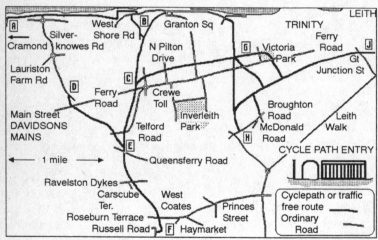

Section C to G
Crewe Toll to Victoria Park.

Get to Victoria Park (play areas) from section H to J by cycling along Stedfastgate (sign) and under Ferry Road. Access also from Craighall Road (path goes underneath). West of Victoria Park spurs not yet surfaced lead to the shore end of Trinity Road (Chain Pier Inn round corner by sea), and towards Canonmills. Going west access from Clark Road, Wardie Road, Granton Road (near south bus stop), Boswall Road, and

Ainslie Park (access through Leisure Centre, childrens fun swim pool, tea room, pirate ship, chutes etc. Phone 551 2400). At Crewe Toll access is just west of the roundabout.

Section H to J

Canonmills to Leith.

Access at the Canonmills end is by the Wm Low supermarket; at the junction of Broughton Road and Rodney St/Canonmills. Further east entry is at Broughton Road and McDonald Road, between the police box and the refuse works; cross the Water of Leith, at the play area turn right by a single storey brick building to join the cycle path by Warriston Road.

Further east access is at Gosford Place; the junction of Coburg St and Couper St, or Sandport Place Bridge by The Shore, where the path ends (feed ducks, see ships). For section C to G turn north at Stedfastgate (signed) and go under Ferry Road and through Victoria Park. The two links further west (see map) may be surfaced in 1996.

Section K

Tollcross to Balerno. (8 miles)

This starts at Leamington Road off Gilmore Place. The narrow sections at bridges are not for wobbly cyclists as they may end in the canal! This gets rural as you travel west. After the second aqueduct, cross a footbridge over the canal & Lanark Road to the disused railwaypath to Balerno - a longer cycle.

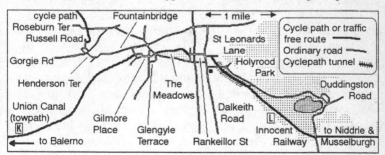

Section L

The Innocent Railway.

Start at the Engine Shed Café in St Leonard's Lane, or from Holyrood Park Rd. The cycleway is a right turn in East Parkside, a left turn before the park - whiz through the tunnel! Cross Duddingston Road to continue east between Bingham & Niddrie to end at Duddingston Park South. There is no access from the cycle path to Duddingston Loch (bird sanctuary), you could use the east pavement on Duddingston Road, then turn left to Duddingston Village on The Causeway. At the Sheep Heid use the lane to the loch. The pavement continues through the Park back to the cycleway tunnel. Reach the Meadows Cycleway using St Leonards Lane, Rankeillor St, cross Clerk St to Gifford Park, left on to Buccleugh St and right through bollards.

Forth Road Bridge to Perth

This is a quiet route, from South Queensferry to Dunning near Perth. It is likely to be useful to long distance tourists going north, but it is also a good bike ride in itself, and mostly on roads with attractive scenery. Total distance 35 miles.

The first four miles round the naval dockyard may be busy, but after this the route becomes increasingly rural. The route goes over the Cleish Hill, which is a steady climb from the south side. The roads in the Ochil Hills are just plain steep; interesting roads though! The route is given in both directions.

Northbound:
South Queensferry to
Dunning (near Perth) (35 miles)

Start in South Queensferry, on the west cycle path of the Forth Road Bridge. Get to this from underneath the bridge, a cycle path leads up. The cycle path continues after the bridge, keep left until you come to a roundabout under the dual carriageway, signed Rosyth Dockyard. Join the roundabout, take the second exit. Immediately after the roundabout, turn left on to Ferry Toll Road. This runs by the dockyard for a mile then crosses a road. Go straight over to Hilton Road, past a modern church. After a mile turn left on to the A985, signed Kincardine Bridge. Follow this for 1.4 miles, taking the second right, just after a brick rail bridge, signed Crossford.

At Crossford turn left into Knockhouse Road by the filling station and first right into Lundin Road. After 1.2 miles turn right to the A907 (Carnock Road). Immediately take the first left, up Craigluscar Road. Turn right at the next cross roads, signed Craigluscar Community Woodland.

There is a gradual climb for 1.5 miles, with a view of the Forth, then it's a left turn on to the A823, signed Crieff, then off it again first right, signed Kelty B915. Keep on the B915 for two miles, taking the second left, signed Cleish 4. There is a steady climb up the Cleish Hill, then a plunge down with a dramatic view of Loch Leven. Watch the road, there's a sharp bend which you see in advance, and then another which you don't!

Turn right at the bottom of the hill (no sign), then left on to the B9097, signed Crook of Devon, after a little bear right off it, signed Kinross 2.5; continue straight on for three miles to Kinross.

In Kinross go down the High Street, continuing straight on to leave the town by a health centre to enter Milnathort. You'll see two churches and the Jolly Beggars Hotel ahead. Go straight over and down the side of the Jolly Beggars, joining a minor road which climbs over the motorway.

Climb steadily through fields, ignore the first left turn but bear left at the second by a monkeypuzzle tree. There's a little descent, at the bottom of which turn left again, signed Path of Condie.

At the steep plunge down to the Water of May ignore the left turn for Path of Condie and zoom over two bridges, signed Dunning. Once you've climbed out of the river gorge there's another T junction, turn left, signed Dunning 4. You thought the drop to the *last* hill was steep? Take time to enjoy the view at the top before descending into Dunning. Make sure your brakes are working properly.

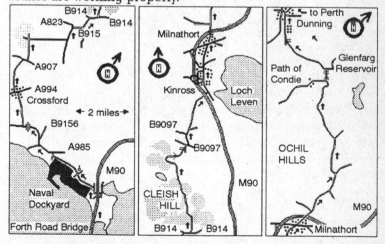

In Dunning cross the river by the post office/shop and turn right down Station Road by the side of the Dunning Hotel to continue north on the B9141. If you are going to Perth leave Dunning on the B934 for Forteviot, just before you get there turn left under the railway line (B9112). Cross the River Earn & turn right. Keep on the B9112, going under the motorway.

It's joined by the A93, half a mile after this you'll be near Perth Youth Hostel (107 Glasgow Road). See also pages 150/151 for the route from Dunning to Perth and Pitlochry.

Southbound:
Perth (Dunning) to
South Queensferry (35 miles)

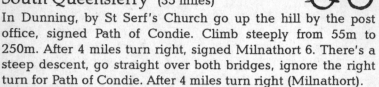

In Dunning, by St Serf's Church go up the hill by the post office, signed Path of Condie. Climb steeply from 55m to 250m. After 4 miles turn right, signed Milnathort 6. There's a steep descent, go straight over both bridges, ignore the right turn for Path of Condie. After 4 miles turn right (Milnathort).

In Milnathort go straight over into South Street, and into Kinross. In Kinross go down the High Street to leave the town on the B996. Just clear of the town turn right under the motorway, signed Cleish. Straight on at the next junction by a white bungalow, at the B9097 bear left, signed Glenrothes. After 500m leave the B9097, turning right, signed Cleish 0.5. Immediately turn left at an unsigned junction up a steep hill.

After the Cleish Hill, turn right on to the B914, signed Saline, then bear left on to the B915 by cottages. Keep on the B915 for two miles, then turn left on to the A823 at a T junction, signed Dunfermline. Half a mile then it's first right off the A823, signed Gowkhall. A mile, then left at crossroads by a sign: Craigluscar Community Woodlands.

Next turn right to join the A907, then take the first left off it for Crossford. In Crossford turn left on to Knockhouse Road (coffee shop), then right by the filling station on to Waggon Road. Next turn left on to the A985, under a brick rail bridge and take the second right, signed Rosyth Dockyard. Follow the dockyard fence, go straight over an access road by a modern church to Ferry Toll Road.

At the end of this turn right at the T junction then go underneath the dual carriageway to join the Forth Road Bridge cycle path. To continue to Edinburgh take the left slip road by the toll booths, descend to under the bridge, then drop to Stewart Terrace in South Queensferry (see page 75).

Where to Stay: Hostels: Perth, 01738-623658; Glendevon (off route) 01259-781206; Edinburgh (0131) SYHA, 447 2994 or 337 1120; Edinburgh independent, 225 6209 or 226 2153 or 557 3984 or 556 6894 or 557 6120. B&Bs in Kinross, Dunning, and Perth. Perth tourist information: 01738-638481. A very pleasant Georgian House bed and breakfast near Dunning is at Garvock House (01764-684287), phone in advance.

Two Routes in Fife

These two routes spill over from Fife into Perthshire, this is so that they can be connected to routes on other pages. Much of the Kinross - St Andrews route is signposted as a bike route by the local council, so it is very easy to follow. Most of it is on quiet roads. Total distance 31 miles, six of these, from the A92 crossing to Ceres are hilly.

The route from Tentsmuir Forest (near Leuchars), to Newburgh is by the Firth of Tay, this gives some fine views. There are a number of options to shorten it, connect it to the previous route, or extend it west to Dunning.

Kinross to
St Andrews (32 miles)

In Kinross High Street bike north. Pass the town hall to a red phone box. 300m after turn right to go round Loch Leven, signed Kinneswood, Scotlandwell. At the next junction turn right, signed Kinneswood and Glenrothes. At Balgedie Toll Tavern (bar lunches), turn *sharp* left, signed Duncrievie and Glenfarg.

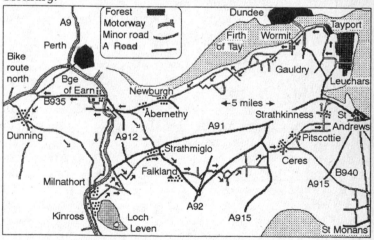

After a mile look for two stone-built houses on your right, and turn right through Gospetry Farm The farmer has no objection to small groups of people biking through. (The alternative, smoother but busier route, is to carry on to the next junction and use the A91 turning right again at Gateside.) At the farm, after two road humps, **walk the cattle grid,** turn right after it. Go up a concrete road to a dirt road T junction and turn left. It's mostly downhill to Strathmiglo with views of the Lomond Hills. In Strathmiglo turn right at The Tavern, then right at the A912, signed Falkland. Falkland Palace (1501) is worth visiting, the town is picturesque (youth hostel 01337-857710).

Leave Falkland on the B936 (Newton Road), signed Freuchie and St Andrews Bike Route. Pass through Newton (food at the Malt Barn Inn). In Freuchie turn left at the Albert Tavern and cross the A914. At Kettlebridge go under the railway then turn left, signed Kingskettle. Turn right at the T junction of Shorehead and South Street, by a church.

At the main A92 turn left, then right up a hill, signed Kettlehill and Burnturk. At the top turn left, signed Kettlehill. In Burnturk turn left at the T junction. After this follow a rolling road along the ridge. Cross a minor road, signed Chance Inn, turn left at the next junction for Chance Inn (no Inn). After Chance Inn, at the T junction at the top of a hill turn left; after 200m, turn right, signed Ceres. Keep straight on in Ceres unless you want to see the Fife Folk Museum.

In Pitscottie or Ceres you can turn right, and use the B940 to reach the former fishing villages of St Monans, Pittenweem, Anstruther and Crail (see map). After crossing the A915 turn right at the sign: Kellie Castle.

For St Andrews turn right at the first road junction after Pitscottie, following the bike route sign.

Tentsmuir Forest
to Newburgh (23 miles)

Tentsmuir Forest has to be reached from St Andrews on the A91. An option for connecting it to the previous route is to go via Strathkinness. The forest is signposted: Kinshaldy Beach.

Leave Tentsmuir and turn right (north) to a minor road. After a mile turn right to join the B945. Follow this road round to the Tay Estuary via Tayport and Newport on Tay (Riverside Coffee Shop on route) to Wormit. After passing Wormit, turn right, signed Balmerino, Newburgh & Scenic route to Perth. The next right turn, signed Balmerino & Coastal Tourist Route takes you down to Balmerino Abbey (Cistercian, 1229, ruined; view from outside only). This is a fast descent, followed by a stiff climb up. To avoid the climb go via Gauldry.

After Gauldry, keep straight on at the next crossroads. Ignore the next two turn-offs, but turn right at crossroads, signed Newburgh & Scenic Perth Route. There a descent then a straighter section. After a sign for geese crossing turn right to the A913 at the Abbey Garage and enter Newburgh. Newburgh has an attractive park with a view of the river, also the Laing Victorian Museum, which is free.

If you are continuing west to Dunning continue straight on to the A912. Turn right then immediately left to a minor road, signed Dron. Turn right at the next crossroads, signed Dron/Kintillo, then first left, signed Balmanno. After this keep straight on passing a church, and up a hill over the motorway. There is a winding descent, then turn left at a T junction with a big house in front (Drummonie House). Turn left to the B935 west of Bridge of Earn, signed Forgandenny. After Forgandenny, at a right bend, keep straight on, signed Invermay Road, to Dunning.

Pitmedden & Blairadam Forests

Two attractive small forests, both quite near Kinross. Pitmedden Forest stands on steep-sided hills between Newburgh and Auchtermuchty. Blairadam Forest is west of Kelty, off junction 4 on the M90. It is less hilly than Pitmedden, but with lots of interesting trails meandering through mixed woodland.

Pitmedden Forest

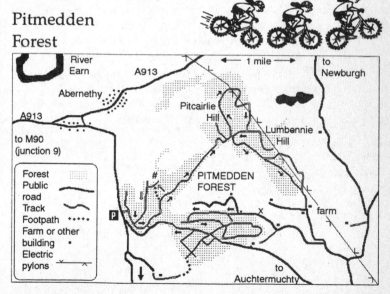

Pitmedden Forest forms a rough circle, broken to the south-east. This could be joined on ordinary roads. Start at the car park on the west side. Climb up the hill and travel south on

the forest road, take the second left near the top of the hill.
Just after this, at a right bend, there is an extra loop (marked
on map), take the path to the left through the woods if you
want to do this.

From the top of the hill there is a descent, with a view of
the Lomond Hills. Just after a bend you encounter a left turn
followed by crossroads. The first left is a dead end but the
second left goes round Pitcairlie Hill. This gives a view over
the River Tay. Half-way round you meet an electricity line, try
to follow the footpath under the pylons! Shortly after this there
is another T junction and you can turn left or right.

Turning left takes you round Lumbennie Hill - great
views, but the track ends under the pylons. The alternative is
to turn right and keep in the forest. For access to the forest
from the road marked X on the map, keep on the road until
you see a small bungalow with a pigeon loft and horses; then
enter the forest where the road takes a sharp turn to the right
up a hill.

Blairadam
Forest

The best part of Blairadam Forest is the east side near junction
4 on the M90. Here the forest is more open and you'll see lots
of beech, birch and oak as well as the usual spruce. The main
forest tracks are fairly easy, but get away from these and there
are lots of interesting bits joining up parts of the main tracks.
Near the forest edge there are good views of the nearby hills.

West of the Cleish Hill road the forest is spruce; Knockhill
racing circuit may be heard. Trails are more limited, the track
to the south of Loch Glow offers a longer run, gates could be
locked. Loch Glow may be busy with anglers.

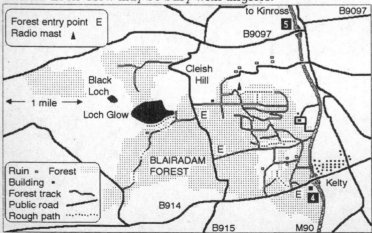

ROUTES TO AND FROM

GLASGOW

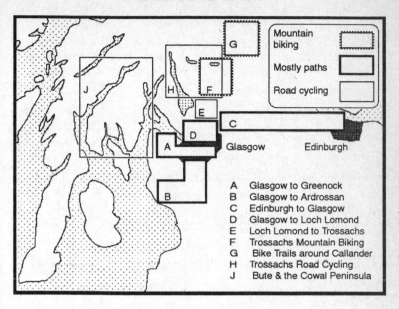

Glasgow Overview

Glasgow to Loch Lomond

Starts at the Scottish Exhibition Centre (SECC). It runs to Clydebank, using a former railway. At Clydebank it joins the Forth-Clyde Canal towpath to Bowling; a bike path to Dumbarton. Minor roads in Dumbarton, then a path by the River Leven to Loch Lomond. The route can be extended to Aberfoyle on quiet roads, and north again on forest trails.

Glasgow to Greenock

Also starts at the SECC but crosses the River Clyde. Quiet streets to Bellahouston and Ross Hall Parks. To Paisley, it's paths and back roads; beyond, the route is on former railway. Short sections on roads at Elderslie and Port Glasgow.

Glasgow to Kilwinning/Irvine/Ardrossan

As Glasgow - Greenock to Elderslie, then it branches south. Mostly bike paths, six miles of quiet roads, Glengarnock-Kilwinning. Sail to Arran from Ardrossan, or bike south.

Forth-Clyde Canal Towpath

While this is used by the Loch Lomond route, you can also use it to travel east, perhaps even as far as Edinburgh!

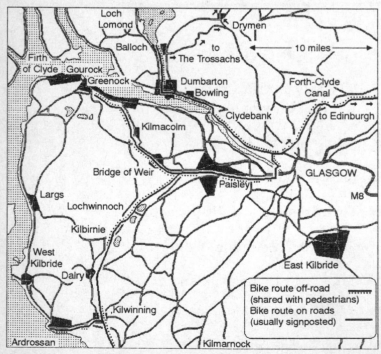

Glasgow to Greenock

This route starts at the Scottish Exhibition and Conference Centre in central Glasgow. It's signposted with the usual blue bike route signs; some of them are not too clear or get turned round - having this guide along with you is a good idea.

Bells Bridge to Bellahouston Park (2 miles)

Starting from the Scottish Exhibition Centre (SECC), cross the River Clyde on Bell's Bridge, and go straight on to Govan Road. Turn left then right, to cross the road and continue away from the river. Turn right into Brand Street, pass a nursing home then turn left into Cessnock Street. Cross Paisley Road at the light-controlled crossing into Percy Street.

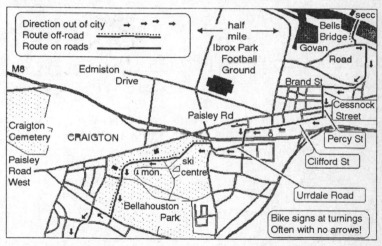

At the end of Percy Street turn right into Clifford Street. Pass a church with a clock, then at the junction with Beech Avenue, turn left over a footbridge leading over the M8 motorway. After the bridge turn right into Urrdale Road, bear right on to the footpath at the other end and cross Dumbreck Road to Bellahouston Park, at the light-controlled crossing.

In the park go on a little way, then turn left through a metal gate to an avenue of beech trees. At the time of writing the bike signs in the park were rather poor. The white line that was meant to indicate the route had mostly worn off, and a number of cyclists (ourselves included) had lost the way. Avoid this by turning right at a classical arch just before the ski slope. Straight on by a striped tree, then bear left at a triangular patch of grass. The monument on top of the hill on the left here, is in commemoration of the Empire Exhibition.

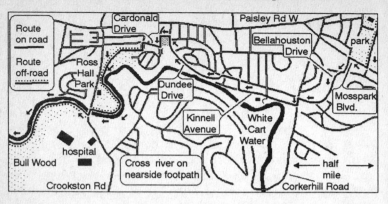

Bellahouston Park
to Johnstone (8 miles)

Leave the park at Mosspark Boulevard. There is a bike route sign here, but it is so high on the post that you are unlikely to see it. No doubt this is to prevent wags from turning it round so that the arrow points in the wrong direction. Turn right on to the pavement, then left over the light-controlled crossing to Bellahouston Drive. At the other end of Bellahouston Drive, carry straight on to cross Corkerhill Road on a light-controlled crossing. Turn left on to the pavement on the other side.

After 20m turn right by a small shop to Kinnell Avenue, left at the other end to Angus Avenue, and first left to Dundee Terrace. This becomes Dundee Drive - a gradual climb then a small descent. Keep left to go completely round the bowling green (Bewick Drive/Cardonald Place Drive). Turn right before the hump bridge following Cardonald Drive. At the end of this cross the railway on a footbridge to Ross Hall Park. Turn left to bike right through the children's play park.

If coming in the opposite direction be sure to bike through the play park, to leave the river.

Going west bike downstream, eventually leaving the park at the railed car park for Ross Hall Hospital. Turn left at Crookston Road to cross the river on the nearside pavement. Immediately after the bridge turn left down a dirt track. This becomes a cycle path following the river. After a while you turn left to a swing park by pylons, then exit near Ben Lawers Drive.

The building on the right is a hospice. Turn right to go round this, join a bike path by the Health Board building, and cross Hawkhead Road to Jenny's Well Road. Another cycle path then it's Whinhill Road, left to Cartha Crescent then right to Marnock Road. Bear left on to Barrhead Road at some lock-ups.

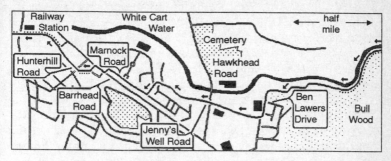

Cross Barrhead Road at a light-controlled crossing near a phone box. By the phone box turn left up Ladykirk Crescent, and opposite No. 5 turn right up a cycle path. This emerges near a cross-roads. Go straight over into Hunterhill Road, eventually joining a bike path at Patrick Street.

You can afford to relax a little now, as the cycling on streets is mostly over. The path goes through a park in central Paisley then joins a disused railway line at Paisley Canal Railway Station. Join or leave the bike route at the Beefeater Pub (Causeyside Street).

Railway paths have easy gradients, so any path that leads steeply up or down off the path, probably isn't part of the route. The path builders may put in a few dips or bends to make it more interesting, but these are quite small.

There is a short on-road section of about half a mile in Elderslie on Main Road. Bike lanes are marked. Going west cross back over to the right-hand side of the road on a light-controlled crossing, this is by a sandstone tenement marked '1910'. After this continue on the other side of the road in the same direction, to join a cycle path leading through a railway arch to open country.

When you see a weir on the river bear left to cross on a bridge. Just after this we come to the main bike path junction near Johnstone. Directions are painted on the ground. Turning right (signed Kilmacolm) takes you towards Greenock. Bearing left (signed Lochwinnoch) leads eventually to Irvine and Ardrossan (see page 93). The other indicator is Paisley which you've probably come from.

Johnstone to Greenock (14 miles)

From the junction near Johnstone the path runs straight through Bridge of Weir without touching any roads. In Kilmacolm there is a very short section on roads where a new mock Tudor housing estate has broken the continuity of the railway line. This starts at the former railway station, now the Pullman Pub (bar lunches). Refer to the map insert.

The path winds its way through rolling farmland and there are a number of interesting sculptures specially made for the bike route. The railway path is broken for half a mile on the outskirts of Port Glasgow. Here you should continue in the same direction using Montrose Avenue, green fields on the left. At the foot of Montrose Avenue turn left then right (see map insert) to rejoin the railway path at Crosshill Road.

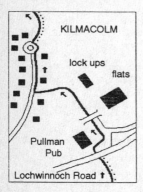

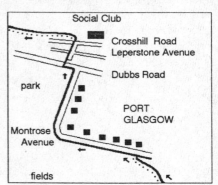

The path now runs high above the Firth of Clyde. The industrial townscapes of Port Glasgow and Greenock form the foreground, the green beauty of the Kyles of Bute stretches away into the distance. Just before you get to Greenock there is a steep descent into Devol Glen. The railway was originally carried over the glen on a sandstone viaduct, but this was blown up by the army when the railway closed in 1966. Perhaps at the time, when a bright new car-owning future beckoned to us, blowing it up seemed a good idea.

The path runs out in Greenock by the side of a children's climbing frame shaped like a helicopter. If you are starting from here, note that the path to take is the one going uphill from the helicopter. The nearest train station is Cartsdyke just down the hill.

Glasgow to Ardrossan, Irvine and Kilwinning

This route is identical to the Glasgow to Greenock Route as far as Johnstone. After Johnstone, instead of going west, this route follows a converted railway line south. The route passes Castle Semple Loch and Lochwinnoch. At Kilwinning the route divides again, one section leads west to Ardrossan; the other part goes south to Irvine.

After Johnstone the path becomes increasingly rural and attractive. Past Castle Semple Loch to Glengarnock, it's nearly all converted railway line with easy gradients - very good for young children. Between Glengarnock and Kilwinning the route is on quiet roads, these are hilly. Kilwinning to Ardrossan is not particularly attractive but can be useful to reach the ferry to Arran. Kilwinning to Irvine is a better day excursion.

Johnstone to Glengarnock (11 miles)

As described in the Glasgow to Greenock route, the converted railway line divides into two near Johnstone, with route directions painted on the ground. Bear left, following the sign for Lochwinnoch.

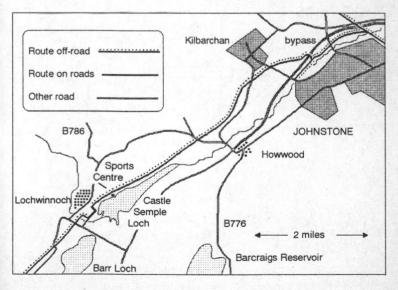

The route runs south, between the A737 Johnstone bypass and the river, Black Cart Water. Cross Barrochan Road on a light-controlled crossing, then shortly after turn right over the dual carriageway, on a high footbridge.

After this the railway path winds past dairy farms, through attractive hilly country. Because it's a converted railway line all the hills on the route itself are very gentle. There is a

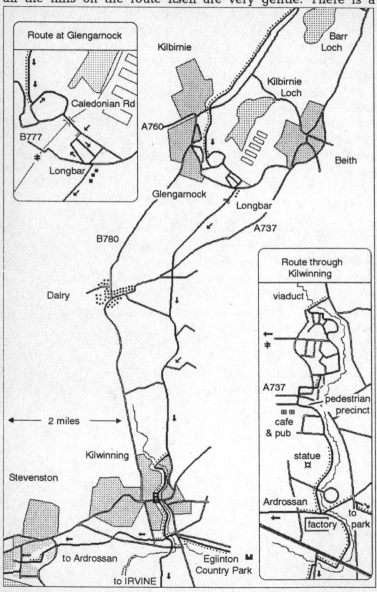

gradual climb, then a gentle descent to Castle Semple Loch. This is popular for sailing and sculling, The water sports centre has toilets, and an information display, but no tea room. There is a tea room in Lochwinnoch village, which is just off the route.

After the water sports centre, the route briefly follows an access road then turns right into a public park. Continue on past the children's swing park, and bear left on to the railway path again. There is another gradual climb, with lots of water channels, to ensure that the burns crossing the path at this point don't flood it. Barr Loch is over to the east, but it's obscured by trees.

The route passes over the A760, and under a number of minor roads. At Kilbirnie you pass under the A760, and run through sports fields to the east of Glengarnock. At the time of writing signs were missing here. Follow the most obvious path which curves round to the left, meeting Caledonian Road at an industrial estate. You have to bike on public roads from here.

Glengarnock to
Kilwinning (8 miles)

Turn left on to Caledonian Road when the bike path ends, and follow it in a wide circle to the north. Kilbirnie Loch comes into view, together with a large number of huge industrial buildings.

Keep on the main road, crossing over a railway line, but look for a bike path leading off to the right. Go down this into a housing estate, going: left, right and left (see map insert). Turn right off the B777, on to a minor road by three modern bungalows; climb up a steep hill.

After this you just keep straight on all the way to Kilwinning. The route runs high on the hill, passing above the village of Dalry. The mountains of Arran can be seen ahead on the right, poking above the lower hills of the mainland. Just before Kilwinning, turn right on to a railway viaduct, and cycle down this to a housing estate.

Getting through the estate seems complicated but just follow the River Garnock (see map insert). You emerge on to the A737 by the river. Cross the road and turn right then left to enter the pedestrian precinct in the town. There is a good Italian restaurant and a pub, just beyond the west end of the pedestrian precinct.

Eglinton country park is quite near Kilwinning, and is accessible on cycle path. To get there carry on towards Ardrossan and Irvine as described next, but turn left over the river opposite a factory, instead of right towards Ardrossan. When you reach the A737, take a bike path 25m to the right on the other side. Do not take the road or path immediately opposite, which leads north-east (see map).

Kilwinning to Ardrossan (8 miles)

Leave the pedestrian precinct in Kilwinning by biking east towards the river, then follow the signposted bike route by the river bank. Enter Alumswell Park, pass a circular statue on the right, ignore the first steel footbridge over the river, but turn right, away from the river, in front of a white factory building by the second bridge. Continuing straight on takes you to Irvine, and turning left over the river takes you to Eglinton Country Park.

Now travelling west, leave Alumswell Park, cross a road and follow a minor road running parallel to the A78 dual carriageway. Pass under a railway then under the A78. After a mile cross the B752 and enter Ardeer Park, cycling by a golf course. You emerge at Moorpark Road East. Turn left, over a railway level crossing and immediately turn right. This becomes a footpath by sand dunes. Pass a caravan park and follow the promenade through Saltcoats to Ardrossan.

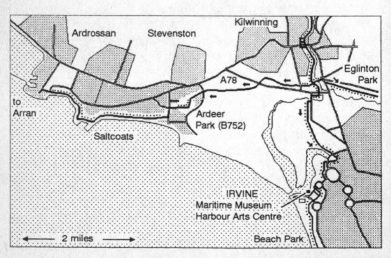

Scott's View, showing the Eildon Hills and the River Tweed (page 41).
(Harry Henniker)

Leaving Snoot Youth Hostel, near Roberton (page 53). (Harry Henniker)

Autumn in the Ochil Hills (page 81). (Harry Henniker)

Looking over the Kyles of Bute near Tighnabruaich (page 117).
(Harry Henniker)

The author taking notes on the Speyside Way (page 122).
(Dave McArthur)

Cyclists need to take to farm tracks near Tomnavoulin at the southern end
of the Speyside Way (page 128). (Dave McArthur)

In Glen Einich (page 139), on the route to Loch Einich. (Harry Henniker)

The old bridge at Carrbridge (page 156). (Dave McArthur)

Pictish symbol stone at Fowlis Wester (page 159). (Harry Henniker)

Glen Lyon (page 163) – one of the loveliest and longest glens in Scotland. (Harry Henniker)

On the off-road route from Arnisdale to Kinloch Hourn (page 179). (Harry Henniker)

First view of Suilven, eight miles from Ledmore on the road to Assynt (page 198). (Harry Henniker)

Entering Portnahaven, Islay (page 209). (Dave McArthur)

The ruined priory on Oronsay (page 211). (Dave McArthur)

The vast stretch of sandy beach at Scarista, Isle of Harris (page 226). (Harry Henniker)

The end of the weekend . . . (Paul McGuire)

Kilwinning to Irvine (6 miles)

This is mostly bike path except for a few short sections on roads. From Kilwinning, follow the directions opposite for Ardrossan, but bear left, instead of turning right in front of the white factory building; do not cross the river.

The route passes under the A78, then briefly joins the B779 to cross the River Garnock. After this it is dedicated bike path to Irvine, where we pass under the A737 (Marress Road) to reach the town. There is a short section on roads just before the Scottish Maritime Museum, then another brief road section on Gottries Road, leading to the Magnum Leisure Centre. After that it's bike path again, passing through Beach Park and on for a mile or two before it ends.

Irvine was the only port for Glasgow prior to 1668, when Port Glasgow was developed. Despite Port Glasgow, Irvine continued to flourish for a further hundred years. When the Clyde was made deeper and wider as far as Glasgow, this had a devastating effect on Irvine; the population fell dramatically.

Irvine was developed as a new town after the war, and since then there has been much restoration of the 18th and 19th century buildings. Visit The Vennell, where Robert Burns came to live in 1781. The Scottish Maritime Museum and the Magnum Centre are also worth visiting.

An Easy Way to Fix a Puncture

Do not remove the wheel, turn the bike upside-down. Rotate the wheel, examine the outer tyre carefully for a cut, or a piece of thorn or glass. Mark the spot and remove the glass etc.

If you have found the cause, expose the inner tube in the immediate area and repair it. Find the exact spot by pumping up the tube and feeling for the leak. If you can't find it, put lots more air in and look again.

If you have not found the cause expose all the inner tube by rotating the wheel. Search for the leak as above. Check the inside of the tyre for glass; check the inside rim of the wheel for protruding spokes, make sure the rim tape is in place.

When you put the tyre back try to do it without tyre levers, push the sides of the tyre into the centre of the rim to make this easier. Make sure the tyre is correctly seated on the rim.

Edinburgh to Glasgow

An attractive way to bike between Edinburgh and Glasgow is to use the Forth-Clyde Canal and Union Canal towpaths. It's 52 miles, and most of it can be done off-road. The Edinburgh end of the Union Canal is best avoided, as it is broken both at Wester Hailes, and by the M8 motorway. An alternative route is given for this section using cycle paths and minor roads.

The Forth-Clyde canal opened in 1790 to link Glasgow to the east coast at Grangemouth. It was closed to navigation in 1963. The Union Canal opened in 1822, and linked Lothian Road, Edinburgh, with lock 16 on the Forth-Clyde Canal.

Towpaths are shared, thank walkers if they give way, stop if necessary. If you come up behind and they don't hear you, slow down and say excuse me. If some sections are busy you should walk, most parts will be quiet. The Forth-Clyde Canal towpath is wider than the Union Canal towpath. The British Waterways Board issue cycling permits for both canals, phone 0141-332 6936 - they will post you one free of charge. Towpaths are not suitable for organised cycling events.

Another bike route between Edinburgh and Glasgow is under construction by Sustrans. When this is complete it will be possible to go a different way. The route here is between Glasgow Youth Hostel, 7/8 Park Terrace (0141-332 3004), and an Edinburgh hostel, 18 Eglinton Crescent (0131-337 1120).

Central Edinburgh to Linlithgow (17 miles)

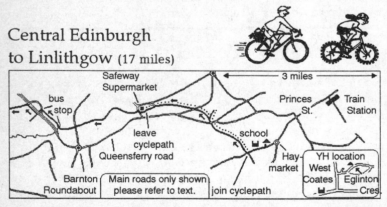

Join the cycle path to Davidson's Mains. This is carried over the road at West Coates on an old rail bridge. From Eglinton Hostel turn right, and bike west to the T junction of Eglinton Crescent and Magdala Crescent (see map insert). Turn left, then right on to West Coates. Face Donaldson's School (playing fields), look left and you will see the bridge. You can join the cycle path from either side of the road.

Bike north on the cycle path to cross the Water of Leith at high level. The cycle path goes under two road bridges, over a road then passes a railway platform; after this you go under Queensferry Road. Immediately after this, when you see Sainsbury's filling station, take the left fork. Pass under two red brick bridges, then under a steel bridge.

The end of the cycle path can be seen, marked with bollards. 100m before the end, turn left on to a dirt track. After a little way you will enter Safeway's car park. Turn right on to Cramond Road South but immediately turn left, opposite a glass building, to Barnton Avenue. Keep straight on ignoring side turnings. The road becomes rough and potholed, then turns into a path. Keep on, passing between two golf courses and enter Barnton Avenue West.

Cross Whitehouse Road, going down into Braepark Road. Keep straight on until you cross the Old Cramond Bridge. Cycle up past the hotel car park, do not enter the main road (A90).

Before the main road, between it and a sign: 'Private No Entry', is a further cycle path. Cycle up here to emerge on a minor road by a bus stop. Opposite this is a pedestrian/cyclists underpass going under the A90 - use it. On the other side, turn left, left and left again to reach the bus stop. Continue up the lay-by and take the left fork, signed Kirkliston.

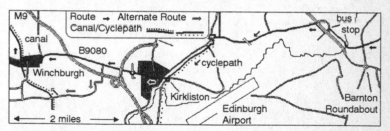

Continue west towards Kirkliston. Pass under a rail bridge, ignore a right turn up a hill. The second bridge over the road carries a cycle path, turn right off the road and left to cross the bridge. After about a mile, where the cycle path crosses a minor road you have to turn off it to enter Kirkliston.

Turn left off the cycle path over a stone bridge, signed Kirkliston. Turn left on to the road, go straight over at the traffic lights ahead, passing through the village and under the M9, using the B9080 to Winchburgh. At the far side of Winchburgh join the Union Canal towpath by turning right opposite a tubular steel footbridge (no sign). A track leads down to the canal on the north side of the road. Turn right through wooden bollards on to the towpath.

Navigation after this point is very easy - just follow the canal. Mostly the scenery is attractive - lots of swans and mallard ducks. When the canal was built the bridges were numbered and these can be seen incised into the stone above each arch. The sequence has to some extent been lost as a few bridges are down and others added. The path is sometimes bumpy, but not so much as to require a mountain bike. The canal bank is mostly wide, but the actual footpath on it is quite narrow; mountain bikers could use the grass to avoid pedestrians. After about five miles of completely flat cycling the spire of Linlithgow Palace comes into view ahead.

Linlithgow to Bonnybridge
(13 miles)

Linlithgow is a good place to stop for lunch. The canal widens here and the basin is used to berth canal boats, nowadays just boats doing short pleasure trips. There are benches to sit on,

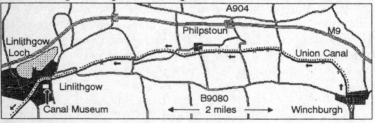

and pubs doing bar lunches not far away. Also here is the canal museum, toilets, and a tea room. One of the surprising things is that even when the canal passes through urban areas it still actually seems quite rural. You get views of peoples' back gardens, often it passes through public parks and the canal is landscaped in.

As it leaves Linlithgow it winds southward following the contour and passes playing fields. The Ochil Hills can be seen to the north, and Grangemouth is just a distant blur as you never go near it. The Union Canal met the Forth-Clyde Canal near Falkirk. Before Falkirk, there is an interesting passage

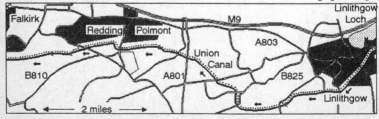

over the River Avon on a high aqueduct. Best to walk as the towpath is quite narrow, and while there is an iron railing, it's a long way down. Shortly after this the canal becomes silted up and full of reeds, this obviously is the limit of the boat trips from Linlithgow.

No such limits apply to bikes though, you roll pleasantly along in open country. Occasionally there will be a barrier on the towpath, mainly to stop motor cycles, bikes are easily wheeled round. It's briefly necessary to leave the towpath to cross the A801, this is a fast straight road so take care crossing. The next town we pass through is Polmont, be sure to keep by the canal bank as a number of other paths lead in the wrong direction. There is a prison on the left as you leave the town, heading towards Falkirk in open country again. An amusing feature near here is a tall bridge with a smiling face high above the water.

Did you bring any bike lights? They are going to be useful in the tunnel at Falkirk. Certainly you can feel your way along in the gloom, and there is a handrail, but a light helps you to avoid the occasional drip from the ceiling. The Union Canal ends abruptly in a public park about a mile after the tunnel.

It is possible to join the Forth-Clyde Canal in the centre of Falkirk but it's best to join it further west at Bonnybridge using the B816. This avoids heavy traffic in Falkirk and misses out sections of the towpath that may be busy with pedestrians. It also allows the possibility of visiting the Antonine Wall (see map). At the end of the Union Canal turn right to go down the hill then take the second left on to Tamfourhill Road (B816). The OS 1:50,000 map shows a track uphill from the canal end leading over the railway but this no longer exists.

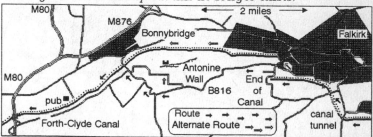

The B816 passes close to the best preserved section of the Antonine Wall. This includes the remains of Rough Castle, one of the forts that were positioned every two miles. The Romans abandoned the wall to the Picts about AD163. The wall originally ran from near Boness on the Forth, to the Clyde. Whether you go to see the Antonine Wall or not, turn right on the B816, to drop down towards Bonnybridge to meet the Forth-Clyde Canal. This is seen just before you get to the town. The video hire shop at the road junction below the canal sells ice cream.

Bonnybridge
to Glasgow (22 miles)

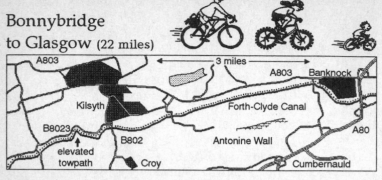

It's immediately obvious that the Forth-Clyde Canal is much wider than the Union Canal. It has locks on it too, though many are non-operational. More relevant is that it has a wide smooth towpath. The first lock you encounter is at Underwood. The lock building is now a pub also providing meals, there are tables outside.

There is a long straight section; the canal goes under the M80 then passes Banknock, the Kilsyth Hills visible to the north. The scenery here in the Kelvin Valley is attractive with lots of mature trees, the canal winding around to keep to a level contour. Just south of Kilsyth, there is a section of towpath that runs quite near to the road (B8023), and is elevated above it. If you have children you might prefer to walk. Shortly after there is an urban section in Kirkintilloch,

then a final rural stretch before reaching Glasgow. Just before entering the city, at Glasgow Bridge, you pass The Stables pub. A place to have a drink or even a meal before continuing your journey. There are canal boat trips, and two restaurant boats also operate from this point.

At Glasgow Bridge it's quite pleasant, you then pass Bishopbriggs Sports Centre to the south. Beside this there is a golf course and on the other side a wilderness plantation.

However by the time you get to Possil Loch (cemetery) you are entering central Glasgow. The canal goes right through though, so no need to cycle on city streets yet. However pay attention, as some navigation will be required of you shortly.

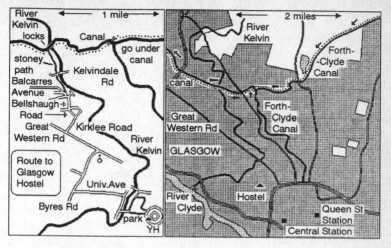

Shortly after passing Possil Loch you pass over a railway line. Very soon after this, the canal splits into two. As you approach the canal junction there is a set of rusty steel girders on the left, forming an old jetty. Opposite these leave the canal towpath, using a footpath leading down to the road below.

Go through the bridge under the canal, **watch out for oncoming traffic**, then immediately turn left up a rough path to gain the towpath on the south side of the canal (see map). Turn left on to the towpath following the sign for Bowling to continue west.

After half a mile you descend steeply, as the canal drops through a series of recently restored locks at Maryhill. Immediately after the bottom lock the canal crosses over the River Kelvin. At this point there is a curved stone wall on the left with a stoney path leading off to the south. This leads towards Kelvingrove, Glasgow University and Glasgow Youth Hostel. Continuing on by the canal will take you to Clydebank and Bowling and then by cycle path to Dumbarton and eventually Loch Lomond (see next route).

Of course if you live in Glasgow you just go home. However to get to the hostel go down the path by the river, cross Kelvindale Road keeping on the same side of the river, then go down a path through a housing estate to emerge on a footpath at the junction of Winton Drive and Bellshaugh Road. Go down Bellshaugh Road by a playing field and turn right on to Kirklee Road.

At Great Western Road turn left (south-west), then after 500m turn right by a church into Byres Road. Turn left down University Avenue after 500m; at the other end you see Kelvingrove Park. Enter the park crossing the river. Cycle through the park, Park Terrace is the road overlooking the park above you. The youth hostel is number 7/8.

For other accommodation phone Glasgow tourist information on 0141-204 4400. Queen Street train station (for Edinburgh) and Central Station are fairly near the hostel.

Glasgow to Edinburgh (52 miles)

Points to watch: leave the Forth-Clyde Canal at Bonnybridge by turning right up the hill on to the B816, about a mile after the lock and pub at Underwood. Leave the Union Canal at Winchburgh, turning left on to the B9080, look out for the wooden bollards (thick posts), and bike up a track to the road. The turn-off is just after bridge 34. If you miss this you will eventually be blocked by the M8 motorway.

In Kirkliston go straight across at the traffic lights, then pick up the bike path on the right-hand side after 300m. After crossing over the A90 dual carriageway after Kirkliston, pick up the bike route at the bus stop. Leave the cycle route after the high bridge over the Water of Leith.

Glasgow to Loch Lomond

The Glasgow to Loch Lomond Cycleway was opened in 1989. It is 22 miles long, and was the first long bike route in the west of Scotland. Mostly it is on purpose-built paths, often on former railway lines. It also uses the west end of the Forth-Clyde Canal towpath; in Dumbarton it uses minor roads.

From the Loch Lomond end it is possible to connect to other bike routes leading to The Trossachs, and from there east and north to Callander and Loch Lubnaig. Further extensions are planned, but the bike routes that already exist provide an excellent safe route out of the city. Loch Lomond itself is not particularly quiet as it is quite near to Glasgow.

Bells Bridge to Bowling (11 miles)

The Renfrew Ferry caters for pedestrians and cyclists only, as since the Clyde Tunnel was opened, there was no need for it to carry motor vehicles. Current charges, adult 50p, child 30p, there is no charge for bikes. The Clyde Tunnel has a seperate section for pedestrians and bicycles. Quite near the Transport Museum (see text) is the Kelvingrove Museum and Art Gallery, this is well worth a visit. Don't forget that Glasgow trains carry bikes. Why not get the train home at the end of your day out.

Forth-Clyde Canal

Yoker

A814

Carscadden

Renfrew Ferry (bikes)

1 mile

RIVER CLYDE

Clydeside Express-way

Victoria Park and Fossil Grove are quite near the cycle route. Victoria Park has a formal garden. Fossil Grove, discovered in 1887, is a 250 million year old geological formation consisting of the stumps and roots of trees which were growing at that time. For exit point for Victoria Park see text..

Partick

River Kelvin

Clyde Tunnel (bikes allowed)

Scottish Exhibition Centre

Bells Bridge

The Bike route starts at Bell's Bridge, opposite the Scottish Exhibition Centre by the River Clyde - this is also the start of the Glasgow to Irvine cycle route. An easily seen landmark near the start is the Finnieston Crane, originally used to lift steam locomotives. On the east side of the river, bike downstream, past the glass Moat House building, to the helipad. Turn away from the river here, and cross over the Clydeside Expressway on a curved footbridge.

The cycleway now runs parallel to the expressway for over a mile. Bike route signs point off it. These are intended to be helpful directions to train stations but often seem to lead cyclists astray. Unless you want go to the place indicated, keep straight on ignoring any side turnings.

The cycleway initially runs beside the expressway, but after a little way there is a narrow park, and the roar of traffic is less obtrusive. A bike route sign points to the right, indicating the way to the Museum of Transport. This is well worth a visit, it has some interesting exhibits including early bicycles. There is a tea room (10am to 4.30pm, Mon to Sat). To get to the museum follow the sign then bear right, don't cross the River Kelvin. To continue to Loch Lomond ignore this turn-off.

A little further on, a path leads to the River Kelvin walkway, ignore this too, also ignore a bike sign pointing to Partick railway station. Shortly after this the cycle route passes under the expressway. It now becomes obvious that the path is running along a former railway line, some of the bridges have been lost and the path dips at these points. There are docks on the left with the Kvaerwer shipyard on the far bank.

Pass Primrose Street (access to Victoria Park and Fossil Grove), Henretta Street, Balmoral Street and then Yarrow's shipyard. Cross over Burnham Road (bike access from Plean Street). Soon after this cross a public road by a food store. Shortly after the path runs beside a rail line. You have to cross the rail line, then immediately turn left before entering Lasswade Street. (If you are coming in the opposite direction look for an old cast iron railway station footbridge and pass under this.)

The path now runs past scrapyards, then turns on to a public road. Look left and see John Brown Engineering. Bike towards this, passing a former railway booking office, then opposite John Brown's main gate turn right to join a cycle path again.

On the left you will notice the modern blue and grey Playdrome building. At the roundabout before it, filter right to ride on cycle path instead of pavement. Bike past the car

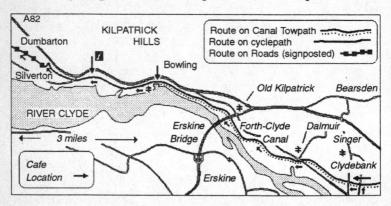

wash, then turn left using the light-controlled crossing to join the Forth-Clyde Canal towpath. Just here, on a small stretch of blocked-off canal, there is the strange sight of a mini ocean liner. It's Monagles Fish Restaurant and it isn't going anywhere. It doesn't have engines and isn't even floating.

Near here too is a large shopping mall, it includes a coffee shop if you don't mind the stares of the shoppers; personally I'd wait until Bowling where there is a café by the canal.

The canal towpath is quite wide with a good dirt surface. It's attractive beyond Clydebank, swans and ducks are frequent, and you get views of back gardens as you roll along. Soon the Erskine Bridge comes into view, then the canal widens, a lock comes into sight, you're in Bowling.

This is where the canal meets the sea, though you can't see it, as railway arches block your view of the outer basin. What you can see in one of the railway arches is a little café - seats outside by the canal. Hot toasties, pies, tea, coffee, and open from 10am to 7pm every day. The large building opposite is the former customs house, an indication of the past importance of the canal.

Bowling to Balloch (11 miles)

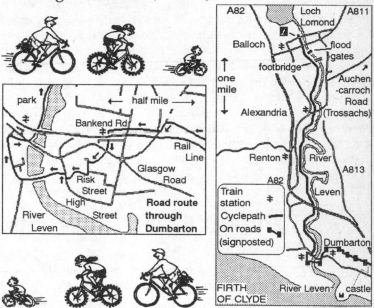

After Bowling you cross the canal then cross a public road. The railway path route starts on the patch of green on the other side. This is a purpose-built bike path. The immediate surroundings are quite pleasant, frequently with lots of trees, but you are sometimes aware of the railway line on your left and the heavy traffic on your right. Just before we enter Silverton, the cycle path passes close to a busy main road and a tourist information office, visit the café next door if you like motorway service stations. Dumbarton Castle can be seen to the left on a rocky spur overlooking the River Clyde (footpath access from cycle path).

The bike route enters Dumbarton at Silverton, turning left into minor roads and paths on a housing estate; look for the bike route signs. There is a short busy section on roads, children should walk. The route crosses the River Leven, then immediately turns right down a minor road to enter a public park. After this it is a shared path with pedestrians all the way to Loch Lomond.

The route follows the west bank of the River Leven. After a mile it passes under the A82 dual carriageway then meanders prettily over little wood bridges, keeping by the river most of the time. The scenery is attractive but this is not always the case with the built environment.

Occasionally the path joins minor access roads, but if you keep by the river you will not go wrong. You go under a curved steel bridge at Alexandria, then a mile after this, enter Balloch, passing under a high-level steel footbridge. If you are intending to cycle on to The Trossachs this is your exit point. Carry your bike up to the bridge on the steps and cross the river. At the public road on the other side turn right then take the second left on to Auchencarroch Road (see below).

To go to Balloch keep straight on, there is a flood control barrier, then lots of small boats and the river widens out into the loch. When you can go no further you have reached the end of the cycle route. Tourist information, train station, boat trips, pubs and tea rooms, it's all right here.

Loch Lomond to The Trossachs

This route is an extension of the Glasgow to Loch Lomond cycle route, going to The Trossachs on quiet roads and forest paths. There is a dismantled railway running most of the way to The Trossachs from Balloch; this is not bikeable. The road route described here is mostly quiet, it's rather hilly. Total distance 20 miles.

Most of the other roads around Loch Lomond are too busy to be worth cycling. In particular the A82 on the west side of the loch should be avoided. The minor road by Balmaha on the east side is pretty, but will have some recreational motor traffic on it. Rowardennan Youth Hostel is at the end of this road. It's mainly used by people doing water sports, and walkers intending to travel north on the West Highland Way. The West Highland Way is not bikeable by Loch Lomond.

Balloch
to Drymen (9 miles)

The route starts at Auchencarroch Road in Balloch. From the Glasgow to Loch Lomond Cycleway this is best gained by crossing the high footbridge over the river, just downstream from the flood control gates. This involves carrying your bike up steps, but it's still a lot easier and safer than getting round on the public road.

Cross the bridge, passing new houses on the far river bank, to the public road on the other side. Turn right here, then second left to Auchencarroch Road. Bike up this past a timber yard to leave the town. The road climbs steadily, then flattens out. There is a good view of Ben Lomond to the north.

Turn left (north) at a crossroads with a sign for Merkins Farm, then take the first right, signed Croftamie. The hills to the right are the Campsie Fells. After a further mile turn right at a T junction, signed Croftamie; then right again at the T junction at Pirniehall (no sign).

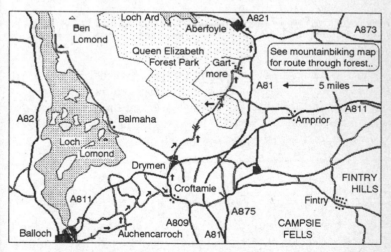

When you reach the main road turn left, signed Drymen. There is about a mile on the A809, you pass over Endrick Water on a stone bridge, then turn left into Drymen. There's a choice of pubs and tea rooms.

Drymen
to Aberfoyle (11 miles)

When you leave Drymen, make sure you do it by passing up the side of the Clachan Inn. Don't take the road for Balmaha. If in doubt look for the steepest hill around - that's the one you're cycling up! The hill is pretty unrelenting, stopping on the way up not only gives you a rest, but also great views of Loch Lomond behind.

The Campsie Fells and Fintry Hills are on the right, Queen Elizabeth Forest Park on the left as you get to the top. Soon you're whizzing down the other side towards The Trossachs. Bear in mind that if you want to travel to Aberfoyle via forest trails from here, you have to turn left *before* you get to the bottom of the hill.

To travel to Aberfoyle or Loch Ard on forest tracks, turn left on to a dirt road opposite a sign: Drymen Road. This is half-way down the hill, at a Forestry Commission car park. The various routes through Loch Ard Forest are described next. For the road route, continue down the hill into Gartmore and turn left into the village. After this turn left again on to the A81, then left again by a hotel into Aberfoyle.

Trossachs Mountain Biking

This is an attractive area, but quite hilly. There are more easy tracks in Loch Ard Forest than in Achray forest. The routes are marked with colour-coded posts. Green routes are longest. Bear in mind that there are other users of the forest: walkers and the timber industry. Show consideration, routes may occasionally have diversions due to logging operations.

Loch Ard Forest

The prettiest starting point in Loch Ard Forest is at Milton, this gives access to all the routes including the easy purple one. Leave Aberfoyle going west, signed Inversnaid Scenic Route. After a mile turn left in Milton, bearing left down the side of a cottage with a hooped steel fence to the forest car park. The red and purple trails are a right turn just before the car park. For the green, or to do the red in a clockwise direction, carry straight on.

110

The simplest thing is to follow the coloured markers. An easy ride would be to cycle the little purple loop by the loch for a picnic. A much longer ride (14x2=28miles) is to the West Highland Way at Loch Lomond (see map, page 116). The track runs by Duchray Water until it leaves the forest - follow the pylons. It then skirts round the north side of Ben Lomond. The West Highland Way is not bikeable at the loch.

The green route is long and technically interesting. Start at Milton, or follow the instructions here to join it via the blue route. Leave Aberfoyle as before but turn left (south) at the crossroads at the west end of the village. After 200m turn right by the Covenanters Inn (blue sign), to a forest road with an overhead phone line. The blue route loops off the main track, north round Lochan Spling and south. Do both loops, south last.

Turn left where the south loop rejoins the main track by a ruined cottage. Bear right at the next junction and follow little bridges with iron railings over the Castle Burn. Pass under an electricity line, aqueduct and white cottage to the right. When you see a right turn over a bridge we are on the green route. Turn right over the bridge to get to Aberfoyle; however keep straight on, deeper into the forest.

Now on the green climb past Victorian water board machinery. Eventually meet a concrete bridge. Turn left here

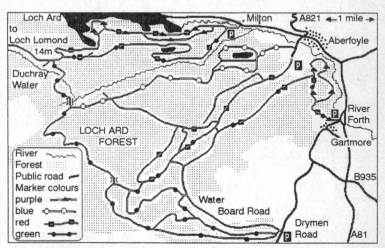

then left again to take the red route, bear right to keep on the green. Climb steeply, views of Ben Venue behind; there is a view across the Forth Valley towards Stirling then a fast descent, the Lake of Menteith far ahead. At the next junction; take either leg and drop down to the public road.

Here there are two options: return on the green, using the opposite leg to the one you came down on, or use the water board road. In the latter case you eventually meet the red route, then either use it anticlockwise (red/green) or clockwise (red only) to return. The first part of the water board road is surfaced. Distances: green 15 miles, both reds 9 miles, both purples 4 miles, blue 7 miles.

Achray Forest

Covering the hills either side of The Duke's Pass, the Achray Forest has long steep gradients making for interesting biking. Again the green route is the longest. Start this just east of Aberfoyle, at the Braeval car park, on the A81. Alternatively start at the Forest Visitor Centre off the A821. A long steep climb takes you to the top of the pass, from where there is a fast descent to Loch Drunkie (toilets).

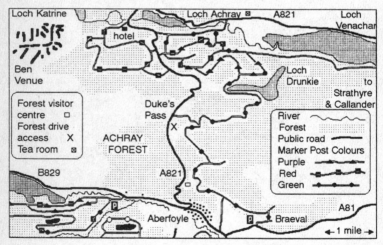

The north end of the western red route starts behind the Loch Achray Hotel, for all the other routes refer to the map. Another bike trail leads along the south side of Loch Venachar towards Callander which gives access to another set of bike trails (see next route). Useful finishing points just east of Loch Achray, on the A821, are the Brig o' Turk Tea Room, or The Byre restaurant. The best tea room in Aberfoyle is at the A821/B829 junction. Distances: Green 13.5 miles. Western Red 7 miles. Others 3 or 4 miles.

Bike Trails around Callander

A former railway line, that of the Caledonian Railway Company, forms the backbone of this route. The railway path runs from Callander to Strathyre (9 miles), it winds initially past the Falls of Leny, through birch and oak, then along the west side of Loch Lubnaig. The cycle path was constructed about ten years ago by Sustrans, the railway path charity.

Cyclepaths along former railway lines have very easy gradients. The same cannot be said of the forest tracks on the slopes of Ben Ledi immediately above. These are marked as mountain bike routes by the Forestry Commission. There are other options too: a quiet route along the south side of Loch Venachar which leads to both mountain bike trails in The Trossachs and a very quiet road cycle round Loch Katrine (see next route).

Callander to Strathyre (9 miles)

The main railway path route starts in Callander, off the main road just north of the Dreadnought Hotel (car park & toilets). It sweeps to the west of the river then crosses the A821 (children take care). After this there are no more road crossings. There is a long straight section leading to the Falls of Leny. Near here the old rail line was carried over the river but the bridge is gone. The cycle path builders elected to keep on the left bank, so the next section is more winding until it meets the old rail line again.

Keep straight on; motor vehicles are prevented from using the next section by a padlocked barrier. It's surfaced here but this runs out again at Forestry Commission chalets. If you are intending to do the purple mountain biking loop here, watch out for coloured marker posts indicating a left turn (see map). The higher trails offer good views towards Ben Vorlich on the other side of the loch but are steep. There is an attractive picnic spot by the lochside, just beyond the chalets.

The path runs by the loch in trees, there is a slight incline when you meet the second (red) mountain biking loop. Shortly after this you encounter a pile of china sinks, these have been here for at least fifteen years to my knowledge and their origin is a mystery, but at least they serve as a marker for turning right (there is also a signpost). The last section at the end of the loch is a rise to meet a minor road, then there is a drop through more trees. Turn right at the junction for Strathyre.

Strathyre to
Balquhidder (4 miles)
and beyond

There is an option to continue northwards on the minor road to Balquhidder. This is very quiet but steep initially, climbing through trees. The last section towards Loch Voil is flat. The little church at Balquhidder is the site of Rob Roy's grave. A fragment of poetry, on a wall in the graveyard, reminds you of your own mortality.

Love all you meet - no season knows nor clime,
Nor, days, weeks, months - which are the rags of time.

After Balquhidder you could visit the Kingshouse Hotel two miles east of Balquhidder; this does bar lunches etc.

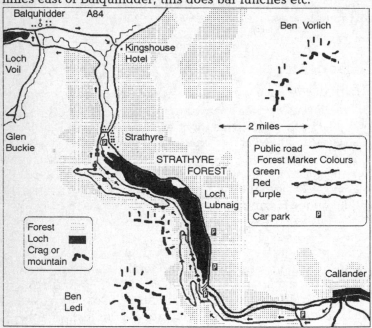

Please note, it is impossible to travel directly between Strathyre Forest and Glen Buckie with a bike. The only route is via Balquhidder.

The track bed of the old rail line is still mostly intact north of Strathyre, hopefully one day this will also be a bike path. Currently it's broken just north of the Kingshouse at a sheep farm. The farmer is quite definite that he doesn't want any mountain bikers trying to find a way through. It's possible to rejoin the rail line the far side of Lochearnhead. A very steep footpath leads up to it, from near the former rail bridge, by the scout station. From here you can mountain bike most of the way up Glen Ogle. Beyond Glen Ogle the line continues into Glen Dochart, meeting the A85 at a caravan site. This is private land, one of the bridges is missing, the way is barred by an electric fence.

Loch Venachar

There is an interesting bike path on the south side of Loch Venachar, this connects to mountain bike routes in Achray Forest. To reach this, bike along the minor road on the south side of Loch Venachar, the cycle path is a signposted right turn about half-way along.

Tourist information Callander, 01877-30342. Killin Youth Hostel, 01567- 820546.

Trossachs Road Cycling

The water board road round Loch Katrine has the unique feature that it has no cars, bikes however are allowed. Add to this, that it is one of the loveliest roads in Britain, and you have thirteen miles of pure delight. Further extensions are possible to Loch Lomond or Aberfoyle via Lochs Arklet, Chon and Ard; on normal roads this time but still very attractive. The pleasure steamer S.S. *Sir Walter Scott* sails on Loch Katrine, and combined cycle rides and steamboat sailings are possible.

Loch Katrine:
Trossachs Pier to
Stronachlachar
Pier (13 miles)

The main route starts at Trossachs Pier, from where the steamer S.S. *Sir Walter Scott* sails. The next shops/tea rooms are in Aberfoyle twenty-four miles away, so if you haven't got food and drink with you, have a cup of tea and a scone here. The first part of the route round the loch is flat and there may be pedestrians. Half a mile thins them out however, and soon you'll be on your own. One mile from the start, looking down through the trees, is Silver Strand beach with Ellen's Isle opposite. This is a good place to stop with little children as the road here ceases to be horizontal.

After this the road winds up and down through trees, close to the loch shore. Do not forget the possibility of the odd water board Land Rover on the road, not to mention some very complacent sheep. While you can't get lost as there is only one road, you should also remember that any support vehicle you might have is forbidden to use the road, so if you break down you have to walk either to Trossachs Pier or Stronachlachar.

A frequently asked question is whether you can cycle right round the loch, using the vehicle track on the south side that is visible from the road. The answer is no. The track stops three miles short of the east end of the loch. This last three miles is so difficult that a German tourist recently abandoned his bike, and all hope of even walking round, and attempted to swim across as dusk set in. Fortunately he was rescued by the water board, who have many similar tales to tell.

Just over a quarter of the way round you come out of the trees for a mile or so, then enter woodland again as the road rises and falls by the shore. Around here you might have the illusion that you are half-way along, as the pier and house at Stronachlachar seem quite close. A steady climb follows, and

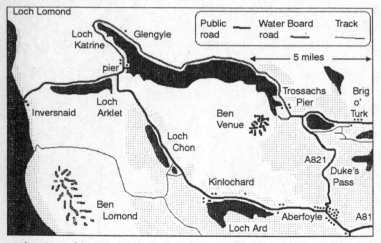

at the top of it you realise that this is plainly not so, as the tail of the loch curves round to the north-west. Also visible to the west is Loch Arklet, the hills in the distance are on the far side of Loch Lomond.

Eventually you drop down again to loch level. The bottom of this fast section is very steep with a sharp left-hand bend. The little graveyard on the small island here is worth looking at. Just before reaching the end of the tail of the loch you pass Glengyle, birthplace of Rob Roy McGregor; if Sir Walter Scott is to be believed, Scotland's own Robin Hood. The final section, travelling south-east to Stronachlachar Pier has hills too. There are toilets and shelter from any rain by the pier but little else.

Stronachlachar to Aberfoyle (11 miles)

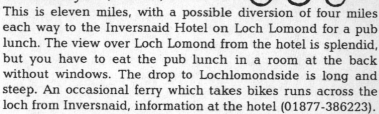

This is eleven miles, with a possible diversion of four miles each way to the Inversnaid Hotel on Loch Lomond for a pub lunch. The view over Loch Lomond from the hotel is splendid, but you have to eat the pub lunch in a room at the back without windows. The drop to Lochlomondside is long and steep. An occasional ferry which takes bikes runs across the loch from Inversnaid, information at the hotel (01877-386223).

The road to Aberfoyle is mainly downhill once you have climbed up to the T junction by Loch Arklet. There is some up and down by Loch Chon. There is a shop and post office at Kinlochard. Soon after this you enter Aberfoyle, the first tea room on the left is recommended. If you have left a car at the Trossachs Pier you will have to return to it via the Duke's Pass, a climb of 210m.

The S.S. *Sir Walter Scott* which sails on Loch Katrine was built by Wm. Denny at Dumbarton and taken in sections up Loch Lomond by barge in 1899, then hauled up by horse and cart from Inversnaid; think of this if you cycle up. The original steam engines are still in use. Sailing times, from Trossachs Pier: 11.00am, 1.45pm, 3.15pm. From Stronachlachar: 12 noon only. Saturday afternoon sailings are 15 minutes later. No Saturday Stronachlachar sailing (0141-355 5333).

Bute and the Cowal Peninsula

Despite being near to Glasgow the Cowal Peninsula is surprisingly quiet. The reason of course is the Firth of Clyde. Tourists generally bypass Cowal, heading north for Oban or Skye. Cowal is hilly but beautiful, and easy and cheap to get to with a bike. This is a weekend ride, but could also be the start of a longer tour starting from Glasgow.

The route starts from Wemyss Bay, catch the Caledonian McBrayne ferry to Rothesay on the island of Bute. A thirty minute crossing, ferries depart from Wemyss Bay at hourly intervals or less (01475-520521). Train service from Glasgow Central to Wemyss Bay, taking a bike on this train is not usually a problem.

Rothesay to
Tighnabruaich (22 miles)

Rothesay has a slightly nostalgic air, the days of trippers from Glasgow going 'doon the water' on paddle steamers are mostly past; it's a lively town though. If you need to buy food for your evening meal get it here. On disembarking turn right and cycle along the A886 to go north, sea on your right. Pass Port Bannatyne and keep north to the ferry at Colintraive. This is a five minute crossing, in summer frequent to about 9pm. The hotel on the Colintraive side does bar lunches, there is no other food stop between here and Tighnabruaich.

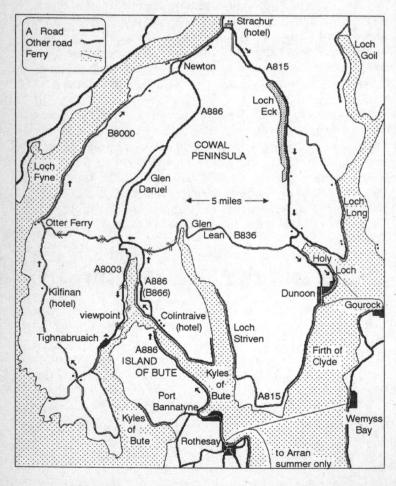

Continue north on the A886 but fork left just after Colintraive, to go by the sea on the B866. Towards the head of the loch both roads merge again. Shortly after this ignore the B836 on the right but turn left on to the A8003, to go south towards Tighnabruaich. There is a stiff climb, your reward is a spectacular view of the Kyles of Bute, the mountains of Arran and the Clyde stretching away in the distance.

It's a fast descent to Tighnabruaich, the youth hostel (01700-811622) is a white house on the right just before you enter the town. There are several hotels, a number of B&Bs, but no tourist office. The tourist office on Bute (01700-502151) would assist.

Tighnabruaich is well known for its sailing school. There are a few small shops, but they always seem to be at the top of a steep hill, and unlikely to be open if you arrive late and leave early. The hostel sells a limited range of tinned and packet food.

If you have plenty of energy left, the minor road which loops south from here (see map) offers unsurpassed views of Arran and the Sound of Bute.

Tignabruaich
to Strachur (27 miles)

The climb out of Tignabruaich is steep, take in the extra loop as above or not, but afterwards head north for Otter Ferry. There is a hotel at Kilfinan and a restaurant at Otter Ferry, now much improved. Otter Ferry is a lovely spot, with a tiny harbour and a pebble beach, ideal for a picnic. It also has a small shop which can produce coffee, ice cream, and a limited range of food.

There is an option to shorten your distance here and head directly east for Dunoon via Glen Lean (see map). Don't be under any illusion that this is easier, there are some fierce hills this way. The route up Loch Fyne is easier if longer.

It's never long enough for me though, for this is one of the loveliest rides in Scotland: flat, hardly any cars, the wind usually behind you; you sail along in beautiful scenery past long shingle beaches.

This flat section ends just south of Newton, where you briefly leave the sea climbing inland. Join the A886 at Newton to continue north along the loch to Strachur. The pub at Strachur, a left loop off the road, does meals, sandwiches, etc; you can sit outside.

Strachur
to Dunoon (19 miles)

The next section is directly south past Loch Eck. Just before Loch Eck, on the left, there is a memorial to Harry Lauder. Loch Eck is notable for a unique species of fish, a fresh water herring which was marooned in the loch when it was cut off from the sea. It has adapted to fresh water but is tasteless.

There is a hotel at the south end of the loch; shortly after you pass the Younger Botanic Garden (tea room, American redwoods) and eventually reach Dunoon for the ferry back to the mainland. Note that both Western Ferries (0141-332 9766) and Caledonian MacBrayne (01475-650100) both operate ferries from Dunoon to Gourock, all the terminal points differ.

Off-Road Cycling

Route is reasonably smooth, not specially hilly; motor traffic is mostly absent. Suitable for young children.

Off-road route on old railway line, canal towpath, etc; a bit bumpy only, could be ridden on any bike.

Mountain bike route, forest trails or Land Rover track, not particularly hilly and not technically difficult.

Mountain bike route, contains steep sections that are hard work to get up and fast or difficult to descend.

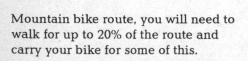

Mountain bike route, some parts not bikeable. You may have to walk up to 20% of the route.

Mountain bike route, you will need to walk for up to 20% of the route and carry your bike for some of this.

CENTRAL HIGHLANDS

MOUNTAIN BIKING

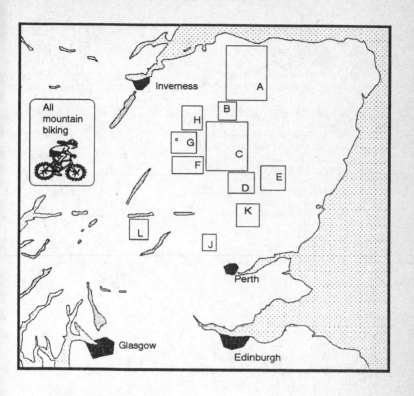

Speyside Way

The Speyside Way runs from Spey Bay to Tomintoul. Bikes are allowed on most of it, elsewhere there are good alternatives. Our route is on former railway line, forest roads, or back roads.

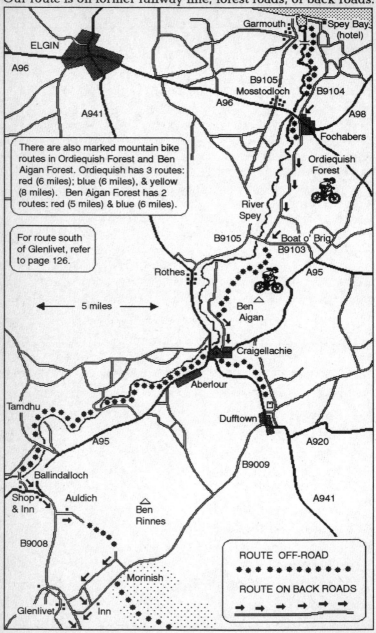

There are also marked mountain bike routes in Ordiequish Forest and Ben Aigan Forest. Ordiequish has 3 routes: red (6 miles); blue (6 miles), & yellow (8 miles). Ben Aigan Forest has 2 routes: red (5 miles) & blue (6 miles).

For route south of Glenlivet, refer to page 126.

5 miles

ROUTE OFF-ROAD
• • • • • • • • • • • •
ROUTE ON BACK ROADS
➡ ➡ ➡ ➡ ➡ ➡

Spey Bay to Fochabers (5 miles)

The Speyside Way starts near the Tugnet Ice House at Spey Bay. You can get to this on the B9104 from Fochabers. Join a stoney track, by Tugnet House, just east of the ice house. A more interesting way to get to the start is from Garmouth by using the former rail viaduct. Take the B9105 from Mosstodloch to Garmouth and join the Spey Viaduct Walk by picnic tables as you enter the village. The former rail line joins the main route just south of the start.

After this keep straight on unless the thistle waymark symbols indicate otherwise. It's easy to miss these on a bike if you are travelling quickly. There is a left fork in trees after a mile, then you meet the river. After passing some fishing huts look for a little ramp leaving the main trail by a horse chestnut tree. Follow a footpath by the river for a little way, then turn left by a bench to the public road. Continue along the road until you see the main road (A96).

Just before the main road turn right on to a grassy track which leads you under the road by the river. If you want to enter Fochabers, you can do this by turning left on the main road, or by following the track which skirts the southern edge of the town. Fochabers is an attractive small town with plenty of places to eat (Quaich Café, Tart & Pie Shop, chip shop).

Fochabers to Craigellachie (13 miles)

This section is hillier, particularly around Ben Aigan. After passing under the A96 on the grassy track, keep by the river, then turn left *before* a little bridge. Cross a road, right to West Street, and rejoin the track by a school. After this the trail gets a bit more technical on a bike. Filter left to avoid steps, duck at the tree! There are a few more steps and you eventually turn right on to a road; after a climb pass Slorachs Wood. There is a scenic picnic spot on the opposite side of the road.

After this there is a steep descent with a tight bend at the bottom, followed by a fierce climb. Following on there is a long descent, gradual at first, to Boat o' Brig, with fine views of the River Spey below. At Boat o' Brig, we cross the B9103 - this can be busy. Turn right, then immediately left up steps by a house with a portico to leave the public road.

Climbing steadily now, turn left at farm buildings, and follow an electricity line into the forest. Turn right uphill again at a gun club sign. The track dips into Ben Aigan Forest, then skirts it giving good views of the Spey valley. After this it enters the forest, and climbs steeply to a forest road. Turn right here. There is an initial drop, a further climb, then a fast descent to leave the forest at a mountain biking sign (see box in map, page 122). Turn left on to the public road and descend further; turn right at the A95 to enter Craigellachie.

The ranger's office is at Craigellachie (01340-881266). You can camp here free of charge - an attractive site by the river. There are toilets with cold water only, and no other facilities. Craigellachie has a Spar food shop, there is a friendly pub with a riverside garden.

Dufftown
Spur (4 miles)

This follows the old Strathspey railway line from Craigellachie to Dufftown up the valley of the River Fiddich; turn left from the ranger's office. It ends at a picnic area just outside the town, easy cycling and very pretty. Dufftown has the Glenfiddich distillery, lots of shops and pubs, and a resident pipe band. The tourist office is in a mini castle in the middle of the town (01340-820501). Balvenie Castle, the impressive 13th century lair of 'Black' Comyn, is next to the Glenfiddich distillery. It was a noble residence for 400 years. Admission £1.20 (75p), or walk round for nothing in the evening.

Craigellachie to
Ballindalloch (12 miles)

This section, on the old Strathspey railway line, is really lovely. There are striking views of the River Spey, it's also surprisingly quiet. Being completely flat with no motor traffic, it's ideal for children.

In Craigellachie, by the ranger's office, turn right on to the old railway line (turning left takes you to Dufftown). The track bed runs under the main road then follows the river bank. There is a small tunnel. Horses are allowed, though we never met any. The route runs through a park in Aberlour, there is a tea room in the old station building. After this the route rolls along by the river through mixed woodland. You pass the former halt of Dailuaine, cross a minor road, then cross the river on a combined 'rail'/road bridge. Left on to the path again.

The track runs by the Knockando and Tamdhu distilleries. You can see a copper still containing 3180 gallons of malt whisky, just ten yards away at Knockando. Visits by arrangement only, but ask nicely and they'll let you use the WC. When we were checking out this route the lady at Tamdhu distillery offered us a free dram, but being eleven in the morning we declined, whereapon she kindly made us a cup of tea. This so overwhelmed Dave that he bought a bottle of the hard stuff - not that he needs much encouragement.

After Tamdhu the path runs high above the river giving lovely views, there's a small viaduct with steps down, pass under the B9102 at Blacksboat, then roll along by wide meanders to the railway bridge at Ballindalloch. Cross the bridge to Ballindalloch Station, now a hostel (no resident warden, phone 01540-651272 to book in advance).

Ballindalloch
to Glenlivet (8 miles)

This section begins on roads, turn left on to the minor road by Ballindalloch Hostel, this joins the A95 at a T junction, turn left here. The A95 is reasonably quiet but there is a rough track on the far side. Follow the A95 for just under a mile past a wee church and shop at Bridge of Avon to the Delnashaugh Inn. If you don't mind slumming it with Range Rovers and BMWs this is a nice place to have lunch.

At the sharp bend in the road by the war memorial, turn right on to the B9008. Follow this for one kilometre, then at the foot of the hill, turn left to a farm road to Auldich. Pass under electricity pylons, shortly after this the farm road becomes a track. The walking route turns right off the track, but *if you have a bike you are not allowed to go this way*, but should keep straight on.

Follow the track to the top of the hill; cross a heathery grouse moor. Ford a burn, and descend the other side to public roads again. Turn right at a white harled bungalow with a wood fence. There is a fast descent with fine views over Strathavon, then a brief climb. Turn left here and descend again to the Croft Inn on the B9009. Turn right (south) for Glenlivet. Alternatively turn left (north) on the B9009 to the forest entry at Morinish for an off-road route south.

It's quite easy to cycle on quiet roads to Tomintoul from here. You should *not* attempt to bike the Speyside Way walking route between Glenlivet and Tomintoul. Instead there are a number of dedicated off-road bike routes created by the Crown Estate - see below.

Glenlivet - Tomintoul

The bike routes between Glenlivet and Tomintoul are interesting to explore in themselves, but can also be used as part of a long distance mountain bike route, connecting the Speyside Way to other routes in the Cairngorms. Do not bike on the Ladder or Cromdale Hills as summit vegetation and wildlife is easily disturbed. The routes are circular so could be started at any point, they are signposted. OS map, sheet 36 is advised. Tomintoul Tourist information 01807-580285.

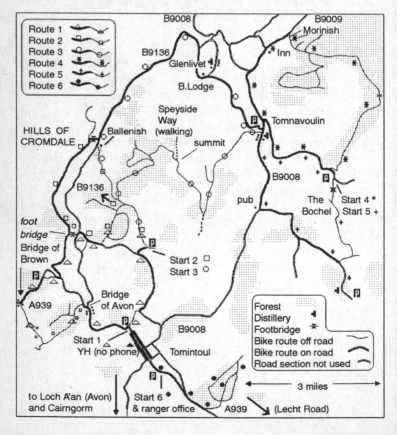

Route 1 (10 miles)

From the start at Campdalmore, take the A939 north-west to Bridge of Avon. Turn left on to a forest road, pass a lodge then Stronachavie, then before a burn, turn right (north) on to a track to Bridge of Brown (tea room), and turn right on to the A939. After half a mile leave it again and turn right by a car park on to a forest track. When you meet the A939 again, go on a little then turn left on to a minor road. Follow this north for two miles, by the west bank of the River Avon to a footbridge. Cross the river, follow a track downstream past a field to the B9136. Join a farm road and travel south-east, past Achlichnie Farm and Tomachlaggan, then turn left (north-east) on to a forest road. The first two right turns are a loop round the hill, take the third right, at the edge of the forest by Chabet Water, and follow this upstream (south). At Glenconglass Farm turn right then left (south), following Conglass Water upstream towards Tomintoul. At a sharp left bend near The Old Kennels join the Speyside Way, passing under an electricity line to the start.

Route 2 (7 miles)

From Glenconglass car park follow a forest road north past two farms. Ignore all left and right turns. Leave the forest on a hill track, passing a ruin then drop to the B9136 at Ballenish. Turn right (north) on to the road but after 100m turn left over the river. Travel upstream (south) for 2.5 miles then cross the river on the footbridge. Follow directions from route 1 to return to your starting point

Route 3 (15 miles)

Start as for route 2 but turn right (north) to cross Chabet Water in trees one kilometre after the second farm turn-off, keeping in the forest. After crossing the river travel two miles in the forest then bear right (south) by the Speyside Way to the summit of Carn Daimh. Join the Speyside Way, re-entering forest. Turn left (north) at the next junction, keep straight on; eventually join a farm road. Turn left (north) on to the B9008 at Tomnavoulin. After a short distance turn left, (north-west) towards Glenlivet. Bear left at Blairfindy Lodge Hotel, then left on to B9136. Keeping on this, curve round to the south. After three miles ignore the right turn over the River Avon, but soon after, turn left at Ballenish House, then continue south up a track, initially through woods then on to open hillside. Keep straight on through the forest following the south bank of Chabet Water to complete the route.

Route 4 (11 miles)

From the car park, head towards Tomnavoulin a little way then turn right into the forest. The route climbs the shoulder of Cairn Muldonich, then descends to cross the Allt a' Choileachain burn, before turning north-west (red squirrel markers) towards the Morinish forest car park on the B9009. Turn left (south-west) on the public road, then left again on to the B9008. Just before Tomnavoulin bear left on to the minor road leading to the start point.

Route 5 (10 miles)

Head south on a farm track from the car park for a little way then cross the River Livet on a footbridge (if you meet a steel gate you've missed the turning). Go south through a field with marker posts, the conical hill of The Bochel to the right. Follow the line of the fence to an electricity line and a house then join a farm track. Go through another gate, pass another house, then turn right through the forest to the public road. Descend to the B9008. The Pole Inn at the junction does good food at reasonable prices. Turn right on to the B9008 and right again just after Tomnavoulin to return to the start.

Route 6 (Quite short)

This is just south of Tomintoul and explores a small area in some detail. At the time of writing trails here were still being developed. The entry point is in Glenmulliach Forest just south of Tomintoul. Mostly on smooth forest roads.

From Tomintoul it is possible to bike off-road, further south towards the Cairngorms. This is described in the next section.

Eastern Cairngorms

A two or three day circular mountain bike route in Scotland's biggest mountains. Take warm waterproof clothing, the weather can change rapidly. If you can't complete the first section in daylight you need to camp. Total distance 57 miles.

Glen A'an to Glen Derry & Braemar
(35 miles)

This is remote country, there is a wet river crossing. You will have to wheel your bike about 5 miles and even carry it for some of this: a rucksack is better than panniers.

Day One: Turn right off the A939 just south of Tomintoul, signposted Delnabo. Follow the minor road, left to a track before the road crosses the River Avon (Queen's View sign, parking). Continue upstream on the east bank of the river, the other road crosses again and you roll along in pleasant scenery thinking: this is easy. The tarmac ends at Dalestie five miles from the start, keep on to Inchrory Lodge.

You can turn east here up a little gorge to the source of the River Don and then follow this, but don't. Continue south past the lodge. Turn right (west) over a small bridge crossing the Builg Burn just before it enters the River Avon. The track passes the Linn of Avon waterfall, then crosses to the north bank at the foot of Glen Loin. Here the track climbs steeply to avoid the waterlogged lower path. On the upper path ignore the right turn to Glen Loin. The pleasant wooded countryside gives way to larger mountains. Continue west on the north bank of the river past the dramatic corrie of Slochd Mor. The small hut here is a useful shelter and a good stop for your first break.

After this the track climbs to avoid a river gorge then descends to cross a burn. Soon, at Faindouran Lodge Bothy, the Land Rover track becomes a rough path. This may be bikeable in places. It crosses a wide valley then leads through a narrow ravine to the rough shelter at the Fords of Avon. You need to cross the stepping stones here to continue south to Glen Derry. If you have time, leave your bike and walk one mile further west to Loch A'an (Avon). This remote loch with its huge cliffs, dropping down from Cairngorm, is one of the most dramatic in Scotland; an interesting place to camp.

Crossing the river when the water level is low is not too difficult; people have been killed trying to cross when the river was high. After this there is a tiny bikeable bit, a smaller burn to cross, then three miles of boulders before the path becomes bikeable again opposite Corrie Etchachan.

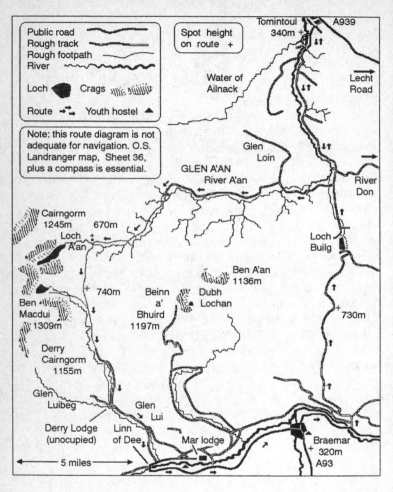

After a further mile the path becomes Land Rover track. Keep on the east side of the river and enter old pine woods at the south end of Glen Derry. When you encounter unoccupied Derry Lodge bear left to go south-east down Glen Lui.

Two miles after, turn right to cross a bridge, passing through more woods to the public road. Turn right to the Linn of Dee then left to travel east to Braemar. It's possible to cycle on the north bank of the river through Mar Estate, however the Victoria Bridge, next to Mar Lodge, is normally locked. This means you have to continue three miles past Braemar to the Invercauld Bridge to cross the river.

Braemar to Glen Builg & Tomintoul
(23 miles)

Day Two: Unlike day one, virtually all of this is bikeable. The exception is the footpath on the east side of Loch Builg. Start at Braemar taking the A93 towards Ballater for three miles, then 200m after crossing the river, turn left, signed Keilloch. After 300m turn left through Aldourie Farm. This becomes a dirt road, there is an electricity line on the left. Shortly after you enter forest and the electricity line ends. Very soon after this turn right up a Land Rover track. If you meet a cattle grid you have missed the turning. Route finding thereafter is easy - just keep going. The biking is more difficult - a big climb, but with panoramic views. The track continues to ruined Lochbuilg Lodge, but leave it and take the footpath on the east side of the loch. The track down Glen Builg is a ten-mile descent to Tomintoul. Hostels: Braemar (013397-41659), Tomintoul & Inverey (no phone). Bike hire, Braemar Outdoor Centre (013397-41242). Braemar tourist info: 013397-41600.

Around Loch Muick

Just south of Balmoral Castle and quite near Ballater, is the shapely mountain of Lochnagar and beautiful Loch Muick. Loch Muick is a typical Cairngorm loch, it's basin scoured out of rock by glaciers.

Loch Muick is best seen on a cold winter's day, with a gale blowing down the loch and snow threatening. Then you get a true sense of its remote beauty. It's not quite the same on a warm Sunday, with cars parked along the road to the glen, and sun loungers by the roadside.

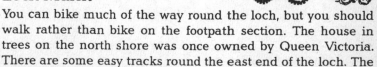

Loch Muick
You can bike much of the way round the loch, but you should walk rather than bike on the footpath section. The house in trees on the north shore was once owned by Queen Victoria. There are some easy tracks round the east end of the loch. The

track shown on the west side of the River Muick (outline arrows on map) is a gentle descent all the way to the B976 near Ballater. Access from the Ballater end is a mile west of the signposted road leading up the glen. There is a red post box at this junction, and a little further up, a sign to deter cars: locked deer gate (not a problem for bikes).

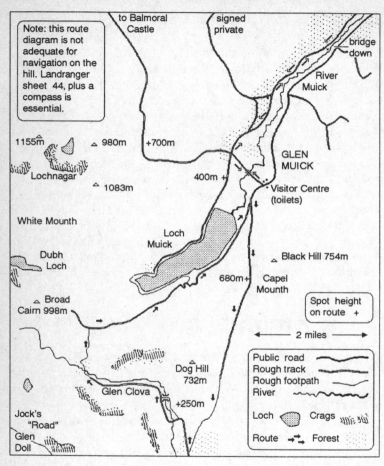

Note: this route diagram is not adequate for navigation on the hill. Landranger sheet 44, plus a compass is essential.

to Balmoral Castle

signed private

bridge down

River Muick

1155m   △ 980m   +700m

Lochnagar   △ 1083m   400m +

GLEN MUICK

Visitor Centre (toilets)

White Mounth

Loch Muick

Dubh Loch   Black Hill 754m

△ Broad Cairn 998m   680m+   Capel Mounth

Spot height on route +

← 2 miles →

Dog Hill 732m   Public road   Rough track   Rough footpath   River

Glen Clova   +250m

Jock's "Road"   Loch   Crags

Glen Doll   Route   Forest

Loch Muick to Glen Clova and Return

(16 miles)

This is an all day route (solid arrows on map). It involves a considerable amount of ascent, first to get out of Glen Muick, then another steep climb to get out of Glen Clova. The greater part of the route is on Land Rover tracks. The part that isn't, the descent into Glen Clova and the climb out of it will involve you getting off your bike. It's best to do it clockwise, if only for the great views over Loch Muick on the return leg. A proper map and compass, and warm waterproof clothing is essential.

The track which runs north-west from Loch Muick, by way of Lochnagar is shown on OS maps as being a footpath for some of the way. In fact it's a steep Land Rover track. At the north end it finishes near Balmoral Castle, summer residence of HM Queen Elizabeth. People do go this way, though the factor of Balmoral Estate is said not to like mountain bikes. What the Queen might think about it is uncertain, however she is patron of the Cyclists' Touring Club.

Glen Tanar & Mount Keen

Glen Tanar is one of a number of side valleys of the River Dee where remnants of the ancient Wood of Caledon are preserved. An important part of the preservation of this type of forest is that old trees are allowed to be blown over in storms, so exposing open soil for seedlings to generate. This however will only occur succesfully where seedlings are protected from deer and sheep. This is why gates should be shut and deer fences not climbed over except where stiles are provided.

There are three suggestions here. A moderately difficult route via the Black Moss; a long difficult route via Mount Keen to Glen Esk; or simply exploring the forest tracks in the Caledonian pine forest.

Black Moss

Route (17 miles circular)

Start at Tombae on the B976, this is opposite the junction of the A97 and A93 on the other side of the River Dee. The track passes a farm (height 200m), and climbs south-west, rising steeply at times. The ascent is continuous, giving a good view of Loch Kinord across the Dee. There is a shallow descent across Black Moss then another steep climb to 535m. At this point Mount Keen and Glen Tanar become visible.

A fast descent follows, this is difficult in places owing to water erosion but is still bikeable. At the foot of the hill turn left at a T junction to go down the glen. A mile after this there is another junction nearer the river, continue down the glen towards the trees. This is a gradual descent, sometimes with gravel and sand surfaces, return to Tombae on the B976.

Biking in the Forest

Glen Tanar is south-west of Aboyne off the A93. Follow the B976 south of the River Dee. The Glen Tanar road starts by a bridge with an adjacent tower and is signposted. Continue up passing a forest car park, then on to a set of farm buildings in

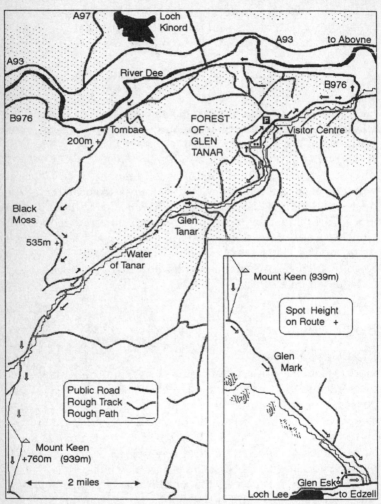

Scottish baronial style. Turn right here following the right of way sign round the farm. Pass a sign saying: 'Ca Canny Doon the Brae', and you are in the forest. The most interesting ride is to follow the track going up the glen by the side of the

Water of Tanar. There is little danger of getting lost in the forest as returning to the river will take you to the exit. If you meet any horse riders stop to let them pass.

Mount Keen to Glen Esk
(16 miles off-road)

This is a hard ride with a lot of climb. Warm waterproof clothing, a 1:50,000 OS map and a compass is essential. The top section will involve some walking.

Start in the forest as before but continue up the Water of Tanar to where the glen becomes steep sided and narrow. At this point turn south towards Mount Keen, crossing the burn. The track continues for a little further then curves round to the west. Leave it here and take the footpath towards the summit, passing to the west of some crags. You will have to walk here as it is quite rocky.

After a further climb the path branches in two, the left fork leading to the summit. Take the right fork, this section is just bikeable, and is a gentle ascent, a flat section, then a gradual descent to a track leading into Glen Mark. Descend down Glen Mark to the public road in Glen Esk.

Unfortunately the youth hostel in Ballater closed in 1995. The other alternative is The Wolf's Hearth, Tornaveen, by Banchory, 01339-883460 (not SYHA). Tourist information at Aboyne (01339-886060) and Ballater (01339-755306).

Braemar to Glen Feshie

Linn of Dee - Geldie Burn - Achlean (23 miles)

This route is not hilly but does cover some remote country. O.S. Landranger map, sheet 43 and a compass is essential. While most is on Land Rover track, and is comparatively easy, there is a six mile section in the middle which is a rough footpath. Parts of this will have to be walked.

Start at Linn of Dee, which is six miles west of Braemar. From the north side of the bridge, take the track which leads west: 'Public Footpath Glen Geldie and Glen Tilt'. The path runs along the north bank of the River Dee, through some Scots pine. After this there are fine open views, you pass a plantation forest, then come to White Bridge.

Continuing straight on will take you up the Lairig Ghru, which is definitely not biking territory; cross the bridge and turn left to travel south on the Land Rover track. You pass another small plantation forest, then meet a fork in the river. Turn west here, and follow the north bank of the Geldie Burn by a corrugated iron roofed cottage. The track becomes slightly rougher but still very bikeable. Keep on for three miles until you see the ruin of Geldie Lodge on the far bank.

The track leads across the burn but don't cross. Instead take a rough footpath to continue west. How bikeable it is will depend on how wet the ground is, we found we could bike about 80% of it. After two miles you see Glen Feshie ahead, but the path becomes less distinct. There is a tiny sign: Glen Feshie, and a few small cairns, but if you miss these just keep on, staying at the same height, until you meet the River Eidart. There is a bridge by a waterfall, search for it if necessary, don't try to ford the river.

After the bridge the path is easy to follow, and after a little, more bikeable. There is a final difficult section and then you are on Land Rover track again. The track follows the east bank of the River Feshie for four miles, passing a bothy, then crosses the river and becomes a surfaced road.

The public road starts at a gate which may be locked to prevent entry by motor vehicles. Continuing on to Aviemore is best done by using the minor road to Inverdruie by way of Feshiebridge; food, etc at The Boathouse at Loch Insh, shop at Kincraig. Glen Feshie Hostel (01540-651323) is a good place to stay; to do this cross the river to Achlean at the second bridge, the hostel is further north on the public road. The Boathouse has a variety of accommodation (01540-651272).

Around Rothiemurchus

Rushing rivers, native pine forests, a variety of mountain biking - you can see why this area is popular. For the adventurous the trip to Loch Einich will provide a technical challenge, and a view of the remote loch long remembered. For families the trails around Loch an Eilein and south of Loch Morlich will provide good days in beautiful scenery, the dramatic backdrop of the Cairngorms never far away.

Loch an Eilein
to Loch Morlich (5 miles)

The description assumes starting from Loch an Eilein but access is also possible from Inverdruie or Loch Morlich. There is a visitor centre at Loch an Eilein giving general information about the Cairngorms, plus toilets and a car park. Loch an Eilein means loch of the island in Gaelic. The castle on the island dates from the 12th century.

Leave the visitor centre, cross the river then bear right following the loch shore. After a mile take a left turn to leave the loch. The other path goes right round, however Rothiemurchus Estate asks that you do not bike round. It is possible to gain access to Glen Feshie via forest paths to the south of Loch an Eilein. If you want to do this walk the short section after the turn-off, as far as Loch Gamhna.

The first problem is a locked gate. People hiring mountain bikes at Inverdruie Mountain Bikes get the key. Those using their own bikes can get a key for a £5 deposit, however you can usually get your bike round or over the gate. If this is too difficult wait a little, someone with a key may be along shortly. After the gate continue east along a sandy trail to the first junction: Lochan Deo. Turn right here (south) to go to Glen Einich, or keep straight on to for Loch Morlich. Left (north) takes you to Coylumbridge.

The journey to Loch Morlich is not entirely smooth as the track gets rough in places. You have to carry your bike over the Cairngorm Club Footbridge. Shortly after the bridge there is another junction in the path anachronistically named Picadilly. The right turn here leads up to the Lairig Ghru, the

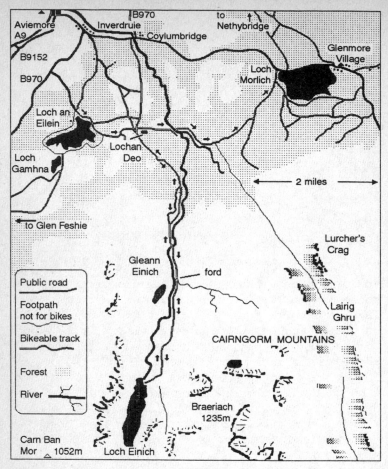

most famous mountain pass in Scotland. This pass takes you from Speyside to Braemar, a distance of over twenty miles. It rises to 835m. Walter Poucher writing in 1947 said that a bicycle was a disadvantage, and this is still true despite improvements in bicycle technology. Blizzards can occur there even in summer.

Continuing to Loch Morlich though there's another locked gate, a more serious one this time with a deer fence. If you haven't got the key, getting over the stile is possible, but it helps if there is more than one of you. Turn left at a forest road leading to Rothiemurchus Lodge. A mile after this you reach Loch Morlich. Turn right just before the public road to gain access to the Loch Morlich trails (see map). There is a shop and tea room by the camp site at Glenmore village.

Lochan Deo to Glen Einich (6 miles)

Unlike the Lairig Ghru the path up Glen Einich is bikeable. The trip to Loch Einich is quite long, and requires you to wade across a river carrying your bike. Keep to the path in the deerstalking season (Sept/Oct).

Get to Lochan Deo as described in the previous section and turn south. The track at first is a steady climb through natural Scots pine forest; eventually this thins out though, giving good views up the glen. Near the edge of the forest the path divides into two. The estate have had to create a higher route as the lower track has slid into the river. The lower track is quicker providing you can negotiate the landslides.

Further up there is a narrow single plank footbridge which needs care. Further on still, a river has to be waded over. Due to a combination of depth, width, and boulders in the river bed, biking across is impossible. Your reward for this is the view over the remote loch with its high cliffs, plunging from the summit of Sgoran Dubh Mhor to the surface of the loch 600m below. Distances: Loch An Eilein to Loch Einich & return 15 miles; Loch An Eilein to Loch Morlich 5 miles; Inverdruie to Coylumbridge via Loch an Eilein 5 miles.

Some useful phone numbers: Loch Morlich Youth Hostel; 01479-861238. Aviemore Youth hostel: 01479-810345. Inverdruie Mountain Bikes: 01479-810787. Aviemore Tourist Information: 01479-810363. Glenmore Camp Site: 01479-861271.

Pass of Ryvoan

The Pass of Ryvoan runs between Glen More near Aviemore, and Nethybridge. It climbs to 380m, mostly through natural Caledonian pine woods. There are good views of the Cairngorm Mountains and Glenmore Forest Park. Experienced mountain bikers will be able to cycle the whole thing; anyone inexperienced, or with another type of bike will have to walk in places. Description is circular starting from Aviemore.

It is usually possible to do this route all the year round provided it is not snow covered. Waterproof clothing is advisable at any time, but in winter you should be prepared for bad weather with extra warm clothing, woolly hat, gloves, etc. Total distance right round 25 miles. Nethybridge to Glenmore via Ryvoan: 10 miles.

Pass of Ryvoan
Circular Route

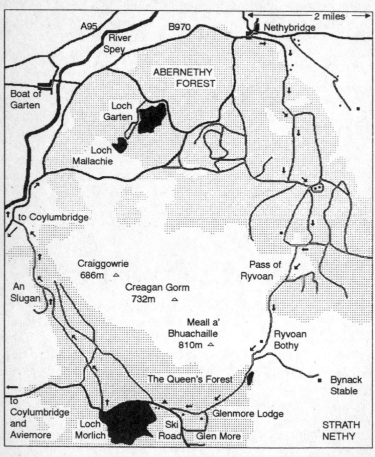

(25 miles from Coylumbridge)
Starting in Aviemore take the ski road towards Cairngorm. After a mile you will pass Inverdruie which has a mountain bike hire shop, the Gallery Tea Room, and Rothiemurchus Visitor Centre. At Coylumbridge, a mile further on, you have the option of turning left, to do the outward journey to Nethybridge on the B970, or continuing on towards Loch Morlich and using trails via An Slugan.

The B970 is fairly quiet with good views. Whether you take the public road or the An Slugan route you can also go via Abernethy Forest and Loch Garten. Abernethy Forest, like Rothiemurchus further south, is a remnant of the native Scots pine forest that once covered the highlands; habitat of red squirrel, wildcat, pine marten and the ubiquitous red deer. Ospreys were re-established near Loch Garten in the 1950s, a helping factor was the free lunch available to them from Rothiemurchus fish farm.

Nethybridge has a tea room/craft shop on the left as you enter the village. Bar lunches at the hotel. In Nethybridge take the minor road between the post office and the River Nethy, travelling west. The road climbs gently, then turns south towards the forest becoming a track. Keep straight on, ignoring any left turns, to a T junction where you can go no further. Turn left here to travel east, then take the second turning to the right (south). If you meet the forest lodge (private) you have missed the turning.

There is a fork in the track at this point, you can take either, the right-hand trail takes a rather higher line on the approach to the pass. It drops down again on a track that may be very muddy. Both paths climb steadily, sometimes steeply, and are now winding and more difficult, rather than just being forest trails.

When you leave the trees most of the climbing is done. Cairngorm will be visible ahead, you may see skiers on it if it's winter and your eyesight is good enough. The path becomes rocky and more Scots pine appear, then after reaching open country again you pass Ryvoan Bothy. Usually there will be someone camping there.

Shortly after this there is a difficult steep descent, more like a river bed than a path, and after this a left turn leading towards Bynack Stable. This is not a stable, but another bothy (rough shelter). The path to Bynack Stable is mostly bikeable, but cycling any further than this, for example up Strath Nethy is completely impossible.

Continuing south the path enters Glenmore Forest Park. Despite being sandy in places it is quite fast (be considerate to walkers) and mainly downhill. Soon you pass Lochan Uaine, steep crags above, then drop to a small bridge. After this at Glenmore Lodge, the track finally becomes a road. Turn right at the ski road to return to Aviemore. Reward yourself with an applestrudel at the Glenmore shop tea room, this is beside Glenmore Campsite.

There are more bike trails to the south of Loch Morlich and in Rothiemurchus. It would be possible to make this route even longer by including these.

Abernethy Forest

The tracks around Abernethy Forest are not too hilly and have quite reasonable surfaces, so would be very suitable for families. Biking round the forest could be combined with a visit to the RSPB hide near Loch Garten to see the ospreys, or a picnic by Loch Garten or Loch Mallachie. Refer to the map.

Craigvinean Forest

Craigvinean Forest is just west of Dunkeld. Access is from the A9, signposted The Hermitage. There are two mountain bike trails, a red route of nine miles, and a blue route of eleven miles. Both are maintained by the Forestry Commission and are well signposted. There are some steep hills but also some flatter sections. There is a tourist information office (01350-727688) and a mountain bike hire shop in Dunkeld.

Red & Blue Routes

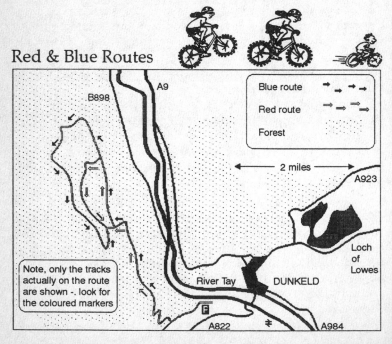

142

Red Route (9 miles)

Both routes start from the first car park right next to the A9. Anyone with children and a car could drive the first section, to a small car park higher up to avoid some of the climb.

Climb through mixed forest to an S shaped bend. Go up the hill to a Y shaped junction and turn left, climbing steeply for about a mile. Climb up 300 metres of steep rough path, ending at a forest road junction. Turn right here, there is a further rough path leading up from the junction - don't join this. There are some gentler ups and downs, then after a little over a mile, turn left on to a grassy track. This climbs steadily, then descends to another junction, where you turn left down a rough path, eventually ending back to the car park.

Blue Route (11 miles)

This is the same as the red route until the end of the 300m of steep rough path. As with the red route turn right on to the forest road, but stay on this for two miles, ignoring the grassy track turn off. After two miles turn left on to a forest road. This climbs steeply, with good views towards Pitlochry. After this there is a slow descent to join the red route again.

Both routes are well signposted, but some of the markers may be obscured by bracken - check the junctions carefully.

Glen Isla to Glen Prosen

A demanding mountain bike route in the Angus Glens. The route starts in forest in Glen Isla, then climbs up Glen Finlet and crosses to Glen Prosen. A short section must be walked. Return to the start is via Glen Uig. Anyone who has children, or who wants an easier day, could explore the forest trails at the start of the route.

Freuchies to Glen Finlet (7 miles)

Start on the B951 just east of Kirkton of Glenisla. To get to this from the south go through Blairgowrie to Alyth. After this follow signs for Glen Isla. The start of the route is a short distance after Highland Adventure Outdoor Centre and is signposted: Glenmarkie Farm Riding Centre.

Follow the track and bear right over the river. At a small car park with a cross country skiing route map, turn left into the forest. Climb towards Loch Shandra, open hillside to the left as the climb steepens; you pass a white cottage, then enter the forest again. The trail gradually levels off, and you meet a crossroads.

If you are not doing the full route you could explore here, otherwise keep straight on. The route sweeps round to the east descending rapidly to a small concrete bridge. Immediately after the bridge turn sharp left up Glen Finlet - a gentle climb.

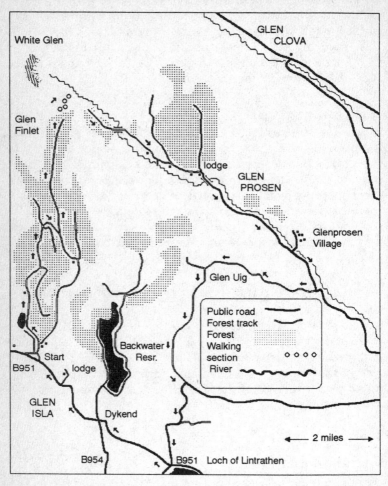

Keep right on to the end of the track in Glen Finlet, passing an end of trail sign for skiers. It ends in a small glade with a burn running through.

Dismount and push your bike, following the burn to the edge of the forest. You will need to cross the burn at several points but this is not difficult. Climb over the stile to open hillside.

144

Glen Finlet to Glen Isla (via Glen Prosen) (24 miles)

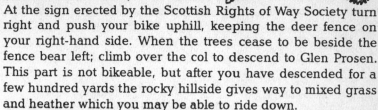

At the sign erected by the Scottish Rights of Way Society turn right and push your bike uphill, keeping the deer fence on your right-hand side. When the trees cease to be beside the fence bear left; climb over the col to descend to Glen Prosen. This part is not bikeable, but after you have descended for a few hundred yards the rocky hillside gives way to mixed grass and heather which you may be able to ride down.

Go straight down the hill to the river (Prosen Water), the high corrie of White Glen to the left. At the river follow the right bank downstream. A grassy surface gives way to a Land Rover track. Eventually you encounter a big steel gate, go through this to a forest road.

Go down this fast bumpy track, crossing the river to the public road at Glenprosen Lodge. A sign here gives notice of deer-stalking periods, access to the hills may be restricted at certain times, 12 August to 20 October is best avoided.

Continue down the public road keeping to the right bank of the river. A left turn over a bridge leads to Prosen Village which has a tea room. Keep on the west bank of the river, following signs for Lednathie and Pearsie. After passing Prosen Village there is a very steep uphill climb, followed by a shorter descent. At a sharp left bend in the road, turn right for Glen Uig, signed Wester Lednathie.

There is a very hilly section then the road becomes a track. Shortly after this there is a fork in the track, take the left fork and descend to the burn, the deep 'V' of the pass ahead.

There is a crow trap at the top of the pass. Turn left here to a grassy track passing through a wooden gate. Ignore the other path which climbs steeply up a hill. This section is bikeable but requires care. After a few miles and a splash across a burn the track meets a minor road.

Turn right on to the minor road and keep on going south until you meet the B951 just north of the Loch of Lintrathen. Turn right, following the sign for Glen Isla. At the next crossroads at Dykend keep straight on to return to the start.

Places to stay: Highland Adventure (interesting lodge) 01575-582238; tourist information: 01575-574097. Pubs and tea rooms: Singing Kettle, Alyth; two hotels and a shop at Kirkton of Glenisla; tea room in Prosen Village; tea room and craft shop at Peel Farm south of the Loch of Lintrathen.

Rannoch Forest

This is one of the most beautiful areas of Scotland, and the routes reflect this, with fine views of the hills, and woods of scots pine, birch and sitka spruce on the lower sections. Two routes are described here; neither of them is signposted. The first route is entirely in Rannoch Forest, except for a road section to return to the start. The other takes you south over the hills to Glen Lyon.

Carie to Bridge of Gaur (22 miles circular)

Start at the car park and picnic site at Carie, three miles west of Kinloch Rannoch, on the south shore of Loch Rannoch. The first part is signposted as a walking route. There was a diversion owing to logging operations. If this is present use the forest road west of the footpath (marked X on map) as the diversion is not bikeable.

Otherwise bike through the car park, then through the picnic area with its rain shelter. A path leads off to the right, bike this following the signs marked Allt na Bogair. After a while the drop to the burn on the left becomes steeper, and spruce, oak and birch are replaced with Scots pine, the terrain becomes more open. Join a forest crossroad (see map insert).

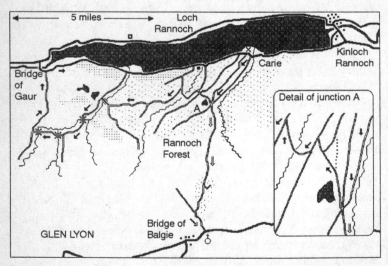

At the crossroads turn right to go north. (The other route is a left turn going south.) The track leading south-west is a dead end. After a short distance you pass a lochan on the left, then bear left on to a wide forest road. Continue downhill, ignoring a track that joins from the right but at the next T junction turn sharp left. A little way after this, at the next junction, bear right to cross the Dall Burn. After the bridge climb uphill to a T junction and turn left,

The track goes upstream on the north bank of the burn and gradually curves round to the west. The forest becomes more open, giving good views of the hills to the south. At a left bend the track turns into a new forest road, keep straight on here to continue west along the older path. Two miles later you drop to another burn and leave the forest. Cross the bridge then turn left (south).

The path winds south then west, between two hills with lots of natural Scots pine, two tracks lead south towards the hill of Garbh Mheall, and these could be explored. Otherwise continue west, crossing three bridges. At the last bridge turn right (north), and descend steeply to Bridge of Gaur on the south side of Loch Rannoch. There is a shop just west of here which has food, tea, scones, ice cream, etc. Return to the start by cycling east on the south Loch Rannoch road.

Carie to Bridge of Balgie (8 miles)

This is the same as the first route as far as the forest junction, but here you turn left to go south. There is a locked gate and a deer fence where you leave the forest and it is necessary to carry your bike over this, using the two metre high ladder provided for walkers.

On leaving the forest the biking becomes more difficult for several hundred metres, but after crossing a burn this is passed. Here you catch your first sight of the Ben Lawers range ahead. The path crosses an old iron fence at its summit, then drops to a wooden bridge. Following this there is a flat section, with the Allt Ghallabhaich burn plunging steeply to your right. You enter forest again after crossing above a waterfall, shut the gate.

The summit of Ben Lawers can briefly be seen ahead before the path plunges steeply into trees. There is another gate, also not locked, and then an easier gradient. Shortly after there is a more recently constructed left fork. You should take the left fork as the older path leads down to the burn where you would have to carry your bike. Finally descend more gently to another gate where you meet the public road.

147

The post office at Bridge of Balgie, one mile west, can provide tea, coffee, home baking and sells drinks and chocolate etc. Otherwise the nearest refreshment stop is the Fortingall Hotel ten miles down Glen Lyon. An attractive option here is cream teas on the lawn in the summer; there are hotels or tea rooms also at Coshieville, Tummel Bridge and Kinloch Rannoch.

To return to the start go back the way you came, or bike down Glen Lyon then over the shoulder of Schiehallion back to Kinloch Rannoch, a distance of 26 miles (map on page 160). If you are doing the route in a northerly direction start east of Bridge of Balgie, by the church and war memorial. There is a signpost, but at the time of writing it had no words on it.

Route Grading Symbols

Road Cycling

Fairly easy road cycling, some hills but they will not be very steep or long.

Varied cycling with some hills, either steep but short, or longer but easier.

Serious hills that are sufficiently frequent that getting off and walking is not really an option. Low gears, and being fit is the only answer!

CENTRAL HIGHLANDS

ROAD CYCLING

This area contains plenty of mountain scenery, but also some busy roads. This chapter tells you how to enjoy the scenery but miss out the traffic. Many of the lochs and glens have roads on both sides, often one side is very quiet. In some areas, for example the Angus Glens, there are lots of quiet roads where you can enjoy highland scenery without too many cars.

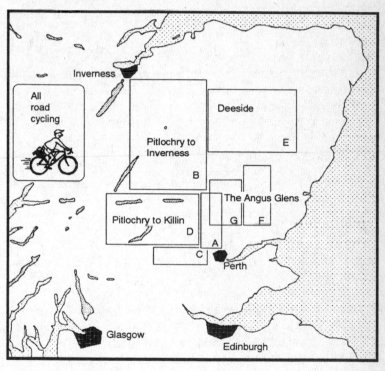

Perth - Pitlochry

Motorists speeding along the busy A9 between Perth and Pitlochry occasionally notice a signposted bike route. The route in this book sometimes follows this signposted route, but mostly it doesn't. Our way is quieter, it completely avoids cycling along the A9. The scenery is better too; it's slightly longer, and a wee bit hillier. The route is given in both directions. At the southern end the description is from Dunning, so that this route can be connected to others from Edinburgh and Fife.

Southbound

(to Perth 31 miles)
(to Dunning 39 miles)

From Pitlochry Festival Theatre travel south on the minor road on the west side of the River Tummel. This road can also be reached by cycling south on Pitlochry main street (Athol Road), until you pass under a rail bridge; take the first right after, go over the river and turn left by a caravan site.

After four miles you arrive at Logierait, turn left on to the A827. After 200m, by the 'thank you' sign, turn right to cross the River Tay using a disused rail bridge. Immediately after this, turn sharp left on a dirt track leading to the B898. Turn left on to the B898, and continue south for six miles, meeting the A9 trunk road.

Look left here, the busy A9 has crossed the River Tay. Taking care, cross the main road, then cross the bridge using the footpath. Leave the road, walk down the right-hand embankment to continue downstream on a forest trail.

Continue south, keeping the river on your right. After a mile you pass a hotel. Keep by the river until the dirt surface becomes a concrete mesh, then bear left on to the access road, taking the first left at some white painted stones. Turn right on to a minor road by a disused gatehouse. This joins the A923, turn right on to this to enter Dunkeld.

Dunkeld is worth exploring, with shops and a choice of tea rooms and pubs; there are benches by the river. To continue south, cross the river again using the old stone bridge, then immediately after, turn left on a minor road, signed Birnam. Go through Birnam and cross the A9 to the B867, signed Bankfoot.

It's mixed farm and woodland for five miles to Bankfoot. On the far side of Bankfoot, turn right, signed Moneydie, Almondbank and Methven. Go straight over at the next crossroads, signed Moneydie and Pitcairngreen, then cross the B8063, to Pitcairngreen. The fine oaks on the green are splendid but unfortunately the pub doesn't provide food.

If you are going to Perth leave Pitcairngreen by the Inn, for Almondbank. After Almondbank turn left (east) on to the A85, to enter Perth.

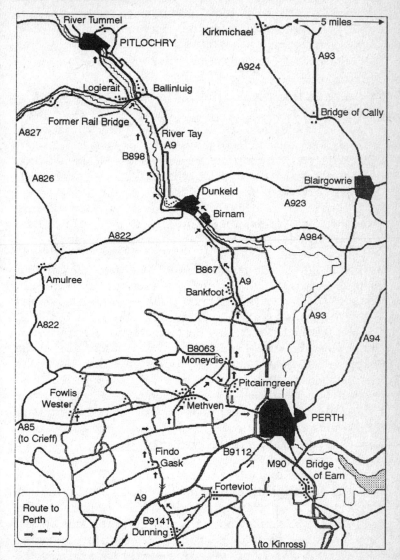

To continue south avoiding Perth, leave Pitcairngreen following signs for Methven and travel west for two miles. Go straight over at the next two junctions for Methven. Enter Methven by Church Road and turn right on to the A85. After a short distance turn left, signed Moss-side. Turn left to Station Road, and turn right at the next T junction, signed Madderty.

At the next junction turn left by the sawmill, signed Findo Gask. Climb, then pass a school and cross the straight Roman Road, signed Dalreoch. There is an amazing view as you plunge straight on down towards Dunning. Cross the A9 on a staggered junction to the B9141. Go under a railway line and continue to Dunning (shops/hotels). To continue south, or for additional accommodation information, see page 82.

Northbound

(from Perth 31 miles)
(from Dunning 39 miles)

To join the route from Perth leave the town on the A85, following signs for Crieff. One mile after passing over the A9 dual carriageway, turn right for Pitcairngreen/Almondbank. In Pitcairngreen follow signs for Moneydie (now see # below).

From Dunning leave on the B9141, by the public toilet. After 1.5 miles pass under a rail bridge. Cross the A9 dual carriageway on a staggered junction, signed Findo Gask. Climb steeply up the hill, ignoring left and right turns.

Next cross the former Roman Road, signed Findo Gask, passing a school. Go straight on for two miles descending again to a crossroads; turn right by the sawmill, signed Perth. Travel east for two miles, taking the second left, signed Methven. On reaching Methven, turn right on to the A85 and cycle east through the village, turning left on to Church Road. Church Road becomes Lyndoch Road. Go straight over at the next road junction, signed Pitcairngreen. Cross the River Almond then at Pitcairngreen turn left just before village green, signed Moneydie.

Cross the B8063, and go on for four miles through farm and woodland. Go straight over at another crossroads to Bankfoot. Turn left to enter Bankfoot on the B867 then continue north for five miles to the main A9. Taking care cross the A9, signed Birnam/Dunkeld. Bike through Birnam, then turn right over the old stone bridge into Dunkeld.

Cycle away from the river down the main street in Dunkeld (A923), pass a stone arch leading to Dunkeld House. Turn left at the next junction and left again at a disused gatehouse. Go straight on until you meet the river, on seeing a hotel bear left on to a dirt track by the river. Go upstream for a mile, river on the left, to the bridge carrying the main A9. Join the main road by climbing the embankment. Cross the bridge and turn right to the B898, signed Balnaguard.

Continue on the B898 for six miles. When the road climbs, then descends look right for an old rail bridge. There is no sign, but a track by the side of a stone cottage with two chimneys and three chimney pots leads to it.

Cross the bridge then turn sharp left on to the A827. After 200m turn right on to a minor road by the Logierait Hotel, signed Dunfallandy. Bike through woods for four miles then take the first left after passing under a railway bridge to enter Pitlochry.

Hostels: Pitlochry, 01796-472308; Perth, 01738-623658. Tourist information: Pitlochry, 01796-472215; Dunkeld, 01350-727688; Perth, 01738-638481.

Pitlochry to Inverness

At the time of writing parts of this route were being surveyed by the cyclepath builders Sustrans, with a view to improving it for cyclists. In 1995 Sustrans was awarded £42.5 million for building cyclepaths from The Millennium Fund, so there just might be some progress!

The main problem with the route at present is that cyclists have to travel on the busy A9 to get through the Pass of Drumochter; a distance of eleven miles between Dalwhinnie and Dalnacardoch. This could be solved by building a dedicated bike path near to the main road, or possibly even routing cyclists through the Gaick Pass, further to the east.

Pitlochry
to Kingussie (45 miles)

Leave Pitlochry on the main street following signs for Inverness, but after passing under the main road continue straight on, using the B8019, instead of turning on to the A9. Ignore the left turn for Tummel Bridge and Kinloch Rannoch, continue north to Blair Atholl using the B8079.

Blair Atholl is a pleasant place to stop. Blair Castle is nearby; seat of the Duke of Atholl, this is open to the public (admission £3). There is an interesting water mill which serves food made from flour which is ground from grain on site. There is a camp site, the BBC TV series 'Strathblair' was filmed in Blair Atholl.

Continue north on the B8079, this passes under the main A9 just before Struan. Struan has a shop, the next food stop beyond Struan is at Dalwhinnie, twenty miles to the north.

Beyond Struan, cyclists are directed along the old road which is now used as a bike route. There may be the occasional car using it for local access, but it will be very quiet. This happy situation continues for six miles until you get to Dalnacardoch; after which at the time of writing, you had to cycle on the main A9 for eleven miles

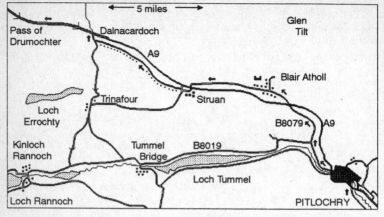

There is a climb of 150m from Dalnacardoch to the summit of the Drumochter Pass. This road is occasionally closed in winter, despite snowploughs being on permanent standby at the car park at the top. Even in summer there may be patches of snow on the surrounding hills. Most of the climb is on dual carriageway. When the long finger of Loch Ericht comes into view the climb is over, after a flatter section turn left towards Dalwhinnie.

Dalwhinnie has hotels, a tea room, and a distillery. In Dalwhinnie turn right on to the minor road for Crubenmore (see map insert). At Crubenmore there is the option of using the old road instead of the busy A9. Doubtless this will eventually be turned into a bike path when the local authority gets its act together. In the meantime the roads department seems to be using it as a dump for sand and gravel, so there may be the odd obstacle in your way. A small price to pay to be safely away from the traffic.

The old road is briefly broken at an access road for Crudenbeg farm steading, just bike along the grass verge to pick it up again. It ends at Ralia picnic site; just north of this there is a tourist information office (01540-673253). Turn left towards Newtonmore, continuing through this into Kingussie.

Tourist information Kingussie, 01540-661297. Hostels: Independent; Newtonmore, 01540-673360; Kingussie 01540-651298. Glen Feshie, 01540-651323. The SYHA hostel at Kingussie is closed.

Kingussie
to Carrbridge (28 miles)

There is some lovely country between Kingussie and
Carrbridge, with Caledonian pine woods and the backdrop of
the Cairngorm and Monadhliath mountains. This is a popular
holiday area but the back roads are mostly quiet. Glen Feshie
is particularly attractive, and is well worth a diversion. The
road on the west side of the glen is the longest and has the
best views.

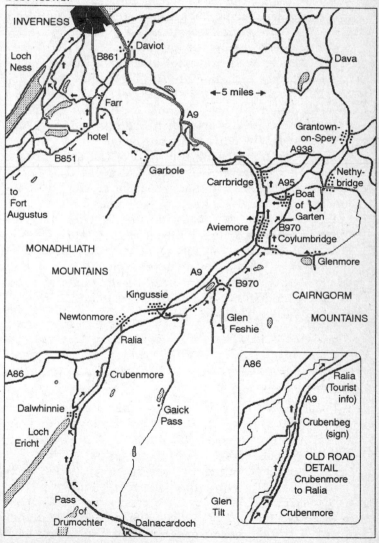

In Kingussie take the B970, between the train station and the public park. This passes ruined Ruthven Barracks, part of the General Wade scheme for pacifying the highlands following the '45 rebellion.

After this the road runs above marshes on the River Spey, an RSPB bird reserve. You then pass the hamlet of Insh, then drop down to Loch Insh. The Boathouse tea room at Loch Insh is an attractive place to stop. They also have a variety of accommodation, ranging from bunkhouse style to self catering chalets (01540-651272).

After Loch Insh the B970 winds through Feshiebridge (turn right for Glen Feshie), then passes near Loch An Eilean. It reaches the Cairngorm Ski Road at a T junction, turn right for Coylumbridge, Aviemore is a left turn.

Architecturally Aviemore is not particularly attractive, but it has every facility, including a youth hostel (01479-810345), tourist information (01479-810363), plus Burger King, McDonald's, swimming pool, ice rink, etc. Further up the Ski Road, at Glenmore by Loch Morlich, there is another SYHA hostel (01479-861238), and a camp site by the Loch.

Continue north on the B970 to Boat of Garten. This road offers particularly fine views of the Cairngorms, and runs through natural Caledonian pine woods for much of the time. A number of attractive quiet minor roads run through Abernethy Forest, and many of the unsurfaced forest roads are sufficiently smooth for a touring bike (see page 140).

Boat of Garten is a left turn over the River Spey, after which you turn left again into the town. To continue to Carrbridge, briefly join the A95, then turn right off it on to the B9153 for Carrbridge (tourist info 01479-841630). There is an independent hostel: 01479-841250.

Carrbridge
to Inverness (37 miles)

Here it is necessary to cycle for about a mile on the A9. After this the route is very quiet. We ride by the River Findhorn, then turn north, climbing steeply through Glen Kyllachy, to travel towards Loch Ness and Inverness.

Leave Carrbridge turning left on to the A938, but at the junction with the A9, bear right to bike along a minor road on the north side of the main road. This passes under the A9 just south of the Slochd summit. Shortly after this, cycling on the main road becomes unavoidable. After just over a mile bear left off the A9, signed Tomatin. Continue along this road until you pass over the River Findhorn on an Egyptian-style bridge (read the enscription). Turn left here for Garbole, to bike upstream on the north bank of the river.

This section is very bonny, with attractive woodland and good views of the river. After four miles, by Garbole, turn north to climb steeply up Glen Kyllachy through plantation forest. This gives way to heather halfway up the hill. The road is single track with passing places, and not very many of them. There is a flat section, then a long twisting descent to the B851 near Farr.

If you want to go directly to Inverness, turn right here, then take the second left to the B861. As you enter the town you pass Inverness youth hostel. Perhaps a better option is to turn left; bike south for just over a mile, then turn right to a minor road which runs by Loch Duntelchaig. Going this way offers good views of Loch Ness which is not visible from the B861. There is also the option of a bar meal at the Grouse and Trout Hotel just beyond the junction (see map). A fuller description of this area is given in pages 174 to 177.

Inverness Hostels: SYHA, 01463-231771; Independent, 01463-236556. Tourist Information, 01463-234353.

A Circular Day Ride near Perth

Pitcairngreen to
Sma' Glen (30 miles circular)

This route starts from the village of Pitcairngreen, just west of Perth, it provides an attractive day out, cycling entirely on quiet roads, with fine views of Glenalmond and the rolling wooded Perthshire countryside. There are some hills, but most are fairly short and easily walked up if necessary. If the total distance is too short or too long for your taste, it would be easy to increase or reduce it.

Being circular you can start this route at any point, but the description assumes starting at Pitcairngreen. Perth is convenient of access from Glasgow and Edinburgh. There is a useful hotel (The Fulford Inn), near Sma' Glen which can provide food. The Pitcairngreen Inn does not serve meals. The only shops on the route are at Methven.

Start from Pitcairngreen with its large village green and

fine oak trees. Take the minor road at the west of the village, signed Dalcrue and Methven, do not turn right for Moneydie. Continue along this for three miles, ignoring a right turn and crossing the River Almond. At a crossroads take a right turn, signposted Glenalmond, Harrietfield and Chapelhill.

Continue along this road for just over two miles and take the first left, signposted Glenalmond and Buchanty. After about a mile you will see the village of Harrietfield and the Logiealmond Hills on your right and Glenalmond College (a boarding school) ahead. The road is straight but undulating for a mile or two, passing more oak trees. After this there is a fast descent to Buchanty and the B8063, with the pass of Sma' Glen visible ahead.

Just before you reach the road junction at Buchanty there is a left turn, signed Fowlis Wester. This is part of the route back to Pitcairngreen, and you have the option here of reducing your distance by turning left, or continuing on, possibly for a bar lunch at the Fulford Inn.

Assuming the latter, ignore this sign meantime and continue, bearing left at the phone box at Buchanty, towards Sma' Glen. You are now on the B8063, and the next road junction is with the A822. This is a busier road. For the hotel, turn left and cycle just over a mile.

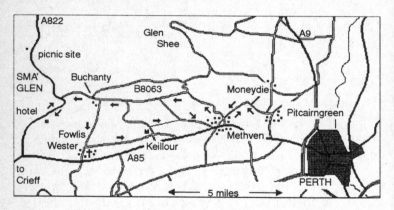

An alternative is to turn right and cycle though the glen, there is a picnic site at the far end. The Amulree Hotel six miles further north on the same road does bar lunches.

The first part of the return journey is to go back to the road junction of the A822 and B8063. After this travel east for just over one mile to the junction at Buchanty, turn right by the white house and fence. Climb south-east for a short distance to the sign for Fowlis Wester and turn right.

There is a steep but short climb and then a fast descent over open moorland, with a wood on the left, followed by a very steep descent to Fowlis Wester. Halfway down this hill there is a left turn. Taking this turn is the way back, but it's recommended you carry on down the hill to see the Fowlis Wester Stone. This will involve you in 60m of climb, but it's worth it.

The Fowlis Wester Stone is a Pictish symbol stone. Not much is known about the Picts, who inhabited Scotland before the Scots came, because they did not have a written language. The stone dates from the time in the sixth or seventh century when the Picts were being converted to Christianity by Irish priests.

On one side are hunting scenes, and on the other a cross, decorated with motifs similar to modern Celtic designs. The stone was found in the church wall when it was being restored in 1927. It is possibly the finest in existence. Until recently the stone was in the village square, but it was recently moved into the church. A fibreglass replacement stands in its place. The church, which is normally open, dates from the 13th century. A leaflet giving more information is available in the church.

Climb back up the hill to the road junction and turn right, after this the climb flattens out. Then begins a long freewheel down the side of the hill lasting for three miles; there are wonderful perspectives over rolling Perthshire scenery towards the Ochil Hills.

At the sign for Buchanty, turn left, and climb up the hill, passing Keillour Castle. Some (small) giant American redwoods can be seen from the road. Very shortly after this you encounter a rough track going off to the right marked: Parks of Keillour, go down this.

Follow this track, which is a right of way, for two miles. Keep straight on, do not take the right bend for Bellour, but continue east on the grassy track, past some kennels, to the public road at the far end. Here you see a brick chimney standing solitary in a field, turn right and descend into Methven.

At Methven turn left on to the A85 at the post office and go along it for 200m. Turn left up Church Road by a pub. Church Road becomes Lynedoch Road. The church dates from 1826 and has an unusual tower. After a little distance you encounter a crossroads. Go straight over, signed Pitcairngreen 2.5. Bear right at the next junction, and you're back where you started.

Pitlochry to Killin

By Loch Tummel and Loch Rannoch the song goes - and so perhaps will you. It's difficult to think of anywhere better than Perthshire for scenery. You can bike from Pitlochry to Killin by Lochs Tummel and Rannoch, and come back via Loch Tay.

All of these lochs have quiet roads on their south shores - too narrow for the tourist coaches - but ideal for cycling. They could make two or three seperate day rides, or they could be connected together for a two or three day tour. Alternatively they could be used to link the Trossachs to further north.

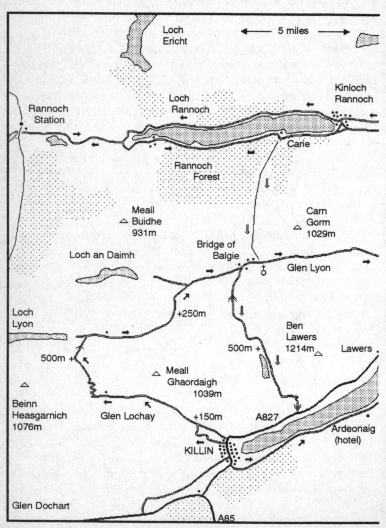

Pitlochry to
Kinloch Rannoch (21 miles)

Start near the access road for Pitlochry Festival Theatre, at the junction between the access road and the main road (A9). To reach this point from the theatre, leave the theatre car park and turn right up the hill. Next to the access road on the north side is a footpath signposted: Loch Faskally Walk. It leads over to a grass area beside the main road, cycle along this.

After a few hundred metres turn left through a gate, then

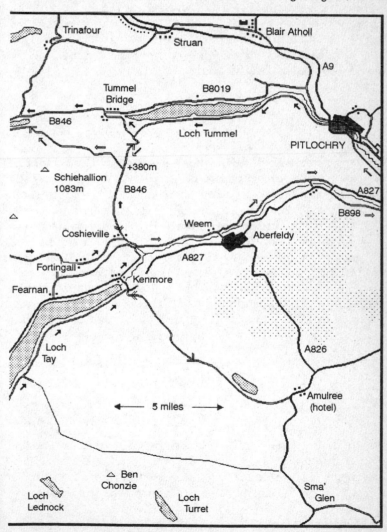

continue in the same direction to an underpass taking you under the main A9. Follow this, you are now on the south Loch Tummel road, which is quiet and more attractive than the road on the north side of the loch. The road passes Loch Faskally, and then winds prettily alongside the river, arriving at Loch Tummel after a short steep hill. Continue west until you reach the other end of the loch, then turn right at the T junction on to the B846. After a short distance you will reach Tummel Bridge. You can buy food and drink here. Distance thirteen miles.

It's a further eight miles to Kinloch Rannoch on the B846, the alternative is the Schiehallion road - a stiff climb. In both cases you arrive at Kinloch Rannoch at the east end of the loch. The Dunalistair hotel in the square does bar meals, you can also carry out drinks and eat your sandwiches on the benches by the door if it's sunny.

Cycling Round
Loch Rannoch (22 miles)

The cycle round Loch Rannoch is very attractive and might be a good option for children. Mostly flat, there are sandy beaches on the north shore at the far end. On the south shore at the far end is a small shop that does coffees, scones, etc, and sells ice cream. Rather more upmarket is the Tallahnd-A-Bheithe Lodge on the north shore which does coffees and cakes, not to mention meals. The accents of the staff will confirm that the German cakes advertised are authentic!

There is also a hotel doing bar lunches at Rannoch Station and a tea room in the station itself. This is a halt on the West Highland Railway Line, but unfortunately most of the trains that use it nowadays are Sprinters with little space for bicycles.

Kinloch Rannoch
to Killin (distances in text)

There are two alternatives here: using the B846 to Coshieville, then turning up Glen Lyon, or reaching Glen Lyon via a mountain bike route which starts from Carie, on the south shore of Loch Rannoch. The latter alternative is described on page 146.

Whichever way you go be sure to bike up Glen Lyon; this

avoids the A827 on the north side of Loch Tay. Glen Lyon is one of the loveliest glens in Scotland as well as being one of the longest. The glen itself is not very hilly. Hotels at Coshieville and Fortingall do bar lunches. The Fortingall Hotel does cream teas on the lawn in summer. Further up, the post office at Bridge of Balgie provides home baking.

If Glen Lyon itself isn't hilly, the same cannot be said of the exits at the top of the glen. You can turn south at Bridge of Balgie, and reach Killin by climbing over the shoulder of Ben Lawers, a climb of 350m. Alternatively continue up the glen to Loch Lyon and climb over the shoulder of Ben Heasgarnich, a 200m climb from the loch. After this you bike down Glen Lochay. Both routes are very scenic but have very steep hills which need extreme care.

Killin has a youth hostel (01567-820546), a tourist office (01567-820254), numerous B&Bs, and several hotels.

Distances: Kinloch Rannoch to Bridge of Balgie via Coshieville, 26 miles; via Carie (off-road) 12 miles. Bridge of Balgie to Killin via Glen Lochay, 22 miles; via Ben Lawers road 14 miles.

Killin to Pitlochry
via Loch Tummel (38 miles)

via Weem (37 miles)

Start this by biking along the south Loch Tay road. This is quiet but has some ups and downs. There are splendid views of the loch and the Ben Lawers range. This section ends at Kenmore which has a choice of tea rooms, hotels, etc. After Kenmore you can go via Coshieville and the south Loch Tummel road.

An alternative is to turn right on the B846 to Weem. At Weem bear left and follow the minor road on the north side of the River Tay. This eventually joins the A827, turn right on to this crossing the river, and then turn left downstream using the B898. Follow this for three miles then cross the River Tay again; this time using a disused railway bridge. The track to it is beside a stone built cottage with two chimneys, one with two chimney pots the other with one pot (see map page 151).

Immediately after crossing turn sharp left into Logierait, and right up a steep hill opposite the Logierait Hotel (signed Dunfallandy/Clunie/Foss). This quiet minor road will take you through Moulinearn, ending up at Pitlochry

Pitlochry Hostel, 01796-472308; tourist info: 01796-472215.

Deeside

The tourist brochures call this Royal Deeside, because Balmoral Estate, summer residence of HM the Queen, is beside the River Dee. The A93 runs along the north bank of the river and is quite busy, but the B976 on the south side of the river is quiet.

South from the River Dee, quiet glens such as Glen Muick and Glen Tanar run into the Grampian Mountains. To the north there is a network of minor roads, running through wooded farming country. There are interesting things to see, and apart from the main roads, it will be fairly quiet.

Braemar - Linn of Dee
(7 miles on public road)

Most of the cycling around Braemar is mountain biking, but the road leading west from Braemar, to Linn of Dee, is worth exploring on a road bike. This runs past the Mar Estate, which has recently been purchased by the Nature Conservancy Council. Previously it was owned by an American millionaire, who it was said, had aspirations to be friendly with The Queen next door.

The public road simply runs up the glen and down again.

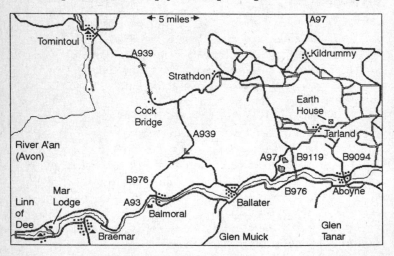

This is a lovely ride in itself, with fine views of the river and hills. Much of the land is covered in natural Caledonian pine woods, but many of the trees are quite old. Excessive numbers of red deer have caused over-grazing, preventing the woodland from regenerating naturally. Presumably the new ownership will rectify this.

It is normally possible to bike through the Mar Estate on the north side of the river, returning to Braemar via the Invercauld Bridge, two miles west of Braemar. This makes an attractive circular tour of just under 20 miles. The Victoria Bridge, immediately next to Mar Lodge, normally has a locked gate, as the estate do not want motor vehicles coming over this way.

Braemar youth hostel: 01339-741659. Accommodation and bike hire also at Braemar Mountain Sports, 01339-741242. Tourist information, 01339-741600.

Balmoral to
Aboyne (21 miles)

Between Braemar and Balmoral you have to travel on the A93, but after Balmoral Castle you can cross the river and bike on the B976. You can tell when you've got to the castle, even if you don't see it, by all the police signs warning you not to stop. Just after crossing the river you pass the distillery at Easter Balmoral. This has a shop and a tea room, as well as offering the normal distillery tour.

Ballater is a pleasant town, worth crossing the river for. It has a good selection of hotels, tea rooms etc. The youth hostel closed in 1995. Just south of Ballater a minor road leads up Glen Muick to Loch Muick, this is a steady climb, but worth it for the views. It is best avoided on summer Sundays as it is a popular drive from Aberdeen. A fairly smooth dirt road goes much of the way round the loch, this would be good for small children. For a description of this area see page 131.

It's a further eleven miles to Aboyne, the road running beside the river most of the time, with occasional easy hills. Just before Aboyne you pass the minor road leading up Glen Tanar, this is a popular destination for mountain bikers who can follow the forest paths in the Caledonian pine woods, see page 133. Aboyne means, place of the rippling waters. It has a large village green and all the usual shops etc (tourist info 01339-886060).

An interesting diversion from the B976 is to go to Tarland. Take the B9119 four miles west of Aboyne and cycle past Loch Kinord, turning right at the A97 junction. Tarland is a quiet village with a fine square. Two miles north-east of Tarland on the B9119 is Culsh Earth House; this is iron age and you can explore it with your bike light. Return to Aboyne on the B9094.

Glen Clova & Glen Doll

This route travels north from Glamis, passing through rolling Angus countryside to Glen Clova, and Glen Doll. It then travels east, by the foothills of the Grampian Mountains to Finavon before turning south to Letham. After Letham we pass south of Forfar on minor roads to return to Glamis.

The route is sometimes hilly. It will take two days unless shortened. There are ample tea stops and lots of historic interest: in particular Glamis Castle, which is everything a castle should be. It was the setting of Shakespeare's play Macbeth. King Malcolm II is said to have died there in 1034. The Queen Mother lived there as a child.

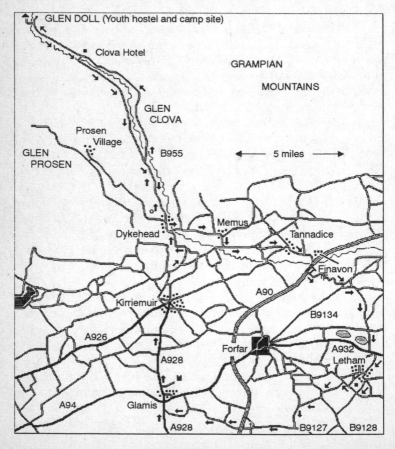

Glamis to
Glen Doll (25 miles)

Start in Glamis and cycle north for five miles to Kirriemuir. The A928 is reasonably quiet, or use minor roads to the west. Kirriemuir is the birthplace of James Barrie, author of *Peter Pan*, you can visit his cottage which includes the wash house, Barrie's first theatre and the inspiration for the Wendy House. The little town is typical of Angus: small stone-built closes and people with time to talk. For refreshments the Pilgrim's Coffee Room is recommended.

Something to eat is a good idea for the next section is longer, involving some ascent. In Kirriemuir follow the signs for 'The Glens', to the B955, after this follow signs for Glen Clova. The road has some descents, but overall there is a steady climb towards Glen Clova, which runs deeply into the Grampian Mountains.

A tower on a hill, the Airlie Memorial can be seen near the left fork running up to Glen Prosen. Access is from the Prosen road. A diversion up Glen Prosen is possible, but it is very hilly. There is a tea room and a shop in Prosen Village.

Glen Clova has a road each side of the river, take the right fork just after a picnic spot to go up the east side of the river. This gives a good view of Glen Doll as you work north. The Clova Hotel near the top of the glen has two bars, one for everyday folk who get there in cars wearing town clothes, and the other at the rear, the climber's bar for people with muddy boots; food served all day.

Stay at the youth hostel at Glen Doll (01575-550236), Glen Doll camp site, or the Clova Hotel (01575-550222). The Clova Hotel has a bunkhouse, the best you can say about this is that it's cheap and handy for the pub. The short trip up to Glen Doll is worth doing as this is some of the best highland scenery in Scotland.

Glen Doll
to Letham (30 miles)

Return down Glen Clova using the road on the west side, this starts directly opposite the Clova Hotel.

Just after Dykehead, in trees, after a sharp left bend, turn left, signed Edzell/Brechin. Pass Cortachy Castle then climb a hill, bearing right near the top. Straight on to Memus, where there is a right bend by a camp site. The road here skirts the hills, giving good views of the Angus countryside. After Memus there is a left turn which you should ignore, keep straight on, past the Drover's Inn (bar lunches), to a T junction and turn left, signed Brechin. After a further two miles turn right, signed Tannadice. After a further mile, bear left at the next junction to enter Tannadice.

Continue through Tanadice on the B957 to Finavon. At Finavon turn left at the bike route sign for Finavon Hill and Bogard, to J G's Diner by the A90. This is a good snack stop, even if the ambience leaves something to be desired. Taking care, cross the dual carriageway on the cyclist's crossing. There is also a cyclist's underpass 300m further west but this may be flooded.

On the other side of the main road turn right on to the cycle path. The path becomes a minor road by some houses. After this turn left at a T junction to a small road that winds steeply south-east up the Hill of Finavon. At the other side of the hill the road descends to the B9134. Turn right on to the B9134, then immediately left off it, signed Pitkennedy. This road goes east, then turns right to go south. It crosses the B9113 by a loch then joins the A932. Turn left here then take the second right, signed Trumperton. Just before Letham we pass Trumperton Forge Tea Room.

In Letham follow a sign for Arbroath, go up a little hill to a cross-roads and turn right, signed Dundee. After half a mile you pass the splendid Idvies House Hotel. This is the place to lunch in style (01307-818787).

Letham
to Glamis (14 miles)

After Idvies continue south-west to a crossroads then turn right, signed Bowriefauld. In Bowriefauld bear left signed Craichie to the B9128. Turn left here, travel south for a little way then take the first right, signed Lour. After a mile turn left in front of gates; after another mile turn right on to the B9127 by a phone box.

Go west for two miles, then at Inverarity, by a church, fork left to pass under the A90 at Gateside. Continue west on minor roads, ignore all right turns. Turn left to circle wooded Hunter's Hill to meet the A928. Turn right and descend to Glamis; take care crossing the A94.

Tourist Offices: Kirriemuir 01575-574097; Blairgowrie 01250-872960.

Glen Isla

Glen Isla is one of those places that always seems to be on the edge of your map. You need to buy three Landranger maps to cover it fully, and even then the part you want is always on the map you open last. Perhaps that's the reason why people say: Glen Isla, where's that? Whatever the reason the roads in Glen Isla are quiet - and the countryside is beautiful.

Pitlochry
to Glen Isla (22 miles)

The only direct route between Pitlochry and Glen Isla is the A924 via Kirkmichael. Despite being a class A road it is fairly quiet. Route finding is easy, follow the sign for Kirkmichael in the centre of Pitlochry. Less easy is the steady climb of 260m from the centre of Pitlochry to the top of the hill, but once you've done it, it's scenic and mostly downhill for eight miles to Kirkmichael. Kirkmichael has a choice of hotels serving food, there is also a shop.

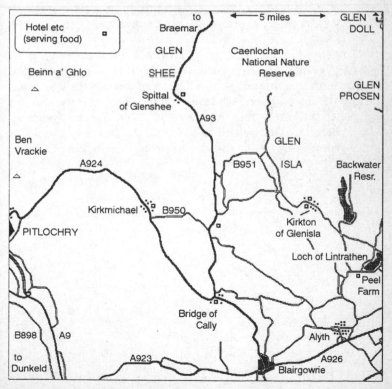

Turn left in Kirkmichael on to the B950. This road starts with a short climb but is fairly flat thereafter. When you meet the A93, turn left to head towards Braemar. The Dalrulzion Hotel which serves bar meals, is near this junction. To get to Glen Isla you can take either the first or the second right. Taking the second right takes you to the top of the glen.

Exploring
Glen Isla

Which route you take through the glen will depend on which options you choose for food and any overnight stop. There are two hotels and a shop in Kirkton of Glenisla. Just south of this Knockshannoch Lodge (Highland Adventure), offers bunk-house style accommodation in an unusual circular building (01575-582238). The tourist office is in Kirriemuir (01575-574097).

All of the roads in Glen Isla are worth exploring with the possible exception of the road immediately west of Kirkton of Glenisla which runs through plantation forest. The dead-end road at the head of the glen is particularly beautiful with the River Isla running by, and good views towards Glas Maol in Caenlochan Nature Reserve.

The area around the Loch of Lintrathen is attractive; there is a coffee shop in Peel Farm to the south of the loch (see map). Alyth is a friendly town, the Singing Kettle tea room, just off the town square is recommended. The next glen to the west is Glen Prosen, this together with Glen Clova is reached via Kirriemuir. Use the minor roads to the north of the A926 unless you decide to use the mountain bike route described on page 143.

NORTHERN HIGHLANDS

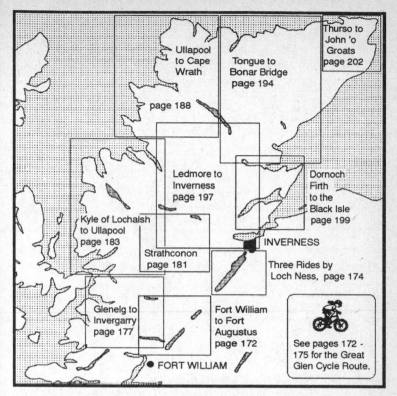

Ullapool to Cape Wrath
page 188

Tongue to Bonar Bridge
page 194

Thurso to John 'o Groats
page 202

Ledmore to Inverness
page 197

Dornoch Firth to the Black Isle
page 199

Kyle of Lochalsh to Ullapool
page 183

Strathconon
page 181

INVERNESS

Three Rides by Loch Ness, page 174

Glenelg to Invergarry
page 177

Fort William to Fort Augustus
page 172

See pages 172 - 175 for the Great Glen Cycle Route.

FORT WILLIAM

The Northern Highlands contain some of the wildest and most beautiful scenery in Scotland. Because of the nature of the terrain there are fewer roads. The area from Fort William to Ullapool is busy with holidaymakers in the summer, so the main roads will not be particularly quiet. Some quiet alternatives and off-road routes are described.

While the scenery in the west is dramatic, the roads are usually hilly, some roads hardly have a flat yard on them. The land around the east coast is gentler with a better minor road network. The area from Dornoch to the Black Isle is interesting. The John o' Groats area is described so that it could be included in a tour of the Orkney Islands.

While there are B&Bs all over, food shops could be less frequent and may be closed on Sundays. Hostels usually have a few basic foods only. Booking your bed a day or so ahead is a good idea. Cyclists without a car may find they can camp on quiet beaches and hillsides providing they are reasonably sensible and can stand the midges (small biting insects).

Fort William to Fort Augustus

(Great Glen Cycle Route)

This route covers the Great Glen, using the Caledonian Canal towpath, quiet roads, and forest tracks. A diversion off the main route, up a quiet road by Loch Arkaig, is also described.

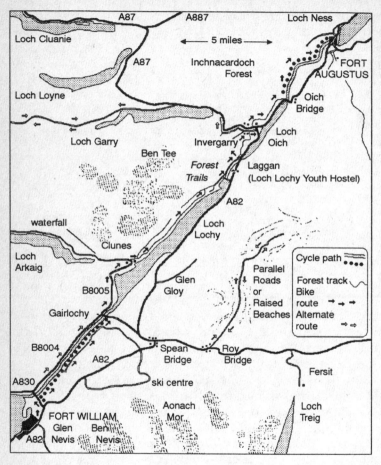

South of Laggan the route is less hilly. There may be pedestrians on the canal towpath so be considerate. Experienced cyclists may prefer to use roads to some towpath sections. The southern part could be done on any kind of bike, a mountain bike would be advisable for the forest tracks between Laggan and Oich Bridge. If you want to keep on roads the whole time you will sometimes have to use the A82. Distance Fort William to Fort Augustus 34 miles.

Great Glen Cycle Route
Fort William
to Laggan (23 miles)

Follow the A82 north out of Fort William, then turn west to the A830, signed Mallaig. This has a cycle path leading to the canal swingbridge at Banavie. Turn right here, taking the towpath on the east side of the canal. This passes Neptune's Staircase, the series of locks enabling the canal to climb from sea level to 30m. An alternate route is to use the B8004, this is fairly quiet and of course hillier than the canal towpath. At Gairlochy you have to leave the towpath anyway; cross the canal bridge and turn right (north) on to the B8005 for Clunes.

At Clunes turn right by forestry workers' houses into Clunes Forest. Keep beside the loch as the higher tracks are not continuous. The gradients are mostly gentle, experienced cyclists could manage it on a touring bike. Towards the north end of Loch Lochy the track turns into a road. At Laggan there is a short cycle path leading to Craig Liath Forest by Loch Oich. Access to Loch Lochy Youth Hostel (01809-501239), which is between Loch Lochy and Loch Oich, is from the A82.

Great Glen Cycle Route
Laggan to Fort
Augustus (11 miles)

After a hilly forest section you emerge near Invergarry. The signposted route takes you via Mandally then on to the A82 to cross the River Garry. Turn left on to the A87. Invergarry has a hotel and a tea room (public toilet). To continue north join a purpose-built cycle path by the public phone box. This climbs steeply then joins a forest road to descend to Loch Oich. After this there is another specially built mountain bike path leading to Oich Bridge. After Oich Bridge the route is on the canal towpath, this takes you right in to the centre of Fort Augustus. Here the canal descends again, through five locks to enter Loch Ness.

Loch Arkaig (13 miles)

An interesting diversion is to explore the minor road by the side of Loch Arkaig. This dead-end road is thirteen miles each way. The loch is beautiful with pebble beaches suitable for picnics. There is an interesting waterfall near the start.

Tourist information: Fort William, 01397-703781; Fort Augustus, 01320-366367. **SYHA Youth hostels:** Fort William (Glen Nevis) 01397-702336; Loch Lochy (South Laggan), 01809-501239. **Private Hostels:** Ben Nevis Bunkhouse (Glen Nevis), 01397-702240; Fort William Backpackers, 01397-700711; Roy Bridge: Grey Corrie Lodge (01397-712236); and Aite Cruinnichidh (01397-712315).

Three Rides by Loch Ness

To bike the length of Loch Ness you can choose between the Great Glen Cycle Route (mountain biking) on the west side of the loch, or road cycling routes on the east side. The Great Glen Cycle Route is being developed by the Forestry Commission and is not yet complete. Between Drumnadrochit and Inverness the route is currently on roads.

The road cycling route on the east side is quiet. You cycle right beside Loch Ness for part of the way. The other part involves a steep climb away from the loch shore to cycle beside some different lochs at a higher level. Both of these routes are very hilly in places.

The alternative is a circular day ride from Daviot, just south of Inverness on the A9. Each route is marked with different arrow symbols on the map.

Great Glen Cycle Route
Fort Augustus to
Drumnadrochit (22 miles)

From Fort Augustus go north on the A82 for 1.5 miles to Allt na Criche picnic site. Turn left into the forest following green mountain biking signs. It's seven miles on hilly forest trails to Invermoriston. There are areas here where the forest has been clear cut - not so attractive, but it does give good views of the loch. There is a long sweep round to the west to make the descent to Invermoriston, then a steep drop to a T junction where you turn right.

At Invermoriston you enter forest again behind the Glenmoriston Arms Hotel. This section is more arduous but has some good views, you climb steeply at first on a surfaced road. After four miles this part ends near Loch Ness Youth Hostel (01320-351274). The next part is ten miles and consists of a stiff climb of 300m, a high level section, then a new link to connect to a minor road leading to Drumnadrochit.

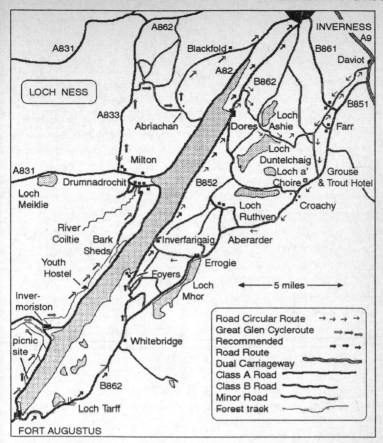

The minor road emerges on to the A82 by the River Coiltie. Turn left and bike half a mile to Drumnadrochit. The Loch Ness Monster Exhibition is in Drumnadrochit. Between Drumnadrochit and Inverness the route is on roads. The Forestry Commission intends that this section too should be off-road, but there is no date for completion.

Great Glen Cycle Route
Drumnadrochit to Inverness (24 miles)

At Drumnadrochit turn left on to the A831 for 1.5 miles, then right on to the A833 to climb, very steeply, out of Glen Urquhart. After five miles turn right for Abriachan following the signposted route. In Abriachan turn sharp left for Blackfold, cross moorland, and drop to the A82 for Inverness. In Inverness cross the canal bridge and turn east to Bught Lane and follow the river to the town centre.

Inverness –
Fort Augustus
(via Whitebridge)

(33 miles)

Travelling on the east side of Loch Ness entirely avoids the A82. It's all road cycling but much quieter. Between Inverness and Foyers the route is fairly flat, but south of Foyers there are serious hills as the road climbs away from the loch shore. The scenery however is quite lovely.

Southbound:

Leave Inverness on the B862 passing near Inverness Youth Hostel (01463-231771); continue upstream by the south bank of the River Ness to Dores. The hotel at Dores does good pub meals and there are tables by the side of the loch. After this you can continue by the lochside to Foyers where there is another hotel.

Beyond this point you have to climb away from the loch shore. This is a steep climb by the River Foyers to Whitebridge. The Whitebridge Hotel here also does food. After Whitebridge there is a high section, then a further climb, followed by a very steep drop to Fort Augustus (Backpackers Lodge 01320-366233; tourist information 01320- 366367).

Northbound:

From Fort Augustus turn on to the B862 by the abbey, and climb north-east towards Whitebridge. There is a very long and steep climb up to Loch Tarff. Loch Tarff is very pretty. Later on you can reward yourself with a drink at the Whitebridge Hotel. After Whitebridge use the B852 via Foyers (hotel, tea room, waterfall) to cycle by Loch Ness.

Another alternative is to avoid Loch Ness by continuing on the B862. This is a lovely road with passing places. You pass Loch Mhor and a craft shop; after this there is an interesting 'Wee Free' church. Just after Croachy you pass the Grouse and Trout Hotel, and shortly after, a herb nursery which also offers refreshments. The minor roads around the lochs here are very interesting and quiet. This is an area well worth exploring in more detail.

After this you should return to Loch Ness at Dores. This is a very fast descent, followed by a gentler climb to take you in to Inverness.

Circular Day Ride
(40 miles - variable)

For those who would like a day ride with attractive views of Loch Ness and other lochs, the circular route: Daviot - Croachy - Aberarder - Loch Ashie - Daviot is recommended. This might suit anyone staying at Aviemore or Inverness who has a car, as Daviot is easily reached on the A9. The route is very quiet and the Grouse and Trout Hotel (see map) can provide bar lunches. The nearby Brin Herb nursery also does food. Just after Dores, on the climb up to Loch Ashie, there is an intriguing small memorial. The poetry is very twee but quite amusing. Tourist Information Inverness: 01463-234353.

Glenelg to Invergarry

(Two Road Routes & One Off-Road Route)

The quietest and most scenic route between Glenelg and Invergarry is via Loch Hourn. There is one slight problem however - an eight mile gap where there is no road.

With this in mind this is described as three routes. A day ride starting from the east (Invergarry); a day ride starting from the west (Glenelg); and a description of the rough track which bridges the gap. The day rides are out and back on quiet roads passing through dramatic scenery. The one way trip Glenelg - Invergarry (including the rough track) can be done in a day.

Invergarry to
Kinloch Hourn (27 miles)

Going west from Invergarry is on the A87 initially. Turn left about a third of the way along Loch Garry, signed Tomdoun/ Kinloch Hourn. This road should be quiet. It runs prettily by the side of the loch for a while, then climbs slowly giving good views. Near the end of the loch the hotel at Tomdoun can provide tea, coffee, etc.

After Loch Garry the countryside becomes wilder with fewer trees. There is a climb to the dam at Loch Quoich, then halfway along Loch Quoich you pass over the Quoich bridge, a long finger of the loch pointing northward towards the high Cluanie Ridge, one of the longest and most exciting day walks in Scotland. Soon after the bridge the road leaves Loch Quoich and starts a 200m descent to sea level. This soon becomes a precipitous plunge.

A few years ago I did this trip with a cycling family from Edinburgh. The mother was biking with her daughter in a child seat. Sensibly, she decided not to descend to sea level as doing this meant a 200m climb back up again. However she made the fatal mistake of giving the pannier containing lunch to her son. He of course sailed down the hill forgetting his mother's lunch. She had to descend the hill but was not pleased. Cups of tea and home-made scones are available at the farm at the bottom incidentally.

Glenelg to Arnisdale
(Loch Hourn) (13 miles from ferry)

Approach Loch Hourn and Glenelg from the north, either by catching the Glenelg Ferry from Skye (01599-511302), or turning off the A87 at Ratagan. The road from Ratagan to Glen Elg is very steep, climbing to nearly 400m from sea level. Once over though there is a long descent with fine views of Beinn Sgritheall to the south. The ferry is a right turn just before the village, there is a coffee shop near here in Glenelg

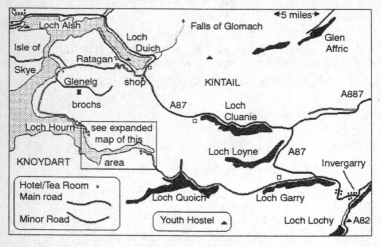

Candles. There are cattle grids, but they are in good condition.

There is a hotel and a shop in Glenelg Village. Just beyond the village a left turn leads up Glen Beag towards the Glenelg Brochs. These are amongst the best preserved in Scotland with walls still over 30ft high. The hollow wall construction of these impregnable towers can still be seen - well worth the two mile diversion.

Beyond this the road continues on towards Arnisdale, climbing at times and giving great views over the Sound of Sleat towards Bla Bheinn (927m) on Skye. As you turn the corner and start to travel east towards Loch Hourn there is a good view of the island of Eigg. To the right of this, the mountains of the island of Rum stick up above the Sleat peninsula on Skye. Currently there is a proposal to re-introduce wolves to Rum to control the deer population. The last native Scottish wolf is said to have died in 1743.

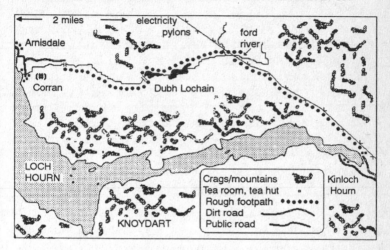

As you turn east there are tremendous views across Loch Hourn towards the mountains of Knoydart. The road eventually drops to the sea at Arnisdale. Keeping on to the end of the road at Corran leads you to the charming lady who runs the tea hut in the village. You have to sit outside, but her gingerbread is worth eating even if it is raining.

Arnisdale
(Loch Hourn)
to Kinloch
Hourn (9 miles)

The off-road section to Kinloch Hourn is best joined just south of Arnisdale. There is a right of way from Corran but it is not recommended for bikes. Just south of Arnisdale the path towards Kinloch Hourn is marked by a sign: 'No Motor Vehicles beyond this Point'.

From Arnisdale the track starts smoothly enough, and is flat as far as the first bridge. After crossing the River Arnisdale it is still bikeable. It soon climbs steeply, rising over 100m in less than half a mile. This is impossible to bike up, in the steeper sections winter rains have washed away all soft material, meaning you have to push or carry your bike up a boulder surface. After this there is a short flatter area, just bikeable, then a steep descent to the Dubh Lochain lochs. A good timber bridge crosses the river again and a path leads round the north side of the first loch. There is a short climb, passing a waterfall, to the second loch.

It's possible to bike round the second loch, indeed you have to if you are not to get wet feet, though this is likely anyway as you probably won't be lucky in all the puddles. At the top of the second loch there is another bridge, then a rough track, still mostly bikeable.

You cross a burn then eventually walk up the north bank of the river, meeting a line of electricity pylons running north-west to south-east. The pylons cross the river, a rough path can be seen on the other side. You have to cross the river to continue south-east. It's best to cross as soon as possible, as biking on the north bank is impossible. There is no bridge but if you pick your spot carefully you should be able to get across by jumping from stone to stone using your bike to balance. Do not cross if the river is high.

The path now follows the pylons. This is a footpath, not an access road. It is however mostly bikeable, and there are several interesting burns to splash through. After two miles there is a view of Loch Hourn far below to the right, then there is a climb to join a wider track. This has to be walked up in places. When you reach the top you are at 280m. There is a very steep drop to Kinloch Hourn over one kilometre. Turn right through a gate into trees and do not continue on the pylon track. Pass by the stalkers cottage to the public road at Loch Hourn.

How difficult is it? A skilled mountain biker could bike 80% of it. If you have a road bike, or serious amounts of luggage you'd be walking much more. One guy on a touring bike said it was interesting but he wouldn't do it again. A lad on a Cannondale mountain bike said it was brilliant - better than anything in Canada.

Other useful information: there is a food shop, a camp site, and a tourist information office (01599-511264) near Ratagan at the junction of the Ratagan road and the A87. Ratagan has a friendly youth hostel (01599-511243) and several B&Bs. If you are cycling between Glenelg and Invergarry on the A87 bear in mind that the only source of food between these two places is the Cluanie Hotel, at the west end of Loch Cluanie.

Strathconon & Strathfarrar

These are two of the loveliest glens in Scotland, but little visited because they are not part of a through route. Mountain bikers can make Strathconon a circular route, but these two glens are so pretty that going up and down is twice the pleasure. This area is sheltered by the hills. The scenery is much like further west, but the rainfall is less. Quite often when Fort William is dull and grey, Strathpeffer is enjoying sunshine.

Strathpeffer or Beauly are the best bases for exploring. Strathpeffer has a youth hostel (01997-421532), both have B&Bs & hotels. Strathpeffer was fashionable in Victorian times as a health spa and has an interesting pump room where visitors came to take the water (tourist info 01997-421415). The Strathconon route starts from Strathpeffer; the Strathfarrar route from Beauly (Strathpeffer to Beauly is ten miles).

Strathconon

(45 miles, returning down the glen)

From Strathpeffer bike south-west on the A834 to Contin. At the junction of the A834 and A835 turn right passing through the village. After a mile turn left to a minor road by the Loch Achilty Hotel. The road passes through trees by the shore of Loch Achilty, then after four miles you meet a little bridge over the River Conon. Turn left over this, then after a further mile cycle over the dam at the head of Loch Meig. After the dam turn right up the glen.

The road climbs gently up the glen on the south bank of the River Meig, then crosses over to the north side at Bridgend. After this the glen turns south-west and becomes steep sided as it cuts through increasingly mountainous territory. There are no serious hills on the road however, and many attractive picnic spots by the river. Parts of the glen are forested and paths in the woods could be explored on a mountain bike; once the paths reach open hillside they cease to be bikeable. The road ends at Loch Beannacharain.

Mountain bikers could take a rough track that leads north-west from Loch Beannacharáin. This becomes a very rough footpath, but leads eventually to the A890 from which it is possible to return to Strathpeffer via Garve. When the railway comes in to view bear right to pass under it. OS

Landranger map, sheet 25 is advisable. To return to Strathpeffer turn right at Achnasheen (train station & hotel).

Returning down the glen is the prettier option. Do not cross the Loch Meig dam but continue on down the glen, following the south bank of the River Meig then the River Conon. Pass Loch Achonachie, meeting the A832 at Marybank. Return to Strathpeffer by turning left, crossing the River Conon on to the A835. Another option is to turn right and follow a minor road for five miles to Muir of Ord to visit the distillery which dates from 1838.

Strathfarrar (49 miles)

Start in Beauly travelling south on the A862. At the T junction south of the village turn right on to the A831. After a mile turn left on to a minor road that crosses the river. Immediately after the bridge over the River Beauly turn right following a line of pylons. After a short climb then a brief descent the road follows the south bank of the river for five miles. After this take a right fork crossing the river again to Struy. This turn off is just after Erchless Castle which you will see on the far river bank. After crossing the river turn right on to the A831, then

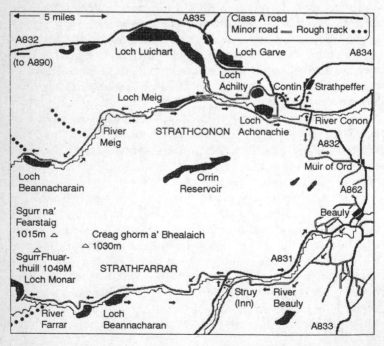

after a very short distance, by the River Farrar, turn left up a minor road leading up the glen. The inn at Struy can provide tea, coffee, meals, etc.

The road up Strathfarrar is closed to motor traffic, the gate only being unlocked at certain times; there are no restrictions for bicycles - just go round the barrier. The road here is maintained mainly for the hydro power station further up, but it gives access to some lovely scenery, with woods of natural Scots pine backed by mountains rising to over 1000m. There are numerous picnic spots on the way, the river tumbling over many waterfalls.

Once you have reached Loch Beannacharan the main climb is done, though there is a fierce final ascent to the dam at Loch Monar. Just before this there is an interesting ford leading to some rough tracks, which the more adventurous might like to splash over. Return to Beauly can be by using the A831 which is reasonably quiet.

Kyle of Lochalsh to Ullapool

This area tends to be busy in summer, holidaymakers of all kinds are attracted by the dramatic scenery. Experienced cyclists should not be put off however; most drivers are tourists who are usually considerate and not in any particular hurry. There are some quieter roads, but even the main roads aren't so busy that they are unpleasant to bike along. Single track roads with passing places force a more relaxed attitude - car drivers can't go fast anyway. Be prepared for some long steep climbs.

Kyle of Lochalsh has most things, but isn't particularly attractive. There is a wholefood tea room, tourist information: 01599-534276. The railway line from Inverness ends here, and there is a new bridge over to Kyleakin on Skye (is it still an island?).

Kyle of Lochalsh
to Lochcarron (22 miles)

To go north from Kyle of Lochalsh, take the minor road leading out of the village towards Plockton. This is very hilly, the railway having appropriated the only flat route by the shore. After two miles the road cuts inland. Shortly after this turn left for Duirinish and Plockton. Plockton is the archetypal pretty highland village and is worth the one mile diversion off route to explore. The working railway station has a café, with tables on the platform.

After Plockton take the first left to join the A890 near Achmore, this involves a stiff climb, then a steep descent to the sea at Loch Carron. Following this continue round the loch

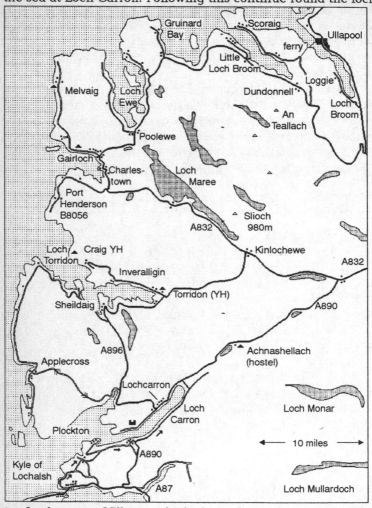

to Lochcarron Village which has shops, a tourist office (01520-722357) and The Bothy Café. The road south-west from Lochcarron leads to ruined Strome Castle. In 1602 a siege of the castle ended abruptly when the cooks made the fatal mistake of putting water in the gunpowder (see the castle information board). The road as far as the castle is fairly flat but becomes hilly afterwards.

Lochcarron
to Torridon

(via A896 22 miles,
via Applecross 50 miles)

After Loch Carron you have the choice of continuing north to Loch Torridon on the A896, or taking the minor road via Applecross. This is quieter and very beautiful but involves a climb of 625m over the Bealach na Ba, or Pass of the Cattle. Some years ago I did this with a friend and my son, then aged ten. It was a Sunday and we decided that there was no possibility of us buying food at Torridon, so it had to be purchased in Lochcarron and hauled over the Bealach na Ba. The deal was if I would carry it, she would cook it. I agreed and she promptly purchased a large and very heavy cauliflower. I felt I'd earned my tea that day!

The climb over the Bealach na Ba is stiff and unrelenting, but the view back over Loch Kishorn is tremendous. Before you reach the highest point on the road there is a view of the islands of Scalpay and Raasay, with Bla Bheinn and the Skye Cuillin Ridge visible in the far distance. Your reward for the climb is a tremendous fast descent with stunning views of Applecross, Raasay and Skye.

If you have climbed the Beallach na Ba on a mountain bike, and the ascent of 625m on the public road isn't enough for you, you could bike up a rough track leading to a radio mast at the very summit of the hill.

When you get to Applecross be sure to stop at the the the camp site and drink a cup of tea in the flower tunnel. This is a great place to stay for a day or two. Applecross has a post office, food shop, public toilets and bike hire. Have a drink at the Applecross Inn and sit at an outside table contemplating the Cuillins on Skye.

Eventually though you'll have to travel north again, leaving Applecross by a long sand and pebble beach, backed by tall stands of beech trees. The road is fairly flat initially, you roll along opposite the island of Raasay, passing a lovely sandy beach at An Cruinn-leum. After a while Raasay drops behind and the Island of Rona is opposite. There isn't too much on the road apart from ruined crofts - signs that before the clearances this land was much more populated.

At Fearnmore (weaving shop) you turn the corner to travel east by Loch Torridon. The road becomes even more hilly. Craig Youth Hostel is just visible across Loch Torridon (no road - taking your bike means carrying it). Finally you meet the A896, turn left for Sheildaig. Sheildaig (Norse for herring bay) has shops (fresh milk and bread three days per week) and a camp site which is free of charge, but a donation is appreciated.

Torridon, eight miles further east, also has a camp site but it tends to be particularly midge infested. Torridon also has a youth hostel (01445-791284) and a food shop that is open seven days a week to 7pm. The road between Sheildaig and Torridon is twin track. The minor road to Inveralligin and Diabeg is an attractive ride though it is very hilly beyond Inveralligin. Craig Hostel is three miles beyond the road end.

Torridon
to Gairloch (30 miles)

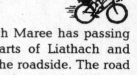

The road up Glen Torridon towards Loch Maree has passing places again, with the towering ramparts of Liathach and Beinn Eighe rising steeply almost from the roadside. The road by Loch Maree is twin track and may be busier, the hills are quite gentle by the loch and there are good views of Slioch, the mountain on the other side.

After Loch Maree the road climbs through Slattadale Forest, passes Loch Bad an Sgalaig, then drops down to sea level by the River Kerry, tumbling waterfalls much of the way. Charlestown and the small villages towards Port Henderson on the B8056 cater for visiting yachts which anchor in the many small bays. Just north of this, Gairloch is a popular holiday centre with all facilities, camp sites, tourist information (01445-712130) etc. The youth hostel of Carn Dearg (01445- 712219) is three miles beyond the town in a quiet location. There is a sandy beach nearby. Private hostels: in town Achtercairn Hostel (01445-712131) or Lighthouse Hostel at Melvaig (01445-771263).

Gairloch
to Ullapool (56 miles)

The road from Gairloch starts with a climb of course, from sea level to 141m just before Loch Tollaidh. After this there is a different view of Loch Maree, seen from the north, before dropping to sea level at Poolewe. Refreshment is available here, but an interesting place to stop slightly further on is Inverewe Gardens (National Trust). The National Trust always seems to do good coffee, and if you like you could take a walk round the 120 year old gardens.

Beyond Inverewe the road runs past Loch Ewe and then Gruinard Bay, the two being separated by the Rubha Mor peninsula. Just here if the weather is clear you start to get views of the Summer Isles, with the mountains of Coigach and Assynt visible in the distance. The Caledonian MacBrayne ferry, sailing from Ullapool to Stornoway may well be seen.

Ullapool as the crow flies is actually quite near, only ten miles away as you start to climb towards Little Loch Broom. By road though, round Loch Broom, it's 35 miles. It is possible to shorten the distance by taking a foot passenger ferry from Altnaharrie. This lands you at the small pier, right in the middle of Ullapool. The ferry is operated from the Altnaharrie Inn (01854-612230) and it is essential to phone first as all sailings are subject to prevailing tides and weather. Part of the route is footpath and may not be bikeable (see map).

Another option is to break your journey at Little Loch Broom. You could stay at the Dundonnell Hotel which is quite posh, but friendly, and serves good food. A cheaper option is the nearby Sail Mhor Croft Hostel (01854-633224). There is a B&B quite near the hostel. These facilities are well signposted.

The road from Dundonnell to Ullapool starts with a steady climb by the Dundonnell River. The massive bulk of An Teallach is obscured by trees much of the time, but is occasionally visible. After this there is a bleaker moorland section before reaching the junction at Braemore. Near here coach parties stretch their legs to look at Corrieshalloch Gorge. It's only a short walk, so you could manage it before continuing north to Ullapool

Ullapool is the terminal for the ferry going to Stornoway on Lewis. There is a tourist office (01854-612135), a youth hostel (01854-612254) and a large camp site. The bike hire shop at 11 Pulteney Street keeps spare parts and does repairs.

Bike Routes Around Ullapool

Altnaharrie - Scoraig (10 miles)

The ferry mentioned earlier, from Ullapool to Altnaharrie, can also be used in the other direction to give access to a bike route leading to Scoraig (map on page 184). From the Altnaharrie Inn go up a steep hill passing a lochan. This leads to a gate where you turn right for the road leading to Badrallach. After that a rough track of about four miles leads to the isolated community of Scoraig. Don't forget to check arrangements with the ferryman for your return.

Lael Forest (4 or 8 miles)

There are signposted mountain bike routes at Lael Forest at the southern end of Loch Broom. Two routes are signposted with red and purple marker posts. The red Upper Glen Route is eight miles and fairly demanding. The purple Riverside Route is easier, being entirely on forest roads, four miles long. The routes start from the signposted car parks. There are some spectacular giant American redwood trees by the roadside but unfortunately the forest itself is mostly quick growing sitka spruce. Perhaps even the Forestry Commission is not prepared to wait 2000 years for trees to mature.

Loggie

On the opposite side of Loch Broom from Lael Forest, a minor road leads to the hamlet of Letters and then on to Loggie. Just beyond this a rough track leads to a vitrified fort (ruin) at Dun Lagaidh. There is also a broch nearby.

Glen Achall

At the north end of Ullapool, by the Mercury Motel, a minor road leads past Loch Achall and eventually to Glen Achall. This track should not be used in the deer-stalking season (September onwards) without checking locally first.

Ullapool to Cape Wrath

Traffic tends to thin out a bit north of Ullapool, many cars travelling on the ferry to Stornoway on Lewis. The minor roads leading to places like Achiltibuie, Drumbeg and Kinlochbervie are well worth exploring, with lovely beaches and views of the hills and mountains.

Ullapool to Loch Bad a' Ghaill (18 miles)

From Ullapool we start with a steady climb by Loch Broom. After this there is a fast descent to Ardmair Bay, which has a camp site with a shop and tea room. The large mountain ahead is Ben Mor Coigach. Three miles after this you cross the River Kanaird. A road leads off to the west from here, leading to a footpath taking you by the shore to Achiltibuie; this is not recommended with a bike.

After this there is a steady climb to the junction at Drumrunie, where the you turn left into Inverpolly Nature Reserve. This is one of the most scenic areas in Scotland, but cycling to Lochinver this way is not easy.

The first section, past the mountain of Stac Pollaidh, and Loch Lurgainn is not dreadfully hilly. Cars will have to wait at the passing places, but the road will normally be wide enough for bikes to pass. The loch has sandy beaches and a number of islets covered in trees - once all of the highlands were like this. A notice board opposite Stac Pollaidh gives information about the nature reserve; the mountain is a popular climb, witness the erosion caused by walkers. At the junction by Loch Bad a' Ghaill turn right for Lochinver.

Loch Bad a' Ghaill to Achininver (15 miles via Atlandhu)

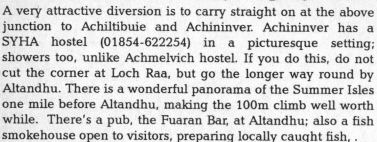

A very attractive diversion is to carry straight on at the above junction to Achiltibuie and Achininver. Achininver has a SYHA hostel (01854-622254) in a picturesque setting; showers too, unlike Achmelvich hostel. If you do this, do not cut the corner at Loch Raa, but go the longer way round by Altandhu. There is a wonderful panorama of the Summer Isles one mile before Altandhu, making the 100m climb well worth while. There's a pub, the Fuaran Bar, at Altandhu; also a fish smokehouse open to visitors, preparing locally caught fish, .

An additional detour on the way is to Old Dornie Harbour, opposite the island of Ristol. On the way too is a shop and craft/coffee shop at Polbain, and more of the same at the village of Achiltibuie. Here also is the the Hydroponicum, growing vegetables without soil, a tour of this is £3.50, though there is no fee to enter the tea room to test the products.

Return to the Loch Bad a' Ghaill junction is best done via Loch Raa. There is a tremendous view of Suilven, Canisp, Cul Mor, Stac Pollaidh and Cul Beag just after Loch Raa. Concentrate on the scenery instead of your legs when you do the next section to Lochinver.

Loch Bad a' Ghaill to Lochinver (12 miles)

The road to Lochinver has some excellent views but there is barely a yard of flat. You should allow at least two hours for these twelve miles. There are only occasional views of the mountains, but the road passes some lovely bays and lochans. On the way we cross the River Kirkaig which is the start of the walking route to Suilven.

Lochinver is an important fishing centre. It also has the Culag Hotel which has a good reputation and which can be competitive in price with nearby B&Bs and does good bar lunches. The SYHA youth hostel is further on at Achmelvich (01571-844480). This is a lovely spot with a white sand beach. There is a camp site by the beach here too. If you are a mountain biker you might be tempted to try a footpath shown on OS maps running between Suilven and Canisp. This is not a good idea; the access point in any case has a 'no bikes please sign'.

Lochinver to Kylesku (25 miles)

North of Lochinver, with Achmelvich near the southern end, is the Drumbeg road (B869). This is possibly the most scenic road in Britain, it is certainly the most hilly. In days gone by you could camp wild on the coast here, but erosion problems have meant that campers have had to be concentrated at two sites: Achmelvich and Clachtoll. The start of the road is signposted Kylesku Tourist Route.

There are a number of minor roads leading towards the Point of Stoer. Just before Stoer you come to a memorial to the Rev Norman Macleod, who eventually settled in New Zealand with his followers. On the way they also tried Nova Scotia and Australia - and this in the days of sailing ships! After Stoer you pass the golden sand of Clashnessie Bay, then up to Drumbeg where there is a hotel. There is another plunge to Loch Nedd; watch out for a dangerous bend just after a sign: 25% descent. There are occasional dramatic views of Quinag along the way. The road ends just south of Kylesku at the A894.

Kylesku to Durness (with optional diversion to Kinlochbervie) (36 miles direct)

Kylesku, just off the main road, has a hotel doing bar lunches, B&Bs, toilets, but no food shop. You can take a boat trip up Loch Glencoul to the Eas Coul Aulin Falls, the tallest waterfall in Britain. Prior to building the bridge in 1983, a ferry which took four cars plied the crossing. After the bridge there is a steady climb, with fine views behind you of Quinag; after a few more up and downs you will be in Scourie. There's a camp site with a tea room here, the Scourie Hotel and a Mace food store. The cafe and store are closed on Sundays.

Going north from Scourie, just before the junction at Laxford Bridge, there is a view of the mountains of Arkle and Foinaven. The road south-east from Laxford Bridge, towards Loch Shin, is just lovely; usually fairly quiet, with what cars there are slowed down by passing places. If you are cycling to the far-north west, this road is one of the best routes. This is covered in the Inverness/Ledmore/Tongue section (page 197).

191

Continuing north, the next road junction is at the head of Loch Inchard, the B801 leading to Kinlochbervie, a six mile diversion. This is another fishing harbour, or rather two, for there is an old one and a thriving new one. The landscape has been described as lunar, but it's much prettier than the pictures from Apollo 5. Along the road to Kinlochbervie is the The Old School House B&B and restaurant (01971-521383). Staff from Edinburgh Bicycle Co-operative report that they recently stayed there, and that it is a fine place.

At Kinlochbervie itself is the aptly named London Store which sells everything; a Spar shop, and a ships chandler opposite the pier. The road continues beyond Kinlochbervie to a number of small settlements. There is a fine beach at Oldshoremore.

Blairmore to Sandwood
Bay (5 miles off-road)
and on to Durness

Sandwood Bay, north of Kinlochbervie is an interesting place to visit. This lovely beach is likely to be deserted. Shipwrecks from Cape Wrath tend to end up here; there was rumoured to be a mermaid living in the off-shore rocks. Most of the route is a track starting from Blairmore. The last mile is a rough path which you will have to walk, particularly if it's been wet.

The final section from Loch Inchard to Durness is a lonely stretch of road, with fine views of the quartzite ramparts of Foinaven. After this there is a long descent to the sea at the Kyle of Durness. The road runs by this for a while, then there is a short climb before reaching Durness.

Durness is strung out along the cliff top. There is a choice of shops, the youth hostel (01971-511244) is east of the village just before Smoo Cave. This is in fact three caves, one including a waterfall. Walking access is to the first cave only, but you can see the second from a platform. To get beyond this you have to use a boat. Information at Durness Tourist Office (01971-511259).

Another place worth visiting near Durness is Balnakeil Craft Village. This is not particularly attractive on the outside as it consists of a collection of concrete huts (the leaflet says: 'imaginatively converted from a military base'). Inside though you will find potters, weavers, enamelworkers, leatherworkers and other crafts people. There is also a coffee shop with home baking. A great place to spend a day if it's raining! Also quite near is Balnakeil Church, an interesting ruin.

Kyle of Durness to Cape Wrath (11 miles)

The route to Cape Wrath is nominally a surfaced road, but it is in such poor condition that cycling it on a touring bike needs a lot of concentration. Mountain bikers get to look at the scenery. Cape Wrath is the most northerly point of Scotland's north-west seaboard.

The track to Cape Wrath is seperated from the rest of the road network by the Kyle of Durness, a foot passenger ferry takes you over (£3.50 with a bike). The only other vehicle on the road will be a minibus that operates a shuttle service. How the minibus got over is an interesting question. The ferry service is frequent in summer, but because the Kyle of Durness is tidal, the ferry can only operate at certain times, phone 01971-511376. Access from the minor road just south of Durness. The hotel by the ferry provides teas.

As soon as you get off the ferry there is a steep climb, then the road contours north towards the head of the loch. After this there is a real pig of a hill when it cuts inland. The views are lovely all the way with dramatic views east and south from the cape itself. Four miles before the cape a track runs down to an attractive beach at Kearvaig. There is an interesting rock stack here, Clo Kearvaig (Cathedral Rock). Return distance 22 miles.

Durness - Loch Eriboll - River Hope (21 miles)

After Durness the road zigzags east past lovely beaches before turning south for the long haul round Loch Eriboll. The road on the west side of the loch is fairly flat for a change; there is a vegetarian tea room halfway down, more or less opposite the island of Eilean Choraidh. The road on the east side of the loch gets slightly hillier as it works its way north. There's a fast descent to the River Hope; this river is only a mile long, and connects Loch Hope to the sea. Here you have the choice of continuing east towards Tongue and Bettyhill (see next section), or turning south on the minor road, to bike by the side of Loch Hope.

I particularly recommend the latter. Visible the whole way will be Ben Hope, the most northerly Munro (mountain over 3000ft), the road is quiet and the scenery lovely. Dun Dornadilla Broch (2000 year old fortified tower) is just off the road four miles south of Loch Hope, and two miles south of that, a Land Rover track leads over to the A838 at Loch Merkland by way of Gobernuisgach Lodge. A locked gate at the south end prevents its use by motor vehicles, but this of course is no impediment to walkers or mountain bikers.

Tongue to Bonar Bridge

In the northern part of this area, the wild mountainous terrain of the far north-west gradually gives way to the gentler landscapes of the Flow Country further east. Long distance tourers can travel to the rail head at Thurso, or the Orkney ferry terminal at Scrabster (see map page 202).

Further south, travellers who originally started at Inverness can cycle by the shore of Loch Shin or via Altnaharra. Whichever way you go, the roads are mostly fairly quiet, and the countryside varied and interesting.

Loch Hope
to Borgie (17 miles)

The gentler gradients of the Flow Country are obviously some way off when the A838 begins its climb eastward from the River Hope to Tongue. When the climb is over the jagged peaks of Ben Loyal will be visible. There is a flatter section by Loch Maovally, then a fast descent to the Kyle of Tongue, which you cross on a causeway and bridge.

An alternative route to Tongue is via the Loch Hope road, then north again from Altnaharra (hotel) via Loch Loyal. This road is quiet too, though like many roads in this area it tends to have a 4pm 'rush' hour. Tongue has a rambling youth hostel (01847-611301) and the usual food shops. Like many settlements here it is a fertile spot and is surprisingly green and wooded.

The A836 from Tongue to Borgie has passing places and there is as usual, a climb out of Tongue. An attractive diversion or day ride is to go via the north coast on a minor road to Skerray, starting from near Loch Buidhe and finishing near Borgie. This is wooded in places, mostly with hardwood, and the road runs past many lochans. There are some fine beaches on the way too. There are two mountain biking routes to the south of the A836, near Borgie and Truderscraig.

Borgie Forest (9 miles)

This is a fairly easy mountain bike route suitable for families, it is marked with blue markers. The forest is one of the Forestry Commission's first plantings in 1920. It includes some 100ft mature trees. Access from the forest road a mile east of Borgie (not at the Borgie junction).

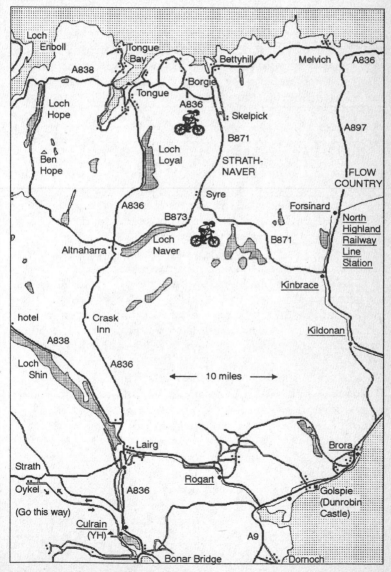

Truderscraig (13 miles)

Another mountain biking option south of Bettyhill is around
Rosal pre-clearance village in Strathnaver. The route is signed
with red markers. When Truderscraig Forest was being
established the surveyors discovered the remains of the
village. To their credit the Forestry Commission decided to
preserve the site. The township covers sixty acres and records
show that people lived there from 1269 until they were evicted
in 1830. Access is off the B873 just south of Syre. The forest
roads lead to another settlement, Truderscraig Village, further
south in the forest. As the area is a protected archaeological
site bikes must keep to forest roads.

Borgie to
Melvich Bay (22 miles)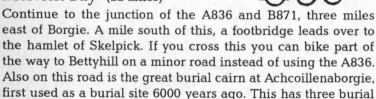

Continue to the junction of the A836 and B871, three miles
east of Borgie. A mile south of this, a footbridge leads over to
the hamlet of Skelpick. If you cross this you can bike part of
the way to Bettyhill on a minor road instead of using the A836.
Also on this road is the great burial cairn at Achcoillenaborgie,
first used as a burial site 6000 years ago. This has three burial
chambers, which you can visit, in a cairn 70m long.

Bettyhill is a small straggling village with a tourist
information office (01641-521342) shops etc. When the
Sutherlands bought their huge estates in the 19th century, the
land around here was populated by thousands of families,
descendents of crofters who had lived there for hundreds of
years.

The Sutherlands wanted their lands empty of people so
that sheep could roam. They employed ruthless men to evict
people from their homes, setting fire to them so they could not
return. The Clan chiefs, whom the people once might have
looked to for protection, were now seduced by the consumer
society, and had no ear for the cries of despair. An eyewitness
in 1819 counted 250 crofts put to the torch in one night.

Strathnaver Folk Museum just east of Bettyhill should be
visited, as it has much material on the clearances mentioned
above, as well as local archeology and history. Another famous
item in the churchyard is the Farr Stone. This intricately
carved cross dates from the ninth century, and is still in fine

condition as the artist, a thousand years ago, was working in hard schist. There are attractive beaches at Farr Bay and Torrisdale Bay which is a bird sanctuary.

After Bettyhill the A836 winds further east past Melvich towards Thurso. East of Strathnaver the scenery is mostly moorland rather than mountain; it is important for conservation reasons but lacks the drama of the hills. Most cyclists are likely to give it a miss unless they are intending to go on to Orkney, or catch a train on the North Highland Line.

Laxford Bridge to Bonar Bridge via Loch Shin (48 miles)

Further south you can travel on the A838, by Loch Shin, to get from the far north-west to Bonar Bridge. This road is hilly further north, but less so by Loch Shin. Cyclists may intend to obtain refreshment at the Overscaig Hotel near the north end of Loch Shin. A number have been refused service at this hotel, a variety of different reasons being given (by contrast the Crask Inn on the A836 south of Altnaharra was welcoming). As you approach Bonar Bridge, Carbisdale Castle hostel is visible on the other side of the Kyle of Sutherland. You are not allowed to cross on the rail bridge. Getting to it means a detour by Strath Oykel or Bonar Bridge.

Ledmore Junction to Inverness

Ledmore Junction - Bonar Bridge (32 miles)

Eastbound: from Ledmore there is eight miles of fairly flat road then a lovely descent into Strath Oykel, the River Oykel tumbling by. Five miles after Oykel Bridge turn right at the sign for Culrain & Inveroykel. After this follow the road past Carbisdale Castle Hostel (01549-421232) at Culrain. This gothic pile more resembles Dracula's castle than anything else. It was built as a divorce settlement for the Duchess of Sutherland. Bonar Bridge has a Spar shop open on Sundays.

Westbound: cross the bridge at Bonar Bridge then follow signs for Carbisdale Youth Hostel. From Carbisdale turn left out the hostel gate and bike north then west for nine miles through lovely wooded scenery. Turn right at a sign Rosehall & Oykel Bridge, then left at the main road.

Eight miles before Ledmore, you pass a loch and get a view of Suilven. Some people call this the sugar loaf mountain but this is lacking in imagination. Really it's a sea-dragon, entombed in stone for a million years. Don't pay any attention to nonsense about Lewisian gneiss.

Bonar Bridge to Inverness

One way to get between Bonar Bridge and Inverness is to use the train, don't forget to reserve a space for your bike. Culrain station, for Carbisdale, is a request stop; signal the driver! To bike it the direct way go via Alness, this is described next. The most interesting way is via the Black Isle (see opposite).

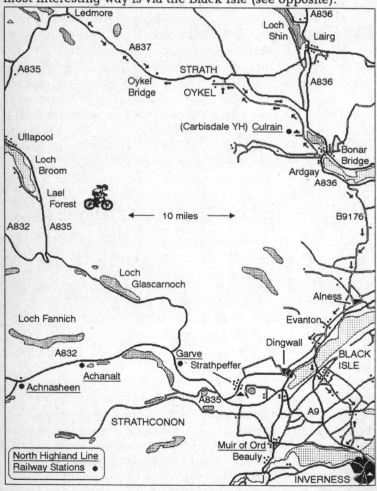

Bonar Bridge to Inverness (Direct Route) (38 miles)

Travel south from Bonar Bridge and Ardgay on the A836. Three miles after Ardgay turn right on to the B9176 to Alness. This is very scenic with good views over the Dornoch Firth, but quite hilly. After Alness, avoid the A9 by using the B817 through Evanton. Join the A9 south of Evanton to cross the Cromarty Firth. Immediately after crossing the Cromarty Firth, turn left off the A9 to Culbokie. After this refer to the Black Isle section for your route into Inverness.

Dornoch Firth to the Black Isle

The North Sea coastline between Inverness and Dornoch is deeply indented by three estuaries, the Dornoch Firth, the Cromarty Firth and the Moray and Beauly Firths. In between is rolling countryside, with forests, farmland, and a network of quiet roads. Some of the forests are signposted for mountain biking. The area has a considerable history with maritime connections to the rest of Europe. There are some lovely beaches and pretty villages. A school of dolphins lives in the Cromarty Firth, and for a change, some of the roads are flat!

Bonar Bridge to Tain (16 miles)

Travelling from Bonar Bridge you can take either the A836 south of the Dornoch Firth, or the A949 on the north side. Thanks to the new bridge across the Dornoch Firth both of these are now reasonably quiet. The road on the north side is slightly hillier, but this gives good views across the firth. An option here is to use the minor road from Bonar Bridge to Spinningdale. This starts from the main road junction in Bonar Bridge.

From the A949 you have to turn south at Clashmore on to the A9 to cross the Dornoch Firth. This has a hard shoulder one metre wide from Clashmore to Tain. Tain is an attractive old town with many fine Victorian buildings and a busy High Street; plenty of shops, tourist information: 01862-892122.

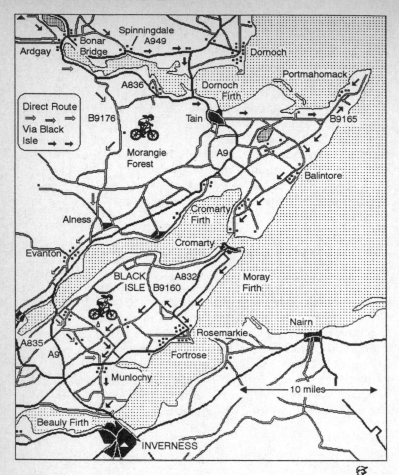

Tain to
Cromarty (25 miles)

Portmahomack is our next port of call after Tain, this is a diversion but worth while. Portmahomack is a restored fishing village, it's the only east coast village that faces west. Recommended is the Oystercatcher Café-Restaurant, which combines the functions of café, restaurant, B&B, craft shop and picture gallery. It's closed Mondays (01862-871560).

After Portmahomack take the B9165 south-west for five miles then turn left (east) for Balintore. This is in fact three small fishing villages: Hilton of Cadboll, Balintore and Shandwick. Their isolated position on the long straight coast gives them a strange air of remoteness. Cycle through all three, then turn inland to the minor road that eventually joins the B9175, leading to the Nigg - Cromarty ferry.

There has been a ferry here since 1309. Now it's run by Seaboard Marine Ltd (01862-871254). In summer it operates half hourly, departing Cromarty on the hour and half hour, and Nigg quarter past and quarter to. It takes two cars, or a larger number of bicycles, fare £1.50. Make yourself visible on the pier! Also evening cruises to see the dolphins.

Cromarty is a lovely historic town over 700 years old. It has had a number of famous people, who's houses you can visit, also an old courthouse and a harbour lighthouse; Florence's Tea Shop is recommended.

Cromarty to Inverness (27 miles)

Leave Cromarty on the A832, but take the first left after a mile, signposted Eathie/Navity. This ridge road is quiet but hilly, and gives views over the Firths. After six miles it joins the the A832 near Rosemarkie, turn left to enter the town.

Rosemarkie is interesting for the Pictish stone art in Groam House. Leave Rosemarkie the way you came, but after 1.5 miles turn left to join the B9160, take the second left down a long straight minor road after a mile.

Go down the minor road for five miles; keep straight on at the first junction near a phone box; straight on again at the first cross-roads; turn left when you come to a second cross-roads (the road layout here is slightly off-set). After a mile turn right at a T junction, bear right at the next junction then cross the A832 to enter Munlochy on the B9161.

Keep on the B9161, but to avoid the A9, fork left to a minor road half a mile after Munlochy. Cross the A9, signed North Kessock (opposite direction sign: Drumsmittal/Kilmuir). The road through North Kessock emerges under the bridge to Inverness. Use the west cycle path to avoid the roundabout on the Inverness side.

Mountain Bike Morangie Forest

Morangie or Ardross Forest is west of Tain and is extensive, with views of the Dornoch and Cromarty Firths. There are some attractive open areas with Scots pine poking through the heather. There are two mountain bike routes here. Morangie Hill route (green markers) is 14 miles long and is graded moderate. Strathrory Route (purple markers) is 22 miles and is graded demanding, part is on public roads. The best way to get to the forest is off the A9 Tain bypass, signed Scotsburn. Access also from the B9176.

Mountain Bike in the Black Isle

Access to this area from a car park on the Munlochy/Culbokie road. The forest is mostly Scots pine, and is on higher ground giving views of the firths. Gradients are reasonable. The signposted route has red markers and is ten miles long.

Thurso to John o' Groats

This section is included for those who want to get to Orkney, catch a train, or go to John o' Groats. The main attraction of this area is coastal scenery. Inland the countryside consists of gentle farmland or lonely moors.

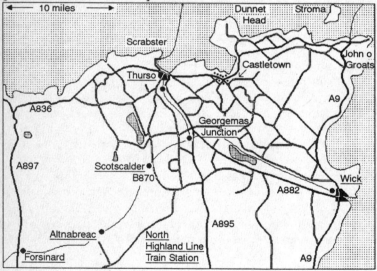

Most tourists heading towards Thurso are going to Scrabster for the Orkney Ferry to Stromness. This is operated by P&O Scottish Ferries (01224-572615). By bike you can take the foot passenger ferry (01955-611353) from John o' Groats to Burwick on Orkney. Go out on one and back on the other. There is a reasonable minor road network in this area so it should not be difficult to avoid the class A roads.

Trains can be picked up at a number of different points, but it is essential to reserve a bike space in advance. Tourist information in Thurso (01847-892371); John o' Groats SYHA hostel (01955-611424).

SCOTTISH ISLANDS

Scotland has nearly 800 islands but only 130 are inhabited. Of these perhaps thirteen have enough roads to be of interest to cyclists, but this still allows plenty of scope. Mull for example, would take several days to explore fully on a bike. The best thing about the islands is their quiet, the rhythm of life is gentler. The scenery is varied, but from the sea cliffs of Orkney to the mountains of Arran, invariably beautiful.

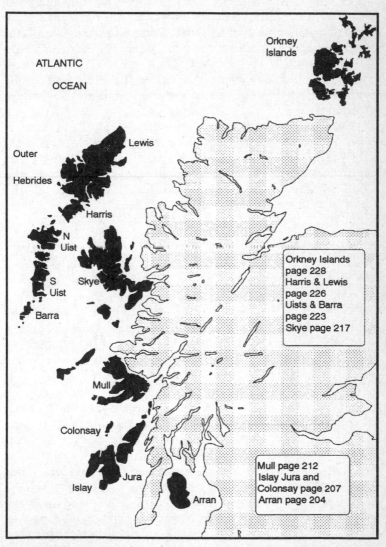

Orkney Islands
page 228
Harris & Lewis
page 226
Uists & Barra
page 223
Skye page 217

Mull page 212
Islay Jura and
Colonsay page 207
Arran page 204

The islands divide into the northern isles, Orkney and Shetland; and the islands of the west coast, from Lewis in the north to Arran in the south. Orkney is a great treasure of early history with monuments dating from stone age times. In the west, tours could include the Outer Hebrides or the larger inner isles, possibly taking in parts of the mainland.

Isle of Arran

Car owners pay substantial sums of money to transport their vehicles to islands, bicycles cost hardly anything. Not surprisingly the Arran ferry often has more bikes than cars. Arran has real mountains and lovely scenery. The roads are quiet, particularly in the west. There isn't a lot of off-road cycling, though a day could be spent on the forest trails in the south. Most of the other paths are too steep, and sometimes too wet to bike.

There are two youth hostels and lots of B&Bs. Visitors generally go to Arran to walk, climb and cycle; the more unpleasant aspects of tourism are mostly absent. The description here is given as a circular route on the coast road (A841), starting from Brodick travelling north. The tourist office is at Brodick (01770-302140/302401)

Brodick - Sannox - Lochranza (14 miles)

Turn right after leaving the ferry terminal, shops, hotels and tea rooms on the left, sea on the right. After a mile you will be clear of the town. Pass the Arran Heritage Museum on the right; this is worth a visit, admission £1.50, child 75p. Shortly after this is the left turn for The String road, this crosses the centre of the island to the west coast and Blackwaterfoot. It climbs steeply and steadily to a height of 234m above sea level, giving good views of Arran's highest mountain Goat Fell (874m). An alternative way of going to Lochranza is to cycle over The String, then cycle up the west coast. This is 24 miles, but either way there will be a serious hill.

Continuing by the sea you pass Brodick Castle which has a tea room, then you go along by a rocky coastline to reach the village of Corrie (shop and hotel). Continue north again by the sea to Sannox; the golf club tea room here is open to passers by. You will need these calories for the climb afterwards. The road from Sannox sweeps round to the north-west, climbing to

199m, before dropping down to Lochranza. There are views of the mountain ridges. Lochranza is a pretty village with a castle by the loch, a post office/shop, a hotel (bar lunches) and a cafe opposite the pier. The youth hostel here is a lovely old house in a beautiful setting (01770-830631). Lochranza is also the terminal for the summer ferry to Claonaig on Kintyre. This can be connected with a short cycle, to another ferry crossing to the islands of Islay, Jura and Colonsay.

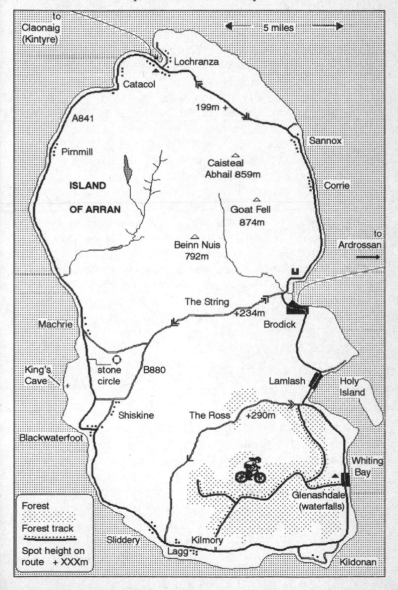

Lochranza to
Blackwaterfoot (17 miles)

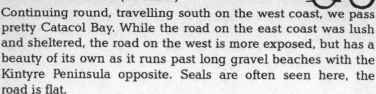

Continuing round, travelling south on the west coast, we pass pretty Catacol Bay. While the road on the east coast was lush and sheltered, the road on the west is more exposed, but has a beauty of its own as it runs past long gravel beaches with the Kintyre Peninsula opposite. Seals are often seen here, the road is flat.

If you started at Lochranza in the morning the tea room at Pirnmill is the right spot for morning coffee. Alternatively the golf club at Machrie, seven miles on, can usually provide some. At Machrie a minor road connects to the B880 String road, enabling you to cut the corner to go to Brodick. Just south of Machrie off the coast road, immediately after crossing Machrie Water, is Machrie Stone Circle. This neolithic monument is along a rough track, easily cycled, and is well worth a visit. It is fairly complete and stands in a fine location.

Just south of this is another historic remnant, but a more recent one; the King's Cave, with its legendary association with Robert the Bruce, one time king of Scotland. It also has Pictish and early Christian carvings. The caves are in a cliff by the sea, isolated from it by a raised beach. Near here too is Arran Outdoor Centre, another place to stay (01770-860333). The next village south is Blackwaterfoot, western end of The String road. It has a comfortable hotel that does bar lunches, a small harbour and a food shop. The hotel has an indoor swimming pool that is open to passers-by, admission £2.50.

Blackwaterfoot -
Whiting Bay -
Brodick (24 miles)

You can cut some of the hilly coast road by using The Ross to get to Lamlash, but this climbs to 290m; the coast road is the prettier of the two road routes. There is a good tea room at Lagg and hotels providing food near Kilmory and Kildonan. The one at Kildonan, which is on a loop off the main road, has a view of the rocky islet of Pladda.

Another option is to bike the forest trails to Whiting Bay (see map). If you do this you will pass the Glenashdale Falls which you should certainly look at. Access to the trails is from a track leading north-east one kilometre east of Kilmory.

Going round the coast you pass Whiting Bay (hostel 01770-700339), Holy Island and Lamlash. Holy Island is occupied by Buddists but it was called Holy Island before this. There is a ferry, and tours of the monastery, so allow an hour or two if you decide to visit it. Out of Lamlash it's another stiff climb to get to Brodick and complete the circle.

Ferry Times. From Ardrossan: 0700, 0945, 1230, 1515, 1800, 2030. Sundays: 0945, 1230, 1515, 1800. From Brodick. 0820, 1105, 1350, 1640, 1920. Sundays: 1105, 1350, 1640, 1920. The Lochranza-Claonaig ferry runs April-October. About 9am to 8pm, 75 minute intervals. To confirm times phone: 01294-463470.

Islay, Jura and Colonsay

Islay is famous for bird life, malt whisky, and being the place where Prince Charles nearly crashed his plane. In many ways it's the ideal cycling island, the hills are mostly modest, the roads quiet, and everyone you meet seems to smile and say hello. Islay is particularly fertile. Otters and seals are likely to be seen. There are many historical things to look at and miles of lovely beaches.

The adjacent island of Jura is more of a wilderness. Mountainous and with only one road, a mountain bike is more suitable for exploring. Here deer outnumber people, indeed the name Jura means deer island. Colonsay can be an attractive day trip from Islay but only on a Wednesday.

Islay

Caledonian MacBrayne sails from Kennacraig on the Kintyre peninsula, to Islay every day of the week (01880-730253). This is convenient if coming from Arran as Claonaig, the termination of the ferry from Lochranza, is only seven miles away on the other side of the peninsula. There are two different arrival points in Islay, Port Ellen and Port Askaig and the ferry from Kennacraig calls at one or the other, not both. Port Askaig is an interesting way to arrive, as you sail up the narrow channel between Islay and Jura. However arriving at Port Ellen gives a good sea view of the distilleries of

Laphroaig and Lagavulin.

There is no lack of distilleries on Islay. It can be a surprise to the malt whisky drinker, who has seen labels such as Bruichladdich and Bunnahabhainn on bottles in bars from Seattle to Sydney, to discover that these are actually places as well. This shock can be tempered though by a visit to the establishment concerned, who will administer the elixir, usually free of charge, and let you see round (phone first).

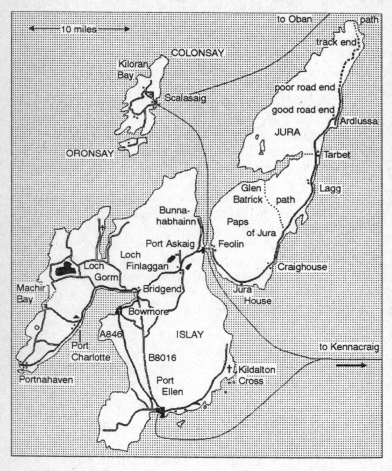

Which routes you take to explore the island will very much depend on where you are staying. Port Charlotte is a good location and the new youth hostel here is very comfortable (01496-850385). There is a wildlife centre immediately below the hostel. Port Charlotte also has the Croft Kitchen café (open all day), and a rural life museum. The hotel at the time of writing was being restored. Bridgend further east is an even more convenient base, there is a hotel that does good bar lunches. The Spar shop in Bridgend is exceptionally well stocked - it has everything you are likely to need in the food line.

Those wishing to stay in B&Bs should contact the tourist information office in Bowmore (01496-810254). There is an attractive camp site at Port Charlotte, and an independent hostel at Kintra Farm, Port Ellen (01496-302051).

Probably the best cycle ride in Islay is around the western peninsula, between Bridgend and Portnahaven. Start at either Bridgend or Port Charlotte and bike south-west on the A847 to Portnahaven. The road runs close by the sea at first but approaching Portnahaven it rises giving good views of the rocky coastline. Portnahaven is a pretty harbour village. The rocky islet of Orsay with its imposing lighthouse is opposite. A new coffee shop, in a converted mill as you enter the village, is reputed to do excellent coffee. There is also a general store.

Leave Portnahaven on the minor road to travel north near the west coast. This rises and falls giving views of the bays and headlands. Watch out for a stone circle about three miles out of Portnahaven. Eventually the road turns south again towards Port Charlotte at Kilchiaran; for a shorter bike ride turn south here.

However for a more interesting time leave the surfaced road at this point, turning left (north) on to a rough track leading steeply up a hill. This leads over the headland to Machir Bay, a lovely beach backed by grass and wild flowers. This is a scenic picnic spot. It can also be approached from the north on ordinary roads. Mountain bike or walk behind the beach to join the public road at the north end. From here you can return to the start going south or north of Loch Gorm.

If going round the north side, which is hillier, you could also explore the road by Loch Gruinart. This is attractive and there is an Early Christian high cross at the north end. The road eventually turns into a rough track leading to the coast on the other side. Near here also is the RSPB bird reserve and visitor centre (no tea room).

However popular Islay becomes with cyclists they will always be outnumbered by the bird-watchers. Islay is home to vast numbers of barnacle and whitefronted geese between October and April. The geese do not restrict themselves to the bird reserve, so Scottish Natural Heritage currently pays £9.50 per goose to the farmers to compensate them for loss of fodder.

Another site to visit is the ruined castle on the island at Loch Finlaggan. Islay was the centre of power of the Lord of the Isles for many centuries. This could be combined with a bike tour on the minor roads to the south.

No visit to Islay can be complete without seeing the Kildalton Cross. This is believed to be the finest in the Hebrides and dates from around AD800. It was carved in local stone by a sculptor from Iona. Considering its age it is in remarkable condition. This is a pleasant ride north-east from Port Ellen.

Jura

Jura is populated by around 5,000 deer and 250 people; there are also a lot of adders. Access is by a frequent ferry from Port Askaig to Feolin. There is no direct ferry from the Scottish mainland. There are two places to stay: the Jura Hotel (01496-820243) or a B&B, Mrs Boardman, Craighouse, near the hotel (01496-820379). There are no camp sites and the estate tends to discourage camping, although cycle-campers should not have any problem.

A mountain bike is the ideal way to get around on Jura. The only road is the A846, mainly a narrow strip of tarmac with passing places. This however progressively deteriorates into a poor road, a rough track, and eventually a footpath. When you get to Feolin you definitely have the impression you've arrived at nowhere. The east coast however is quite different. Craighouse, the only significant settlement on the island, is in an attractive situation overlooking Small Isles Bay. The Jura Hotel is here, plus a Spar shop, the distillery, and the Antler Café.

Worth a visit near the southern tip of Jura is Jura House, which has a famous walled garden with exotic plants. There are a number of attractive walks nearby (leaflet in the house). North from Craighouse the A846 has grass growing down the middle. It follows the coast north past Tarbet to the tiny settlement of Ardlussa. Just after Lealt it becomes a rough track to lonely Kinuachdrachd. George Orwell lived near here in 1948 while writing his prophetic novel 1984.

It is possible to take a mountain bike to the very northern tip of Jura, the last two miles are a rough footpath. Just north of here is the Gulf of Corryvreckan, a famous whirlpool said to be the second largest in the world.

The other off-road route on Jura is Evan's Walk, a five-mile footpath starting from the public road four miles south of Lagg (grid ref: 550 731). It leads to Glen Batrick on the west coast. The adventurous might like to try this but I have no information as to what proportion of it might be bikeable. There is also a short footpath across the narrow part of the island from Tarbet (grid ref: 605 828) to the west coast at the head of Loch Tarbet. Tarbet has an interesting old churchyard.

Colonsay
and Oronsay

You can travel to Colonsay from Oban on the Caledonian MacBrayne ferry on Monday, Wednesday or Friday. Alternatively you can take a day trip from Islay on Wednesdays only, arriving at 11am, departing at 5pm. This is long enough for a cycle tour, but you'll want to stay longer!

One of the first things you see on arrival at Colonsay is the Pantry Café. They have a good selection of home-made cakes and can provide packed lunches. Even if you aren't hungry it's a very good idea to call here because they will tell you the state of the tide. This is necessary if you are going to visit Oronsay.

For a clockwise trip round Colonsay take the first left after the harbour (no sign) and head towards Oronsay, the island to the south. Some guide books refer to a tidal causeway between the two islands, but in fact you have to bike on wet sand for about a kilometre to cross over to the other island. Assuming you've checked on the tide it's worth crossing over. If you don't want to get salt water on your chain and components it might be better to walk.

The main attraction on Oronsay is the ruined priory. You can still see the cloisters and there are human remains (skulls) under the stone alter. If this memento mori hasn't put you off this is a scenic place to picnic. There is also an exhibition of monumental stones owned by Historic Scotland. On return to Colonsay you could visit the Barn tea room just above the beach.

Continue clockwise round the island passing attractive coastal scenery then some lochs. Near Colonsay House, there is an interesting detour to visit Kiloran Bay. This has been described as one of the finest beaches in the Western Isles.

After this, complete the circuit on the main road, or detour through the grounds of Colonsay House before catching the ferry back to Islay.

Island of Mull

Mull is arguably the best Scottish island for cycling. It vies with Skye for dramatic scenery but is quieter. Single track roads with passing places ensure that tourist coaches are mainly limited to the journey between Craignure and Iona. It would take about three days to bike all the roads.

There are mountain biking possibilities in the forests, but going to Mull to bike in plantation forests is silly when there is such lovely coastal scenery. There is some great mountain biking on Ulva with wonderful views of the cliffs, and the islands of Staffa, Fladda and Eorsa.

Humans reached Mull about 6000BC. Iona, where St Columba built a wattle and wood monastry in AD563, is Mull's most famous small island. The Vikings dominated Mull until the 13th century, after which it became part of the Lordship of the Isles. The castles date from then. Subsequently it was run by the Maclean clan and then the Campbells.

Emigration started in the 19th century at the time of the potato blight, this combined with the clearances reduced Mull's population from 10,000 to its present number of around 4,000. Mull has a reputation for being rather anglicised, many of the tourist facilities are run by incomers as the locals have a tendency to regard catering for tourists as a second-class occupation, compared to fishing and farming.

Mull, Loch Linnhe and Ardnamurchan

A three day circular bike ride, with five ferry crossings. On day one (25 miles) the route uses the Island of Lismore to avoid busy roads near Oban. Day two is on Mull with three choices of route (22, 45, or 48 miles). Day three (50 miles) is on the remote and lovely Ardnamurchan peninsula by the shore of Loch Sunart; the final ferry crossing is at Corran. The route is hilly at times.

Most of the route is on single track roads with passing places, but these need not cause you any delay. Overnight stops in youth hostels or B&Bs in Oban and Tobermory, camping is possible. The description assumes starting at Ballachulish, but it would be possible to start at Oban.

Day One -
Loch Linnhe & Lismore (25 miles)

Leave any car in Ballachulish, in the visitor information centre car park, three miles east of the bridge (toilets). A friendly bike shop, Mountain Madness (01855-811728) is just along from the car park. A convenient youth hostel near the start is Glen Coe (01855-811219), there is a camp site here too.

From Fort William, getting to the start involves cycling down the busy A82(T). This can be avoided by cycling on the A861, a single track road with passing places on the other side of the loch. Cross over from Fort William on a foot passenger ferry to Camusnagaul (01397-703701, no Sunday service), return to Ballachulish on the Corran ferry.

At the roundabout south of the Ballachulish bridge, take the A828, towards Oban. This first section could be busy in summer. The route runs along the shore of Loch Linnhe for three miles, them dips inland for 2.5 miles. On your return to the shore cycle five more miles to Shuna Island.

Look for Castle Stalker on a tiny island on the right. One mile after, turn right to a minor road for Port Appin and Lismore Island. There is a shop and sea-food restaurant (recommended) in Port Appin. The ferry is two hourly, charge 70p (01631-730217). Any ferry after 2pm is probably too late.

The ferry from Lismore to Oban is a left turn after five miles, signposted Achnacroish Pier, you have 90 minutes to get there. Just time possibly for tea and cakes at The Old Schoolhouse on the way. The ferry leaves at 0945 and 1545. Additional 1745 service on Tues/Fri and 1145 service on Tues/Thurs/Sat. No Sunday service. Ferry fare £1.80.

Oban is the major departure point for ferries going to all the Western Isles. The tourist information office is near the ferry terminal (01631-563122). There are two bike shops, Oban Cycles, Craigour Road, (01631-566996) and David Graham, Combie Street (01631-562069). For Oban Youth Hostel turn left after the pier and cycle half a mile by the shore. Advance booking is recommended (01631-562025).

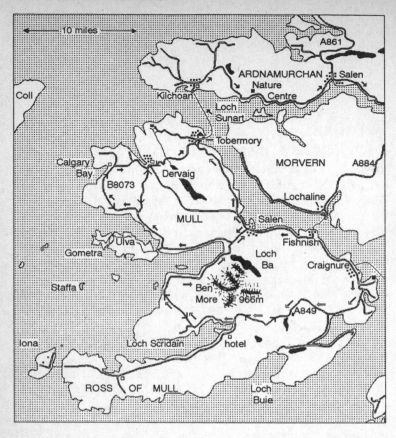

Day Two -

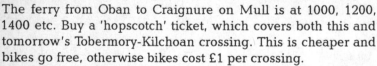

Mull (Choice of Distances)

The ferry from Oban to Craignure on Mull is at 1000, 1200, 1400 etc. Buy a 'hopscotch' ticket, which covers both this and tomorrow's Tobermory-Kilchoan crossing. This is cheaper and bikes go free, otherwise bikes cost £1 per crossing.

Just before entering Craignure there is a dramatic view of Duart Castle, with Ben More (966m) behind. A picnic lunch? There is a shop by the pier. Today's cycle is to picturesque Tobermory. Allegedly a Spanish armada galleon is sunk in the bay. The short route is directly up the east coast via Salen (22 miles), an attractive cycle ride. The shop further up the road at Salen is closed on Sundays as is the restaurant, The Puffer Aground. The hotel at Salen is generally open and does bar lunches, tea and scones, etc.

214

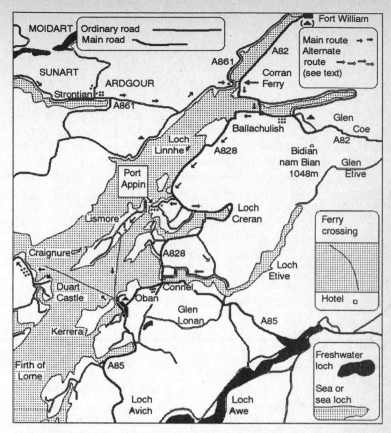

Another choice (solid arrows on map, 45 miles) is to turn left at Salen and cycle round the north-west coast by the island of Ulva. The scenery here is cliffs and waterfalls, with lovely beaches and plenty of birdlife. Otters are sometimes seen. No camping on the shores of Loch na Keal, the first section, but the farmer on Ulva generally gives permission to cyclists, and there appears to be no objection to it above the cliffs opposite Ulva. Explore the waterfall that plunges over the cliffs here, but take extreme care. You can reduce the distance by going directly north to Dervaig, but this misses out a beautiful beach at Calgary Bay. The road near Loch Frisa is mostly through plantation forest.

There is no hotel or shop between Salen and Calgary Bay. The Carthouse Gallery just beyond Calgary Bay does cakes and coffee, bar lunches in the Bellachroy Hotel in Dervaig. The bookshop in Dervaig does coffee and sells food. There is a neolithic stone circle just beyond Dervaig, on the climb towards Tobermory; this is now in forest.

215

It is possible to do some of the route between Dervaig and Tobermory off-road. Turn north on to a rough track opposite the Loch Frisa Salmon Farm sign (see map). This diversion takes in Glengorm Castle, view from the outside only.

Another alternative (outline arrows on map) is to turn south at Craignure. Cycling all the way to Iona, then reaching Tobermory in one day is too far for most people, but Craignure-Loch Scridain-Salen-Tobermory (48 miles) is more reasonable. There are some serious climbs but the gradients are less steep than the northern loop. There is a hotel that does bar lunches one mile beyond the road junction at Loch Scridain on the Iona road. There will be tourist coaches travelling from Craignure to Iona, timed with the ferries. In the afternoon, the views of Staffa, Ulva, and the other islands as you descend are tremendous.

Whichever way you go, end at Tobermory (Tourist Info: 01688-302182). Tobermory hostel (01688-302481) is basic (no showers). The Mishnish Hotel nearby may allow showers (£1). Bikes are wheeled through the hostel to the back yard.

Day Three -
Ardnamurchan (50 miles).

Turn left from the hostel door for the ferry terminal. The 0820 ferry will allow a leisurely lunch and still enable you to complete the circle by teatime; the alternative is the 1000 ferry. Sunday service is only July/Aug, and no 0820 service. At Kilchoan take a right turn after half a mile. By the time you get to the next junction (right again) you have done the major climb. There is an undulating section, then a fast descent to sea level, with views of the islands and inlets of Loch Sunart.

At the shore you meet Ardnamurchan Natural History Centre, it's got to be morning coffee time by now. Press on afterwards, it's still a long way to go. The lochside road is pretty, but winding and undulating. Turn right on to the A861 at Salen. Pub lunches in Salen or Strontian, if you are at the Natural History Centre at lunchtime you are in trouble!

After Strontian you are joined by the road from Lochaline. Keep straight on, there is a climb through Glen Tarbert, with a fast descent to Loch Linnhe. The final section to the ferry at Corran is flat; cars pay, for you it's free. The ferry service is continuous. The A82 back to Ballachulish is narrow and busy and needs care. Another option of course is to extend your ride via the west shore of Loch Linnhe, and then go on to the Great Glen or even to Skye.

Mountain Biking on Ulva

As mentioned earlier there are a number of tracks on Ulva that make good mountain bike routes. The main track which follows the north coast, leads eventually to Ulva's companion island Gometra. This is not too difficult, the path on Gometra crosses over to the south side of the island and overlooks Staffa and the cliffs of the Ross of Mull. Another track, which starts easily, but becomes more difficult, leads over to the south side of Ulva.

Ulva is very rocky, as you bike around there will be stunning views across Mull and the minor islands. The island is owned by a lady farmer, her son operates the small ferry that takes you over. They also run a small restaurant/tea room by the ferry crossing. If you want to camp it is important to ask permission. The farm occupies the fertile eastern end of the island. You can take a boat trip to Staffa to see Fingal's Cave.

Isle of Skye

Occasionally people ask me about mountain bike routes in Skye. The logic seems to go like this: they've heard about Skye, and that it has mountains. They like mountain biking, therefore there must be mountain bike routes on Skye. Do yourself a favour, if you want to do a lot of mountain biking - go somewhere else.

There is no doubt that Skye has some of the most beautiful and dramatic scenery in Britain, particularly the Cuillins rising from the sea, and the Trotternish peninsula. Skye has some incredibly lovely back roads, but connecting them up means cycling on main roads that will be busy in summer. There are only two mountain bike routes that I can really recommend. A good plan is to dip into Skye as part of a longer tour, or explore the remoter parts on foot.

Armadale - Broadford (18 miles, via A851)

A popular way to arrive on Skye is via the Mallaig - Armadale ferry, this is a half-hour crossing. The heavy traffic to Skye does not come this way so the A851 here is quite reasonable to cycle along. You can also bike south towards the Point of Sleat. This is quiet but becomes very hilly as you work south. The road ends at the Aird of Sleat, two miles short of the point. This gives a good view of Eigg, but for a full view of Rum you have to continue on a rough track and path to the lighthouse.

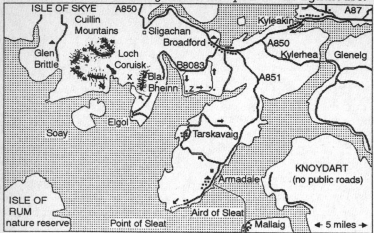

The best bike ride on the Sleat peninsula is via Tarskavaig on the minor road just north of Armadale. This starts just north of Armadale Castle, now the Clan MacDonald Centre (restaurant). There is a steady climb to 188m, then a fast scenic descent past Loch Dhughaill to Tarskavaig Bay. After this there is another smaller climb over to Tarskavaig (take either fork), then a drop to the sea near Tokavaig.

Here you get your first really good view of the jagged ridges of Bla Bheinn. Despite its impressive appearance, technical climbing gear is not necessary to reach the summit. Bla Bheinn has recently been bought by the John Muir Trust, and so will now be preserved for hill-walkers and climbers.

On a headland here is Dunscaith Castle, though it is difficult to detect, because it is so ruined that it appears a natural formation. Here in legend, the Queen of Skye is said to have taught the Irish the art of war. After this there is another short climb, then a descent to the sea again by Loch Eishort at Ord where there is a hotel. The return to the A851 isn't quite such a long climb as before, just 113m this time.

Continuing north on the A851 the road cuts inland for a time, touches the sea with more fine views of the mainland, then heads towards Broadford where it joins the A850. This is Skye's main road, now connected to the mainland at Kyle of Lochalsh by a toll bridge. Biking along this is difficult to avoid, it's not too unpleasant, and the views are fine. Personally if I've come a long way, I don't want to spend much time on roads like this, mixing it with motor traffic. One way to avoid some of the A850 is to come via the Glenelg - Kylerea ferry crossing, you have to like hills however!

Broadford has a tourist office, 01471-822361; lots of B&Bs; a youth hostel, 01471-822442; and a mountain bike hirer. Armadale Youth Hostel, 01471-844260.

Broadford to Elgol (15 miles)

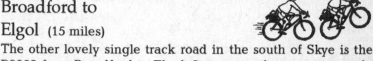

The other lovely single track road in the south of Skye is the B8083 from Broadford to Elgol. It runs south-west, past reedy Loch Cill Chriosd, where Bla Bheinn appears again. Soon after you pass the Skye Marble quarries and descend to Loch Slapin. After this the road skirts the head of the loch then runs down the west side, eventually climbing away from the sea to 134m, before dropping to Elgol.

Be careful on the descent to Elgol for it is extremely steep. As you come round the bend there is the additional distraction of the Cuillins. The Victorians considered the Cuillins to be ugly. Nowadays people would not agree; but on a dark day you can see why they felt this, for they soar blackly out of the sea to over 1000m, almost satanic in appearance.

There is a small shop selling ice cream, sweets, etc, just before Elgol, plus toilets and a tea room on the descent to the sea, at the shore you can take Donald's boat to Loch Coruisk. There is a rough footpath along the shore to Camasunary. Do not try to bike it.

Mountain Bike to Camasunary (3 miles)

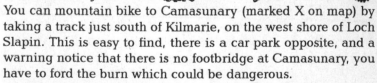

You can mountain bike to Camasunary (marked X on map) by taking a track just south of Kilmarie, on the west shore of Loch Slapin. This is easy to find, there is a car park opposite, and a warning notice that there is no footbridge at Camasunary, you have to ford the burn which could be dangerous.

If you are travelling with a bike you should not go any further than Camasunary. It is possible to walk north from Camasunary to Sligachan, but it is usually so wet that biking is impossible. In addition biking would do unacceptable damage. The John Muir Trust, which has recently bought the estate, is putting a lot of effort into footpath repair. If you want to do more mountain biking, try the next route.

Suisnish Loop
(9 miles)

This route starts from the same road as the Camasunary route, but on the east side of Loch Slapin. Begin just east of the Skye Marble quarry, signed Kilbride. Cross a cattle grid, view of Bla Bheinn ahead, bear left through a gate when you see the quarry. The route passes the quarry to the sea at an undersea cable station. After this it is a good quality rough track as far as the clearance village of Suisnish (marked Z on map).

You can return from Suisnish, but it is possible to follow a path east along the shore to the second clearance village of Boreraig. These were the last two villages to be cleared of people in Skye. The sheep are still here, the people have never returned. The shore path is only partly bikeable, and depending on conditions, you may have to carry or push for about 20% of the way. From Boreraig the path becomes fully bikeable again providing it's not too wet. It leads north back to the public road just east of Loch Cill Chriosd. This route should be avoided in lambing season.

Broadford
to Portree (28 miles)

Continuing north requires you to bike along the A850. If you are travelling with a car, or don't mind the traffic - fine, the scenery is impressive enough. You have to go this way to Uig for the ferry to Tarbert (Harris) and Lochmaddy (North Uist). The main road has some long steep hills, one of these can be avoided by taking the shore road at Loch Ainort, signed Moll.

The island of Raasay is a worthwhile diversion, with lovely views of both Skye, and Applecross on the mainland. You can stay at B&Bs, Raasay House Outdoor Centre (01478-660266) or the youth hostel (01478-660240), ferries from Sconser five times a day.

After Sconser, at the head of Loch Sligachan you pass the Sligachan Hotel and camp site, much used by climbers. Here you can fork right for Portree, or left for Dunvegan. Either way there will be a serious hill. Portree is the only town on Skye and it has the facilities you would expect. This includes a good bike shop, Island Cycles (01478-613121) who hire touring and mountain bikes. There is a private hostel, Portree Backpackers (01478-613332), and an indoor swimming pool.

Glen Brittle to Glen Eynort (6 miles)

Cyclists often visit Glen Brittle, usually staying at the youth hostel (01478-640278). The best view of the Cuillins is on the way there, rather than from the glen which is too close.

An option for mountain bikers is to bike through the forest on the west side of the glen. Enter just north of the bridge, a mile north of the hostel to cross over to Glen Eynort. Return can be via Glen Eynort to make a circular route, OS map advised.

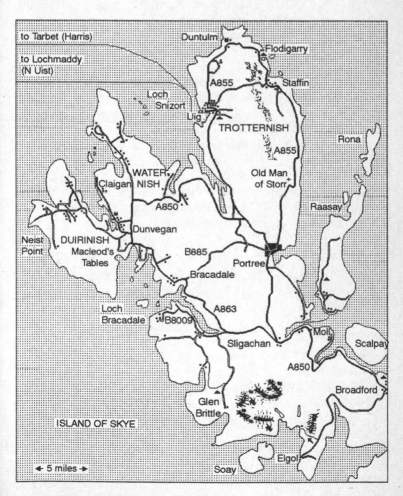

Trotternish

(Portree - Uig - Flodigarry -
Staffin - Portree: 48 miles)

Trotternish is the most scenic part of north Skye. Clockwise from Uig there is a steady climb, with views over Loch Snizort. You pass the Skye Cottage Museum at Kilmuir. Shortly after, on a little loop off the main road, there is a memorial to Flora MacDonald, who saved Bonnie Prince Charlie from the English. The memorial is a replacement, the previous one was entirely removed piece by piece by tourists.

You pass Duntulm Castle and hotel; then as you turn the corner to travel south, the scenery becomes more and more fantastic, with the rock formations of the Quirang above the road. Just before this the Flodigarry Hotel is an attractive coffee or lunch stop. The independent Dunflodigarry Hostel (01470-552212) next to the hotel is an economical place to stay. The hostel is pleasant and residents will still be welcome in the hotel for bar meals. Camping is allowed and campers can use the hostel facilities.

An alternative approach to the Quirang is by using the minor road that cuts across from Uig. This is a stiff climb up, a flatter section across moorland, then a steep descent right through the Quirang with amazing views. There is a food shop at Staffin. Down to Portree is another scenic ride, past the tall pinnacle of the Old Man of Storr.

Waternish and Duirinish

Waternish and Duirinish have quiet back roads, but the A850/A863 around Dunvegan Castle will be busier. Dunvegan Castle has a long history, but as a castle building it's not particularly impressive - lovely garden though. North of Dunvegan at Claigan there are coral beaches. Biking round Duirinish is pleasant, a good thing to do when the clouds roll in and cover the mountain scenery. There are fine sea cliffs on the west coast, seen from Neist Point. The flat topped hills known as Macleod's Tables are seen from all over.

Other places to stay in north Skye: lots of B&Bs, but particularly around Uig. Tourist information at the ferry terminal (01470-542404). Uig youth hostel (01470-542211) is a little way south of the town up a steep hill, it has great view however!

Barra to North Uist

There aren't many Gaelic words that have made it into English, but machair is one. It means the land behind the beach. There are lots of beaches. Quiet stretches of shell sand, deposited by countless Atlantic rollers, behind: a profusion of wild flowers. On a sunny day, the sea over the white sand is more shades of blue and green than you can imagine.

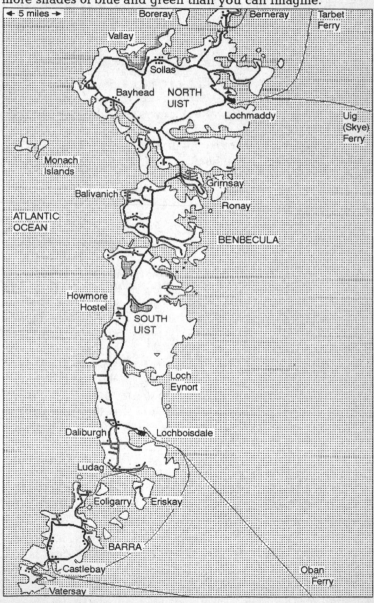

Barra

If you are arriving in Barra from Oban you'll probably be cycling down the Cal-Mac gangplank shortly after 8pm, and the immediate need will be to find a bed. The tourist office (01871-810336) opens to meet the ferry and they'll find you a B&B. There is wild camping at Ledaig at the east side of the bay, there is no hostel. There are several hotels, two shops, a co-op, a post office, bank and tea room in Castlebay.

Barra is quite hilly and its beaches rival those of North Uist. Exploring on a bike takes less than a day, the best beach is at Tangasdale. Bike over to Vatersay on the new causeway. This was built after the local bull drowned on his annual swim to impregnate the cows of Vatersay. Barra and South Uist are Roman Catholic, but relaxed about it. When the time comes to go, take your bike on the small ferry from Eoligarry to Ludag on South Uist (01878-720233).

Lochboisdale to
Benbecula (21 miles)

The description here is northerly, starting at South Uist and ending in North Uist. Doing the route north to south is fine too. Wind direction tends to be unpredictable; winds from the north are likely to be drier than the prevailing Atlantic south-westerlies, so if you are cycling north and there is a head wind, at least it's likely to be dry!

Causeways join South Uist, Benbecula and North Uist. If you are going north from Barra you can get food at the shop at the junction at Daliburgh. Lochboisdale has shops, a bank and a tourist office (01878-700286). South Uist is the hilliest of the islands and the road climbs as it works north. There are diversions west to attractive beaches, some marked as danger zones due to the nearby missile range. The main danger from this though is from army drivers rushing home for tea.

The youth hostel at Howmore is a small crofthouse with a thatched roof, pretty but primitive; handy for the beach however. It is run by the Gatliffe Hebridean Hostels Trust. You need a full sleeping bag, instead of just the sheet sleeping bag normally used at SYHA hostels. The nearest shop is one mile away. There is no telephone and advance booking is not possible.

Benbecula
& North Uist

The shop with the best choice in Benbecula is the army NAAFI at Balivanich. This is open to the public, although it, like some other parts of the military establishment, is under threat due to the ending of the cold war. There is a little loop you can do to the east on Grimsay island, which is on the causeway between Benbecula and North Uist.

North Uist is equally land, lochs, and beaches. Near Lochmaddy it often seems as if there is more water than land, and that doesn't include the sea! The beaches in the west are not particularly attractive. The beaches in the north, opposite Harris are just wonderful. Particularly so is Vallay Strand with its long finger stretching out towards Berneray, Vallay island in the bay.

The fertility of the machair behind the beach is due to the mixture of peat and windblown sand. Peat is normally infertile owing to poor drainage. You should do the full circuit of the island, but also be sure to bike the minor road that short-cuts the west-most loop, try to do it in a northward direction. The northerly spur, leading to the small ferry from Newtonferry to Harris (via Berneray) is worth cycling, even if you don't catch the ferry.

Lochmaddy has a SYHA youth hostel (01876-500368) with a friendly warden, plus the usual shops, tourist office (01876-500321), hotel, etc. It is also the ferry terminal to take you to Uig on Skye or Tarbert on Harris, but the little ferry mentioned is much the best for cyclists going to Harris. There is also a shop at the southern road junction, and just north of this a specialist fish shop. Shops also at Bayhead further north and at Sollas just east of Vallay Strand.

Ferry Services. Caledonian MacBrayne provide a car ferry service calling at Oban (mainland), Castlebay (Barra) and Lochboisdale (South Uist). On some days it calls at Mallaig (mainland). The voyage will take between five and seven hours and is very scenic. The timing and places called at vary from day to day but the most frequent service leaves Oban mid-afternoon, getting in to Barra at around 8pm and South Uist two hours later. (01878-700288 or 01631-66688).

Cal-Mac also operate a service between Lochmaddy (North Uist), Tarbert (Harris) and Uig (Skye). Timings vary, sailing time from Lochmaddy to Uig is just under two hours. (01876-500337 or 01470-542219)

The foot (and bicycle) ferry between Newtonferry (North Uist) & Leverburgh on Harris operates twice daily, mid-June to September, but only Monday, Wednesday and Saturday in other months. The ferry calls at Berneray which is attractive and has a croft type hostel similar to Howmore. (no advance booking, shop half mile). Ferry phone 01876-540230 if no reply phone 540250.

Harris and Lewis

Harris and Lewis are two islands joined by a narrow isthmus. Confusingly the name Harris applies to the southern island, and the southern part of the northern island. Harris turns into Lewis at roughly 58.03 degrees north. North of this the terrain tends to more open moorland, while the south is mountainous. Harris is more scenic, the east coast is rocky with hundreds of small lochans. The west coast is flatter, with vast sandy beaches. Harris is also the source of Harris Tweed, although nowadays more of this is produced in Lewis.

Harris

(Leverburgh - Tarbert
via west coast: 22 miles)

Possibly the best place to arrive in Harris is at Leverburgh. The village itself, called after soap magnate Viscount Leverhulme, is nothing special, but you will have come from North Uist via lovely Berneray - ahead of you on the west is a vast stretch of shell sand: Scarista Beach.

The road on the west coast of South Harris is fairly flat, running along through the flowers of the machair, although there is a steady climb when the road eventually turns east. You can stop almost anywhere for a picnic. The east coast is different, rocky and barren but with delightful little coves and hundreds of small lochans full of water lillies.

On the way up the east coast is St Clement's Church at Rodel. Dating from the 16th century it has some outstanding medieval stone carvings. The road twists and turns past small hamlets perched on the Lewisian gneiss that all these islands are mainly made from - the oldest rock in Europe. The road is rarely flat but eventually you will arrive at Ardvey on Loch Stockinish. Turn right here for Stockinish Youth Hostel (01859-530373) or keep straight on for Tarbert. Going via the hostel also takes you to Tarbert via the lovely Golden Road. The hostel is basic, no food store, it does have blankets!

Tarbert, the terminal for the Skye ferry, has B&Bs of variable quality, several hotels, and a tourist information office (01859-502011).

An interesting place to stay is at Rhenigadale on Loch Seaforth. This was once the most remote community in Britain, accessible only by sea or over a hill track. There is a croft-type hostel in the village (no phone, no advance booking). The overland route is now a road which makes it easy to get there.

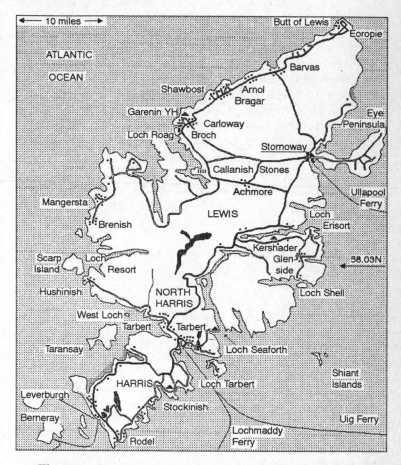

There is plenty to explore around North Harris. Go along the side of West Loch Tarbert past Amhuinnsuidhe Castle to Hushinish. The castle is for let if you can afford it. Several rough tracks, passable on a mountain bike, lead north into the remote mountains of North Harris (restrictions in stalking season).

Lewis

(Tarbert to Stornoway 37 miles)

Going north from Tarbert to Stornoway is a one day ride, passing fiord-like Loch Seaforth. At first it's hilly, with a mountainscape more like Norway than Scotland. Once you have passed Loch Seaforth the cycling gets easier.

Lewis is a vast moor covered in lochs and peat. Many loch names end in 'vat' revealing their norse origin. The west coast is interesting with many things to see, notably the broch at Carloway and the standing stones at Callanish.

Brochs are impregnable towers, usually near the sea. There are brochs all over Scotland but none elsewhere; built from 100BC to AD100, their origin is a mystery. One theory is the reason for their construction lay in the Roman occupation of southern Britain. Areas on the periphery were raided by sea to obtain slaves. The Picts had at least one ingenious mind that was able to devise a defence - see a broch for yourself.

At Arnol is the Black House Museum. This display of how things used to be was lived in up to 1964. North again is Eoropie, the most northerly village in the Hebrides. The 12th century church of St Moluag is here, key in the shop. A mile north again the road ends at the Butt of Lewis lighthouse.

Stornoway, the largest town in the Outer Hebrides, is the centre of Gaelic culture. Caledonian MacBrayne ferries (01851-702361) sail from here to Ullapool (2.5 hours). It has the usual hotels, B&Bs and tourist office (01851-703088). Hostels at Kershader (01851-880236) and Garenin (no phone).

The Orkney Islands

Whatever your taste you are likely to find something to interest you in Orkney: the dramatic hills and sea cliffs of Hoy; the birds, puffins, arctic skuas, kittiwakes, guillemots to name just a few. Most intruiging is the mystery of Skara Brae and the Ring of Brodgar: neolithic monuments erected by a people who pre-dated the pyramids.

The cycling is mostly easy, with no serious hills except in Hoy. Because of the northern latitude there will be long hours of daylight in summer, and it can be quite warm. Bear in mind though, that there is very little shelter in Orkney because there are few trees. If the weather is poor (Atlantic depressions can still occur in summer) you will need good waterproofs.

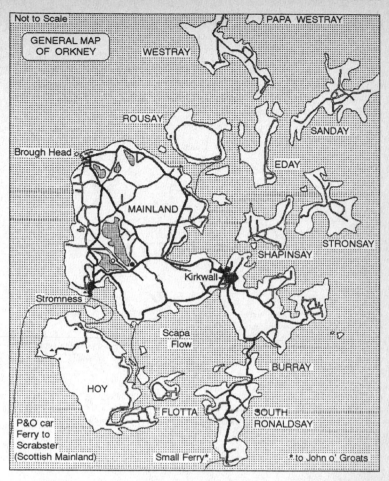

Not to Scale

GENERAL MAP
OF ORKNEY

PAPA WESTRAY

WESTRAY

ROUSAY

SANDAY

Brough Head

EDAY

MAINLAND

STRONSAY

SHAPINSAY

Kirkwall

Stromness

Scapa
Flow

BURRAY

HOY

FLOTTA

SOUTH
RONALDSAY

P&O car
Ferry to
Scrabster
(Scottish Mainland)

Small Ferry*

* to John o' Groats

West Mainland (43 miles)

This route starts from Stromness and travels north on the west
side of Orkney Mainland, taking in the cliff scenery of
Yesnaby, the neolithic village of Skara Brae, and Brough
Head. The route then turns south-east to Kirbuster Mill, then
south-west round Greeny Hill. After this you go south by the
Loch of Stenness to the Ring of Brodgar before returning to
Stromness. The route mostly avoids the main A967 running up
the west coast using minor roads to the west of it.

Stromness is an attractive town, huddled close by the
harbour with winding streets and narrow closes. Leave on the
A965 (Dundas St/Victoria St) out of Stromness, then turn left

on to the A967. The traffic on the main road should be quite light. One mile north of the A967/A965 junction, loop west off the main road, past farms at Newhouse and Kirbister. We rejoin the A967 at the north end of the Loch of Stenness.

After this the main road takes a sharp right turn, ignore this and keep straight joining the B9056. Take the next left to the cliffs and sea stacks of Yesnaby. This is a good place to see the power of the Atlantic and has some of the best coastal scenery in Orkney. A 20-minute walk south along the cliff tops reveals a distant view of the rock stack, the Old Man Of Hoy.

From Yesnaby retrace your way on the minor road and turn north again on the B9056. Keep on the B9056, ignoring all right turns and after three miles, at the Loch of Skaill, turn left for Skara Brae. Skara Brae is one of the most remarkable things in Orkney. This prehistoric village was occupied from 3100BC to 2600BC. Around 45 centuries ago the village was overwhelmed by a sand storm. It lay there, preserved by the sand, until another severe storm in 1850 caused it to become exposed again.

Skara Brae gives a unique guide to the lifestyle of the people of the village. Perhaps you thought the damp proof course was a recent invention. Not so, it was in use 5000 years ago in Orkney, together with water tanks, beds, dressers, cupboards and jewellery all of which can be seen here. One of the rooms is a workshop and was used to make pottery in sizes up to 60cm.

On leaving Skara Brae continue north on the B9056. Just north of here there was a tea room at Northdyke serving fresh spiced bread which should still be open. Further north the nature reserve at Mar Wick has rare primula.

Turn left about a mile after passing the conical hill of Vestra Fiold. Turn left here also for the cliffs of Marwick Head, in early summer the breeding grounds of thousands of guillemots, razorbills, kittiwakes and fulmars; puffins and peregrine may be seen too. The cliffs lie up a steep footpath at a road end (see map). Here too is the Kitchener Memorial, and north of Mar Wick, off the A967 at the north of Boardhouse Loch, is the Barony Hotel which does lunches.

If you are going to Brough Head turn left on a minor road before you get to the A967/A966 junction. It is just possible to mountain bike over to Brough Head if the tide is out. Otherwise, go south-east on a minor road on the north side of Boardhouse Loch, past The Barony, to Kirbuster Farm Museum, turning right (south-west) at the junction here. At the next junction turn sharp left then keep right to skirt Greeny Hill.

Cross the A986, then turn left (south) on to the A967. Travel for a mile on the A967 then turn left on to the B9055 to pass between the Loch of Stenness and the Loch of Harray. On your right, just before the narrow strip of land between the lochs, is the Ring of Brodgar. This is one of the finest stone circles or henge monuments anywhere. An estimated 4700 cubic metres of rock were moved to make it in the third millennium BC. Exactly what these people believed is unknown but they had precise astronomical knowledge.

On leaving the Ring of Brodgar continue south to the A965 and turn right to return to Stromness. The distance can be shortened and traffic avoided by taking the first left after the A965/A964 junction, but this involves more climb. If you've looked at everything on the route you will have had a long day!

East Mainland & Rousay (55 miles)

With this route we start from Kirkwall and travel up the east coast of Mainland to Tingwall Pier, using minor roads. After this it's over to Rousay, to cycle round the island, visiting a broch and a chambered cairn. On returning to Mainland we go inland (west) to return to Kirkwall via the Loch of Harray, Maes Howe and the Loch of Kirbister.

Start at the youth hostel in Kirkwall, which is in Old Scapa Road, south of Kirkwall bus station. Turn north on to the A964 towards the High Street but take the first left into Glaitness Road. This becomes Old Finstown Road. Continue west along this between Wideford Hill and Kellylang Hill (radio masts).

There is a road leading to the top of Wideford Hill on the right two miles after leaving Kirkwall. This gives an excellent view of the northern isles, and is well worth the climb up if the weather is clear.

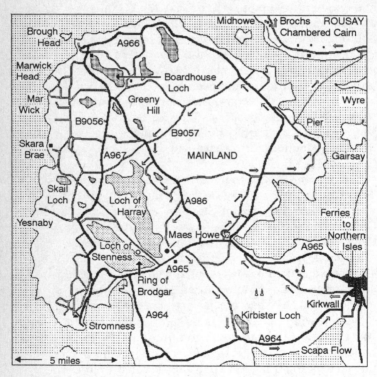

After this continue west, ignoring any right turns until you meet the A965. Turn left on to this and continue straight on past the A966 junction. Take the first right after this on to a minor road leading north round a tidal pool. Keep straight on for three miles by the side of the hill until you come to a T junction. Turn right (east) here, left (north) at the main road, then immediately right (east) on to another minor road. Follow this for five miles, ignoring any turn-offs and passing the small island of Gairsay. The large island you see will be Rousay and the ferry to it is a right turn 1.5 miles after the bend in the road opposite Gairsay island.

Ferries are quite frequent. There is a café on the pier on Rousay, also a hotel doing bar lunches two miles west of the pier. Rousay is very pretty, there is virtually one road only, the circuit of the island is 13 miles. Rousay is fairly littered with chambered cairns, neolithic burial chambers, but probably the best to visit is at Midhowe (3500BC) because this also enables you to visit a broch (see page 228 for information on brochs). Access to both of these is along a track by Westness House (see map). This can be cycled, or alternately use the footpath further along.

There is the remains of a crannog, an artificial island, on the Loch of Wasbister in the north-west corner of Rousay. Rousay was once well populated until the people were cleared off in favour of sheep, look for evidence of runrigs, narrow strip fields, as you cycle round. There is a shop in the north-east corner of the island.

On returning to Mainland turn right (north-west) after Tingwall pier, rejoining the minor road which meets the A966. Continue up the A966 for two miles then turn left inland on the B9057. If you have plenty of time there is an attractive beach near here, and another broch, opposite Rousay; access is just south of the A966/B9057 junction.

Otherwise keep on the B9057 for five miles, passing south of Greeny Hill, until you meet the A986. Turn left (south) here, but after a mile loop right towards the Loch of Harray. This returns you to the A986 after two miles. Continue south for a half mile then turn right again on another minor road towards the loch. At the end of this road you meet the A965, Tormiston Mill, and Maes Howe.

Maes Howe is possibly the finest architectural achievement of neolithic Europe. Despite dating from 2750BC it is completely intact. Before visiting it however you might like to fortify yourself at nearby Tormiston Mill visitor centre which has a tea room.

Maes Howe is a burial chamber although no bodies were found in it. Possibly they were cleared out by the Vikings who broke in during the 12th century. The interior of the chamber bears Viking grafitti - pictures of a serpent and a walrus, plus a number of runes - even a joke about pompous women. The vikings removed treasure, the runes say, but they did no real damage to the tomb itself. After they left, Maes Howe remained undisturbed until 1861. That it has remained intact over such a long period is evidence of high quality construction. The chamber is 4.5m square with a narrow passage. On the shortest day of the year the interior is briefly illuminated for a few minutes by the setting sun.

On leaving Maes Howe cycle east for one mile then turn right (south) to return to Kirkwall via Kirbister Loch. The final junction, near the shore of Scapa Flow, is a left turn on to the A964 for the last six miles to Kirkwall.

Island of Hoy
(about 30 miles of road)

The name Hoy is derived from the Viking word for high island. Hoy is quite unlike the rest of Orkney, geologically it is a detached part of the highlands which just happens to be

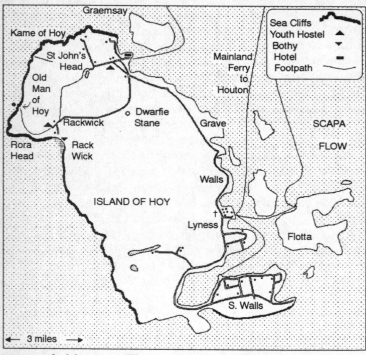

surrounded by sea. The north and west coasts are bounded by spectacular cliffs which are seen on the ferry crossing from Scrabster to Stromness. The most famous feature is the Old Man of Hoy (137m), an impressive rock stack on the west coast. This is however not visible from any road and requires a two to three hour walk (mountain biking not recommended). The other feature of Hoy is the large amount of wildlife, particularly birds. Inland there will be curlews, red grouse, meadow pipits, golden plovers, dunlins and red throated divers. On the sea cliffs, fulmars, shearwaters and puffins. Otters may be spotted on the east coast in the morning, hares are common inland.

The road network on Hoy is fairly limited so no detailed route is given. The obvious plan is to arrive on one ferry, say from Stromness, and leave on the other. This will avoid having to cycle along the hilly east coast road twice. Which direction you do it in is not important. Any serious amount of walking on Hoy is likely to require an overnight stop, staying at one of the two hostels or one of the B&Bs. There is a dry bothy at Rackwick near the beach where you can stay for nothing, no shop though.

It will be necessary to do some walking if you are to see anything of the cliff scenery. The most accessible cliff scenery is a short walk along the coast, just west of the northern tip of the island. This gives good views of the Kame of Hoy. Slightly further round is St John's Head (351m), the highest vertical sea cliff in Britain. The walk to The Old Man of Hoy starts at Rackwick, and is a three hour trip. Taking a mountain bike along this path would be anti-social as you would cause damage to the narrow path in anything but very dry conditions.

On the road to Rackwick is the Dwarfie Stane, an isolated hollowed out block of sandstone dating from around 3000BC. It has two chambers, a passage and a block for preventing entry. Other places that could be visited are Lyness Interpretation Centre (naval museum), the naval cemetery at Lyness, and Betty Corrigall's grave on the east coast road. The main attractions of Hoy however are the dramatic scenery, and the huge numbers of birds, both on the sea cliffs and in the hills.

Southern Islands

(21 miles, Kirkwall to Burwick pier)

Probably most people will do this route on their way back to mainland Scotland. The small ferry from the southern tip of South Ronaldsay to John o' Groats on the Scottish mainland makes an attractive alternative to the car ferry. The road which links the four islands to Mainland runs along the Churchill Barriers. These were built on the orders of Winston Churchill, when he was First Lord of the Admiralty early in the Second World War. This followed the sinking of the

235

British battleship HMS *Royal Oak* by a German U boat. Royal Oak, together with ships of the German high seas fleet from the First World War, still lie under the waters of Scapa Flow.

Many of the 74 German ships that originally surrendered have been salvaged, but three battleships and four light cruisers remain. Nowadays they are a mecca for visiting divers. An interesting stop, just before the first barrier, is the Commodore Motel. This has a display of the building of the barriers, which was eventually completed by Italian prisoners of war, coffee available too. Just south of the motel, at the other end of barrier one, is the Italian Chapel, built by Domenico Chiocchetti between 1943 and 1945. This beautiful interior inside two Nissen Huts is one of the most visited monuments in Orkney, it was gifted by Chiocchetti to the Orcadian people in 1961.

After barriers one to three is Burray island. A diversion here could be to the small islet of Hunda on the west coast which has a seal colony. Burray Village is attractive, with a bar and restaurant in the old fisherman's store. Much sand has built up on barrier four between Burray and South Ronaldsay, but several blockships, meant originally to stop submarines, are still visible. South Ronaldsay is particularly attractive. The picturesque village of St Margaret's Hope lies in a bay at the north end. This has the Creel Restaurant and two museums.

The ferry to mainland Scotland runs from Burwick, this operates in the summer only. The village of Herston on the west coast is worth a visit and puffins can often be seen on the rocky coast near here. If you have time before catching the boat there is a chambered cairn just beyond Cleat on the south-east tip of the island. The small island of Swona to the west of Burwick is uninhabited except for wild cattle.

Orkney Phone Numbers: **P&O Ferries**, 01224-572615 or 01856-850655. **Small ferry to John o' Groats,** 01955-611353. **Tourist Information,** Kirkwall, 01856-872856; Stromness: 01856-850716. **SYHA Hostels**, Stromness, 01856-850589; Kirkwall, 01856-872243; Hoy, 01856-873535 ext 2404. **Independent Hostels**. Brown's Hostel, Stromness: 01856-850661; Trumland Farm, Rousay: 01856-821252; Wheems Bothy, S Ronaldsay, 01856-831537.

APPENDIX

Scottish Tourist Board
23 Ravelston Terrace,
Edinburgh EH3 4EU
0131-332 2433 (Written and telephone enquiries only)
The Scottish Tourist Board publish a booklet which lists
cycling holiday operators in Scotland.

Scottish Youth Hostels Association
7 Glebe Crescent,
Stirling FK8 2JA
01786-451181
As well as providing economical accommodation for people
of all ages, the SYHA also organise cycling holidays.

Dales Cycles   Central Cycle Hire
Dobbies Loan,   13 Lochrin Place,
Glasgow   Edinburgh
0141-332 2705   0131-228 6333
Both of the above firms hire quality touring bikes as well as
mountain bikes.

Cyclists' Touring Club
69 Meadrow,
Godalming,
Surrey GU7 3HS   Phone: 01483-417217
Long established as the organisation which represents
touring cyclists in the UK, the CTC also run cycling holidays.

British Rail (Scotrail)
Travel Centre Manager,
Edinburgh Waverley Station,
Waverley Bridge, Edinburgh EH1 1BB
0131-556 2451
Some trains can only take two bikes, reserve a bike space
early. This can be done by telephone if you have a credit
card.

Caledonian MacBrayne
The Ferry Terminal,
Gourock PA19 1QP
01475-650100   Fax: 01475-637607
Caledonian MacBrayne operate ferries to most of the
inhabited Scottish Islands except Orkney and Shetland.

Sustrans
35 King Street,
Bristol BS1 4DZ
0117-926 8893

Sustrans
53 Cochrane Street,
Glasgow G1 1HL
0141-552 8241

A registered charity, Sustrans designs and builds bike paths all over Scotland and the UK, often in conjunction with local authorities. Development of new routes is funded by the membership. Recently Sustrans have been successful in a bid to the Millennium Fund, however this money will only be forthcoming if it is matched from other sources.

Spokes
The Lothian Cycle Campaign,
232 Dalry Road,
Edinburgh EH11 2JG

Campaigning for better facilities for cyclists in Scotland's capital city, Spokes has had many successes over the years. Spokes has a variety of different groups, building cycle paths, publishing newsletters, and organising campaigning events and cycle rides. If you would like to help you would be welcome. Send a *large* stamped addressed envelope to the above address and you will receive a lot of information!

Glasgow Cycling Campaign
53 Cochrane Street,
Glasgow G1 1HL

Glasgow Cycling Campaign campaigns for better facilities for cyclists in Glasgow. If you live in or near Glasgow, and would like to help, they would like to hear from you.

Edinburgh Bicycle Co-operative
8 Alvanley Terrace,
Edinburgh EH9 1DU
0131-228 1368   Fax: 0131-229 4447

There are many excellent bike shops in Scotland, I mention this one because this book would never have been written without their support.

The BikeBus
4 Barclay Terrace,
Edinburgh EH10 4HP
0131-229 6274   Fax: 0131-229 4447

The BikeBus is a transport service for cyclists, mostly catering for local people who would like a day out; it will also be of interest to *groups* of cyclists requiring transport within Scotland. The BikeBus is not a holiday company and does not provide regular scheduled bus services.

Major Ferry Routes

Orkney, Hebridean and Clyde Ferries.

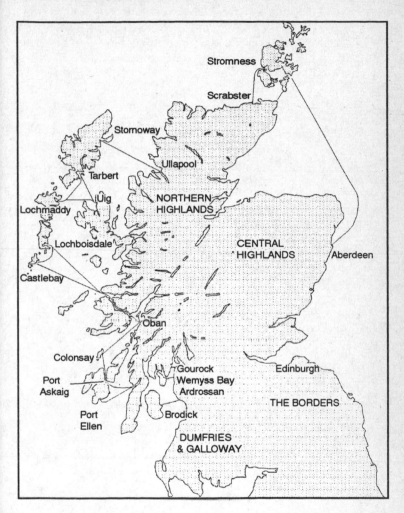